THE BURDEN OF RHYME

THE BURDEN OF RHYME

Victorian Poetry, Formalism, and the Feeling of Literary History

Naomi Levine

The University of Chicago Press   Chicago and London

The University of Chicago Press, Chicago 60637
The University of Chicago Press, Ltd., London

Published 2024
Printed in the United States of America

33 32 31 30 29 28 27 26 25 24 1 2 3 4 5

ISBN-13: 978-0-226-83496-2 (cloth)
ISBN-13: 978-0-226-83497-9 (paper)
ISBN-13: 978-0-226-83498-6 (e-book)
DOI: https://doi.org/10.7208/chicago/9780226834986.001.0001

The University of Chicago Press gratefully acknowledges the generous support of the Frederick W. Hilles Publication Fund of Yale University toward the publication of this book.

Library of Congress Cataloging-in-Publication Data

Names: Levine, Naomi (Literary historian), author.
Title: The burden of rhyme : Victorian poetry, formalism, and the feeling of literary history / Naomi Levine.
Other titles: Victorian poetry, formalism, and the feeling of literary history
Description: Chicago ; London : The University of Chicago Press, 2024. | Includes bibliographical references and index.
Identifiers: LCCN 2023057836 | ISBN 9780226834962 (cloth) | ISBN 9780226834979 (paperback) | ISBN 9780226834986 (ebook)
Subjects: LCSH: English poetry—19th century—History and criticism. | Poetics. | Criticism—History.
Classification: LCC PR591 .L48 2024 | DDC 821.809—dc23/eng/20240105
LC record available at https://lccn.loc.gov/2023057836

♾ This paper meets the requirements of ANSI/NISO Z39.48-1992 (Permanence of Paper).

For Greg

Contents

Introduction

Anyone who loves poetry will tell you that the charisma of a favorite poem is elusive: we experience it, we *know* that we experience it, we can point to the efficacy of this or that detail, and yet we still can't quite explain it. We can return to the same poem year after year (or semester after semester) and find its charm entirely undiminished. Repeated readings don't dull the effect; they may even intensify it. For the professional poetry scholar, teaching the poem, analyzing it, researching it, and writing about it don't dull it either. Why?

I don't know. But that kind of tantalizing not-knowing can be a spur to poetic theory. It was for the Victorians, who were passionately curious about how poetry works and who tried to satisfy their curiosity—or perhaps sustain it, prolong it, enjoy it—by turning their questions about the effects of aesthetic forms into questions about the genesis of aesthetic forms. I call this affective and historicist orientation toward form *genetic formalism,* and I argue in this book that we can't appreciate the significance of Victorian poetry—or understand the history of literary studies—without it.

A central claim of my book is that literary history *was* literary theory in the nineteenth century; poetic theory participated in the historicism that conditioned so much of the period's intellectual life. Historiographic stories about the origins and development of poetic forms were a way to theorize authorial expressivity, readerly affect, and, above all, poetic technique. These genetic stories were everywhere in the nineteenth century: in dedicated works of literary history and aesthetic theory, in public lectures and literary reviews. They were also absorbed into Victorian poems, not just as thematic material but as the prosodic effects that have come to seem most distinctively, even egregiously, Victorian. Foremost among these is rhyme. Victorian rhyming practices (which included couplets, stanzas, assonance, blank verse, free verse) were shaped by historiographic hypotheses about the geographical origin and transnational development of rhyme. One influential hypothesis that I discuss traced English rhyme backward through Italian and Provençal poetry to medieval Persian and Arabic love lyrics. Such stories, which emerged from "general" (rather than national) literary historiography, and which theorized rhyme as a multicultural palimpsest of poetic feelings, taught Victorian poets how to read and write rhyme.

It shouldn't be surprising that, in a moment of acute historical consciousness, poetic theory had a historical inflection.[1] But this is not how we tend to think of Victorian poetry and poetics. Two intellectual and institutional developments have interfered with our recognition of genetic formalism: the shift from generalist to specialist literary historiography, which erased a transhistorical and transnational conception of form; and American New Criticism's still powerful orthodoxy that form is "intrinsic" and literary history is "extrinsic" to a work of literary art.[2] Genetic formalism frustrates the dominant methods of the discipline, the formalisms and historicisms that continue to guide scholarly work. I suggest that the mismatch between Victorian poetry and twentieth-century methods is no accident: New Critical formalism was designed not only to professionalize literary criticism and its pedagogy but also to wean our taste away from Victorian poetics, with its unwieldy historicisms. In this regard, the reception of Victorian poetry is the business of all literary scholars who use and think about literary methods.

The Burden of Rhyme works to reanimate nineteenth-century literary historiography and to show how it determined Victorian experiments with form. It is my hope that a better understanding of genetic formalism—that is, a better understanding of the historiographic thinking and feeling in Victorian poetics—will encourage a reassessment of Victorian poetry itself, which remains a surprisingly minor subfield of literary studies, despite decades of brilliant critical work. But this book has aims beyond contributing to the project of Victorian poetry's revaluation. In presenting an unfamiliar prehistory of New Critical formalism, it revises both the history of literary studies and the concept of form. These revisions have consequences for interpretation. Reading for genetic formalism means reading differently, and for a different kind of form and a different kind of history than we're used to. In this case, it means reading for (and feeling for) the now doubly historical feelings in Victorian poems: the feelings that Victorians thought *they* could feel in historical forms. This mode of reading requires us to reconsider both historicist and formalist methods, in the past and in the present. And it asks us to reimagine the relationship between scholarly knowledge and the ineffable charisma of a poem.

HISTORIOGRAPHIC RHYME

The genre of scholarly knowledge that I explore in this book is literary historiography. I mainly use the phrase "literary historiography" to mean literary history as it was written and imagined in the eighteenth and nineteenth centuries: as a set of theories and wishes about the long, transnational history of literature; as a way of speculating about beginnings and what beginnings determine; as a view of aesthetic forms in relation to social institutions; as a means of approaching literary objects, in their technical and affective dimensions. I borrow Hayden White's inflection, "historio*graphy,*" to highlight the discursive practice of literary history, its status as writing and ideas, and as an imaginative and "poetic" orientation to the always limited data of history.[3] When I say that the Victorian model of form was genetic, I mean that nineteenth-century literary historiography, with its deep mythologies of poetry, offered Victorians a language for conceptualizing form.

At this point, it is an all but dead language. Although literary history remains a major—perhaps the dominant—literary method, its scope and its aims are not the same as they were in the nineteenth century. Then, literary history was often continuous with history proper: with a synoptic view of human activity over the *longue durée*. Now, literary history tends toward the study of influences, or the immediate contextualization of an author or text, rather than toward the creation myth or the story of culture. Neither more recent model attempts the kind of historically or geographically synoptic view characteristic of nineteenth-century literary historiography, although that earlier historiography often included in its purview both synchronic context and diachronic influence and development.[4] There are good reasons why we no longer practice the style of literary history writing that conditioned Victorian literature: it relies on grand developmental narratives that tend to favor European history; its uneven attention to evidence is incompatible with our scholarly and institutional norms. But the generalist character of nineteenth-century literary historiography made it possible to see poetry differently than we do now, especially within English departments.[5] Its picture of literature—even English literature—was international and multilingual. And literary forms like rhyme were accordingly allowed richer, longer, and more cosmopolitan lives.

In the twentieth century, the New Critics promoted rhyme as technique itself, an icon of ahistorical form, and that remains our working model insofar as we consider rhyme at all. But in the nineteenth century, rhyme was a historiographic form. It held a privileged place in nineteenth-century histories of literature, because its story was also the story of literary-historical development writ large. In the generalist literary historiography of Germaine de Staël, August Schlegel, J. C. L. Simonde de Sismondi, Arthur Hallam, and others, the medieval invention of rhyme marked a break between classical and modern, or "romantic," poetics in Europe. According to these histories, the subsequent fortunes of rhyme helped account for the shifting tastes and sensibilities that differentiated one era from the next. Because theories of rhyme were inextricable from theories of literary history, transmission, and periodization, Victorians saw in rhyme the intrinsic historicism of poetic forms. Thus, Victorian poets working with rhyme had a sensitive historiographic instrument. Rhyme's connection with literary modernity and with a repertoire of medievalist, Italophilic, and orientalist myths about love, loss, and poetic longing meant that the form of rhyme had *content*. Through a range of prosodic techniques, poets entered live debates about rhyme: whether it began in the East or West, how it moved into English literature, whether it signified spiritual achievement or cultural decline, and how it expressed and elicited emotion.

In light of this nineteenth-century culture of rhyme-thinking and rhyme-feeling, *The Burden of Rhyme* rereads a set of canonical poets from the period 1830 to 1910. It shows Arthur Hallam and Alfred Tennyson mining Arabist historiography for evidence of rhyme's affective powers; Elizabeth Barrett Browning deriving a capacious "rhymatology" from her study of European literary history; William Morris using rhyme's association with Provençal love to eroticize his verse; Coventry Patmore imagining, via the history and theory of the ode, a future for English poetry. These poets were not the only ones who turned genetic formalism into historiographic experiments with prosody, but they represent a dominant line of Victorian poetics—a line initiated by Hallam's and Tennyson's discovery of Romantic literary-historical thought and culminating in Ezra Pound's philological rediscovery of troubadour poetics.[6] All these poets had a scholarly and creative relationship to literary historiography, they all engaged explicitly with the story of romantic literature, they all devised forms that theorized *prosodically* about the history of rhyme. They also wrote some of the poems that mattered most to nineteenth-century readers—poems that haven't been adequately recognized as historiographic forms.

Needless to say, the genetic and affective view of rhyme that this book describes was not the only approach to rhyme in the nineteenth century—one has only to think of the comic rhymes of Gilbert and Sullivan or the sinister rhymes of Robert Browning's "My Last Duchess" to realize that Victorian rhyme had many tonalities. And yet, I would argue that deviations from this romantic model of rhyme often operate *as* deviations, deriving their comedy or frisson from their conspicuous refusal to feel like romantic rhyme.[7] As subsequent chapters show, stories about the origins of rhyme were at the center of rhyme theory in the period; they constituted a common, and felt, knowledge about poetry for Victorians with a literary and historical education. That those stories have not been part of our education—that twentieth-century criticism educated us away from them—has meant for us a loss of access to the inner lives of Victorian forms.

FEELING INTO FORM

How do we resensitize ourselves to Victorian poetic forms? Through careful reading and detailed historical scholarship, to be sure, but also through a process of *Einfühlung*—a quasi-philological *feeling-into* a formalism that is not our own. New Critical formalism sought to disentangle literary form from literary history and literary feeling. In order to read Victorian forms for the history and feeling they carried, we can't just rely on formalist or historicist methods, or even on New Formalist strategies of historicizing and contextualizing form; nor can we rely on an untutored aesthetic response. We need to bring historical, technical, and affective knowledge to bear on a poem, and to let those kinds of knowledge and intuition illuminate one another.

The critical practice of *Einfühlung* has its own history. In the eighteenth century, J. G. Herder theorized it as a historical method, an empathic erudition that acknowledges the "gulf" of historical and cultural difference and nonetheless makes the willingness to *feel into* a precondition of historical knowledge.[8] In the nineteenth century, Walter Pater (and later, Vernon Lee) developed an aestheticist variation on *Einfühlung*.[9] For Pater, the "first step" to knowing the aesthetic object was asking what it is "to *me*"—an interrogation of felt aesthetic experiences as "the original facts with which the aesthetic critic has to do." But as Pater's case studies demonstrate, the aesthetic critic's goal wasn't just self-knowledge; it was also a more profound and immediate understanding of the history and meaning of art.[10] In fact, Pater's method strove for an integration of formal, historical, and affective intelligence, valuing "theories which bring into connection with each other modes of thought and feeling, periods of taste, forms of art and poetry, which the narrowness of men's minds constantly tends to oppose to each other."[11] In the mid-twentieth century, Erich Auerbach returned repeatedly to the historicisms of Herder and his precursor Giambattista Vico, insisting that empathy and personal intuition (in addition to "a scientific encounter with the material") are central to philological inquiry, and especially to the difficult task of historical synthesis.[12] At the beginning of the twenty-first century, Edward Said wrote movingly of Auerbach's own philological *Einfühlung* as a model of sympathetic and creative humanistic scholarship.[13]

My approach in this book is neither aestheticist nor philological, and I am not advocating an uncritical return to these older scholarly practices. But what I borrow from them is a conviction that feeling and knowing together constitute a powerful means of accessing historical poetry.[14] Sometimes the residuum of an obsolete poetic theory is the poem that believed in it, so getting as close as possible to the poem's form is one way toward that lost theory. The technical analysis of a poem, but also an intuitive and affective response to it—the recognition of what it is "to *me*"—can lead to a "scientific encounter" with historical material.[15] Conversely, sometimes an obsolete theory generates surprisingly viable possibilities for interpretation; thus, an openness to outdated (even debunked) forms of knowledge can yield a more immediate experience of the poem.[16]

I have endeavored in these pages to combine more familiar styles of historical scholarship and close reading with a historicist-formalist *Einfühlung* that is responsive to the methodological strangeness of nineteenth-century poetics. One feature of that strangeness is the inseparability of form and history; another is the assumption that forms have feelings. For the nineteenth-century writers I discuss, rhyme is not simply a medium between the expressive poet and the affected reader. Because of its structure (the interplay of similarity, difference, proximity, distance) and because of its history (its imagined origin in medieval scenes of love and sorrow), rhyme yearns for, desires, remembers, misses, grieves for, lusts after, and loves its partner rhymes. These are *prosodic* feelings. Such feelings may be mimetic of or parallel to human feelings, but they are not reducible to the author's intention or the reader's experience.[17] Poets can work to cultivate rhyme feelings, and readers can respond to them, but in between the feeling poet and the feeling reader is the feeling form. Heavy with affective and historical meaning, rhyme was a way for Victorian poets to empathically access and reanimate the literary past. A wager of this book is that reading the strange formalism of Victorian rhyme demands a similarly empathic method: a willingness to experience those prosodic feelings and to treat them as historical information.[18]

It should be clear from the foregoing paragraphs that my own use of "feeling" closely follows my Romantic and Victorian materials. The method of *feeling-in,* the concept of feeling form, and many other invocations of *feeling* and *affect* in this book escape the taxonomies of contemporary affect theory because they predate them.[19] Eighteenth- and nineteenth-century writers of literary history and poetics drew on a broad affective vocabulary, using words like "feeling," "emotion," "pathos," "passion," "sentiment," and "sensation," if not exactly interchangeably, then with a generative nonsystematicity. The vagueness of this vocabulary, in addition to suggesting what Arthur Hallam calls the "innumerable shades of fine emotion," registers the open-endedness of their projects to explain the experience and history of poetic form.[20] At the same time, such words often had strong genetic connotations, pointing to the manifold origin stories from which Victorian poetic theory was made.[21] I have tried to preserve both the looseness and the historical specificity of these terms.

THE BURDEN OF RHYME

My title, *The Burden of Rhyme,* is meant to evoke the literary concept of *burden,* or *burthen,* as both form and content: a temporal figure of repetition or continuity (a refrain, an undersong) and also a theme or idea.[22] Freighted with fantasies of poetic origins, with a burden of history and feeling, rhyme was more than a prosodic device in the nineteenth century. For Victorian poets, it was an enabling idea about what forms could say and do and mean. If my title also suggests a long tradition, revived in the twentieth century, of viewing rhyme as itself a burden—an impediment to creative freedom—this last connotation can help emphasize the others. The aesthetic value of rhyme changed when rhyme became a form without a content.

This book has two main parts. The first, "Genetic Formalism," develops a theoretical and intellectual-historical argument; while the second, "Historiographic Forms," unfolds a sequence of case studies from Victorian poetry. A word about these terms: "genetic formalism" signifies for me a methodological precursor to the ahistorical formalism prevalent from the 1930s onward. By using the slightly ambiguous adjective "genetic," I am reactivating a term from both eighteenth- and nineteenth-century historicism and mid-twentieth-century criticism. In those contexts, it referred to the explanatory value of origins, where "genetic" had to do with the historical genesis of a phenomenon and pointed to the ongoing meaningfulness of beginnings—or, eventually, the error of believing in such ongoing meaningfulness (as in the genetic fallacy). Readers today likely have other, more immediate associations with the word "genetic," both inside and outside of the humanities. My aim, however, is to recover the term's significance for the history of literary studies. The phrase that structures the second half of the book, "historiographic forms," concerns poetic practice. Whereas "genetic formalism" names an unfamiliar complexion of formalist thought, "historiographic forms" denotes the poetic manifestation of that thinking: the experiments in prosodic and stanzaic form that emerged from nineteenth-century ideas about the international history and expressive capacity of poetry.

My first chapter, "Old Historicism, New Criticism, and the Feeling in Form," argues that what we call "form" should really be understood as dehistoricized form, in order to account for the dehistoricizing effort fundamental to the concept—both explicitly, in the moment of its New Critical theorization, and implicitly, in our ongoing practices of formalist reading today. The chapter demonstrates that this newer idea of form was a reaction against the older genetic one inherited from the nineteenth century. I show that some of New Criticism's signature concepts—the division of "intrinsic" from "extrinsic" approaches, the famous intentional and affective fallacies—were meant to undermine genetic formalism as a method. Examining the connections between history, form, and feeling in Romantic literary historiography; in the poetic theory of René Wellek, Austin Warren, William K. Wimsatt, and Monroe Beardsley; and in a Tennyson poem, this chapter proposes that we need a pre-twentieth-century concept of formalism both for approaching Victorian poetic forms and for understanding the origins of our own methods.

If the first chapter in this section attended to the twentieth-century reaction against genetic formalism, the second attempts to reconstruct it from within. Chapter 2, "Arthur Hallam and the Origins of Rhyme," considers the early and influential use of literary-historical thinking as a resource for Victorian poetics. The chapter centers on Arthur Hallam, who is now best known as the subject of Tennyson's *In Memoriam* (1850) but who was a significant poet and essayist in his own right. I argue that Hallam's criticism connects Romantic literary historiography and Victorian poetry and thereby establishes the theoretical background for many of the poetic innovations that follow. Hallam used the genetic narratives of "general" or "world" literary history (especially the Arabist theory from Sismondi's *Historical View of the Literature of the South of Europe*, 1813) to conceptualize rhyme as an instrument of feeling, and I suggest that this borrowed historiography is the key intertext for Hallam's important review of Tennyson's early poetry. Through its examination of Arthur Hallam's poetic theory and the philosophical and historical writings of Sismondi, Hegel, and Arthur's historian father Henry Hallam, this chapter describes a passionate Romantic debate about rhyme's origins and recovers a lost genre of literary history and criticism.

Part 2, "Historiographic Forms," turns to Victorian poetry itself, beginning with Hallam's direct influence on Tennyson's poetics. My third chapter, "Alfred Tennyson's Lyric Stanza," tracks Hallam's thought into the poet's career, which spanned the remainder of the nineteenth century and yielded some of its most canonical poems. Focusing on *Poems, Chiefly Lyrical* (1830), I demonstrate Tennyson's serious engagement with Hallam's Sismondian idea of affective prosody. In the stunning technical and tonal variety of *Poems*, I find Tennyson thinking, along with Hallam, about the Arabic and Provençal roots of modern lyric: the medieval ideal of matching form to feeling and the burst of stanzaic invention that resulted from it. The melancholic rhymes of "Tears, Idle Tears" (1847) and *In Memoriam* (1850) represent a more mature if less transparently historical development of affective form. By turning general literary history and its genetic thinking into an interpretive and creative method, Hallam and Tennyson devise a Victorian historiographic poetics.

While Arthur Hallam was a minor Victorian literary historian who is nonetheless remembered for his impact on Victorian poetry, his father, Henry Hallam, was a major one whose contributions have been forgotten. Chapter 4, "Elizabeth Barrett Browning's Unblank Verse," reads Barrett Browning's infamously bad rhymes and her blank verse as related stylistic responses to her study of the elder Hallam's *Introduction to the Literature of Europe* (1837–39), the first large-scale work of general literary history in English. Studying Barrett Browning's heavily annotated volumes of Hallam's history and her own literary history writing, I show that she had a vexed relationship with his work. On one hand, Hallam was a model for her historiographic scholarship, and his book represented an extraordinary trove of information about literary history; on the other, she felt excluded from his kind of scholarly authority and vehemently disagreed with his critical judgments. Although Barrett Browning rejects Hallam's neoclassical taste, she nonetheless draws on his historiographic plots to authorize her poetic experiments. I argue that Hallam's transnational historiography—

particularly his accounts of Spanish assonantal poetry, and of the historical convergences of epic and sonnet in Italian and English—allows her to see blank verse as, counterintuitively, a subspecies of rhyme.

Chapter 5, "William Morris's Fleshly Rhymes," investigates the shared historiographies of rhyme and love, and their significance for Morris's Pre-Raphaelite poetry. I follow the historiographic concept of the *romantic* through the work of Thomas Warton, Germaine de Staël, August Schlegel, G. W. F. Hegel, and Walter Pater to reveal the multivalent meaning of what Hegel calls "romantic rhyme." The conflation of rhyme with romantic love in the period was not just a matter of analogy; it also had a historical logic. Because rhymed poetry was thought at its medieval origin to be a language of bodily desire, it presented itself to nineteenth-century poets as a way to speak about love apart from any particular thematic material or stanzaic form. William Morris exploits this historiographic connection to imbue his medievalist poems in *The Defence of Guenevere* (1858) and *The Earthly Paradise* (1868–70) with an eroticism associated in the nineteenth century with romantic poetics. This chapter seeks to recover the particular kind of historical and erotic content that Victorians like Morris found in, and worked to draw out of, the "fleshly" form of rhyme.

Chapter 6, "Coventry Patmore's Passionate Pause," turns to the prosodic theory and poetry of an important later Victorian. I argue that Patmore's synthesis of Romantic literary historiography, ode theory, and Tennysonian formalism allowed him to develop his quasi-scientific system for putting feelings into poetic forms. Examining Patmore's 1850 review of *In Memoriam*, his influential "Essay on English Metrical Law," and his late elegiac odes, the chapter explores the historiographic aspects of Patmore's prosodic thought. I see Patmore's prosody intervening in the conversations about rhyme and the nature of the ode that he began to engage in his *In Memoriam* review. Was the ode, as Edmund Gosse believed, a transhistorical genre rooted in Greek poetry, or was it, as J. G. Herder had argued, a dynamic idea about how individual poetic cultures, with their particular cultures of feeling, express themselves? And what was rhyme's role in a truly English ode? In the elegiac odes of *The Unknown Eros* (1877), Patmore puts his historiographic and affective theory to the test, constructing coherent systems of feeling from irregular patterns of rhyme and pause. In doing so, he aspires to a new poetic idiom—distinct from both classical and romantic prosodies, and suggestive of modernist free verse—where form and feeling might be more perfectly in tune.

The book ends with a brief coda on early twentieth-century poetry and Ezra Pound's *The Spirit of Romance* (1910), a work that appears to conjure New Critical reading methods from the fading world of nineteenth-century literary historiography.

PART I

Genetic Formalism: A Theory and Its Histories

1

Old Historicism, New Criticism, and the Feeling in Form

This chapter presents a theoretical argument, in the form of a historical argument, about the relationship between formal and historical approaches to literature. It argues that both the methodological models that separate history from form and those that seek a compromise between history and form have made it difficult to understand the historicism internal to Victorian poetic forms. They have also made it difficult to acknowledge the ways historical methods shaped the apparently ahistorical and antihistorical formalisms of the twentieth century.

Stories about the discipline of English studies, especially the ones about the fate of formalism in the American academy, tend to describe a long contest between history and form.[1] First there was literary history (often retrospectively called "the old historicism"), then form triumphed over history (New Criticism), then history triumphed over form (New Historicism), then came the various returns to form or promises of reconciliation between form and history.[2] This narrative has resulted in an almost complete forgetting of the nineteenth-century context from which twentieth-century poetics emerged. The problem has to do with our ways of talking about that initial event: the triumph of form over literary history.[3] In my reading, New Critical formalism didn't represent a shift from historical to formal (or "extrinsic" to "intrinsic") approaches to poetry. It represented a shift *away* from literary-historical explanations for poetic form. In other words, what changed with New Criticism was not that form became the object of literary theory for the first time, but that literary history was no longer the primary means of theorizing literary form, as it had been throughout the nineteenth century. New Critical formalism was a reaction against literary historiography's ways of knowing literary form. It has consequently limited our sense of Victorian poetry and poetics, whose primary model of form was historical. For this reason, I think the distinction between form and history that literary studies has often assumed to be a natural state of affairs would have looked counterintuitive, even incomprehensible, to nineteenth-century poets, poetic theorists, and readers. This is not an argument against the thing we call *form*; it is an argument for knowing that thing better, both in the nineteenth century and after.

Let me reiterate why rhyme is at the center of an argument about literary historiography, the aesthetics of Victorian poetry, and the history of our methods. One answer is recursive: rhyme binds all of these together. Rhyme was a battleground for modernist poetics, and it remains closely identified with Victorian poetry and its excesses.[4] Rhyme was also, relatedly, a site of negotiation for New Critical formalism; the polemics of close reading relied on the ahistoricity of rhyme, on an idea of rhyme as pure form.[5] This idea of rhyme was a rather violent departure from nineteenth-century poetic theory, where rhyme was a historiographic form. In the nineteenth century, rhyme was not just a detail of literary historiography's narratives. It was a figure for literary history itself. Rhyme represented the end of classical poetics and the origin of modern European literature; it was a periodizing force, marking out literary history's subsequent progression; it was both an agent and measure of cultural change. Victorian rhyme, as a technical feature of Victorian poems, was rich with these meanings.[6] The story of rhyme theory across the nineteenth and twentieth centuries—rhyme's transition from a historiographic to an ahistorical form—is an untold story about how we read and think about literature.

In what follows, I examine the ideas of form and rhyme developed in American formalism in relation to the eighteenth- and nineteenth-century literary-historiographic models they were meant to displace. First, I will address the meaning of form in contemporary method debates, and I will show that, despite ongoing efforts to retheorize the concept, we are still relying on a New Critical paradigm. That paradigm, of an ahistorical formalism, is best illuminated by the American New Critics' redescription of rhyme as an "intrinsic" element of poetry and its redescription of literary history as "extrinsic" background and by W. K. Wimsatt and Monroe Beardsley's still powerful critical "fallacies." I will show that the New Critical evacuation of literary history from rhyme was correlated to a novel view of form as objective rather than affective. Cutting form off from literary-historical thinking also meant cutting it off from a whole repertoire of feelings associated with historiographic form—and rendering those formal feelings, including the ones encoded in Victorian poems, hard to read. In the last part of this chapter, I reflect on the significance of these methodological developments for the field of Victorian poetry.

DEHISTORICIZING FORM

In order to begin measuring the distance between nineteenth- and twentieth-century literary formalisms, we need first to acknowledge that there has been some consensus about what form has meant for professional literary studies. But it has become conventional to emphasize the open-endedness of the word, the problem that *form* is both ubiquitous and elusive. In the introductory chapter of her 2007 book *On Form*, Angela Leighton tracks form's shifting meanings for Romantic and post-Romantic aesthetics, celebrating the word's "dense and crowded," "pliable" character, its "multiform potential."[7] Leighton confronts this confusion with a chronologically ordered catalog of definitions, opting for an etymological narrative of usage instead of a synthetic definition. Abigail Zitin's *Practical Form* (2020) likewise traces the history of the idea across eighteenth-century aesthetics, recovering an overlooked pre-Kantian concept of form derived from art practice and its theorization. Zitin argues that "what looks like a constant is actually a variable: aesthetic form is not the same, in the 1790s, as it was in the 1740s."[8] Caroline Levine's *Forms* (2015) is less an etymology or an intellectual history than a polemic for opening the word to wider usage still, to all manner of social and institutional arrangements, in order to export the skills of close reading to political analysis. But she still relies on a familiar idea of form's "conflicting, sometimes even paradoxical meanings" to license her polemic. In literary studies, she says, "the vocabulary of formalism has always been a surprising kind of hodge-podge," so the word "form" need not be restricted to the aesthetic at all.[9] In their essay "Form and Explanation" (2017), Jonathan

Kramnick and Anahid Nersessian survey such "versions of form" on the way to a polemic against the kind of polemic that makes us choose one "form" over others. They argue that what appears to be inconsistency and contradiction across usages is in fact proof that the concept of form is "inquiry relative," and that literary studies tolerates, indeed, thrives on, a range of meanings for the word.

Collectively, these metaformalist arguments remind us that form has meant many diverse things in both the history and the prehistory of the discipline. But I don't think it follows that we need to abandon specifying what form is, what its common ground of meaning might be. Why do we understand one another when we name disparate literary objects as forms? Kramnick and Nersessian suggest that we recognize as form that which the formalist attends to and explains; form is "an entity known by occasion, through encounters with its subsidiary phenomena."[10] This answer is appealingly generous, but to my mind it overstates the range of objects that literary scholars have called forms. I want to insist that "form" *does* have a consistent meaning for literary studies. The understanding of form that scholars generally share is that form is the literary object separated, however provisionally, from what in the nineteenth century went by the name of literary history: all those histories—intellectual, biographical, aesthetic, linguistic, cultural, political, economic—involved in the existence of literary works.

This separation of form from history characterizes the aesthetic formalism that has no use for history; it also characterizes the "activist" or "historically informed" formalism that puts form and history in relation to one another.[11] For unhistorical formalism, an essential separateness from history is the point. For historically informed formalism, the same separateness from history is the premise from which the New Formalist critic begins the project of making history and form converse. To read a sonnet, a rhyme, a foot, a plot for history is always form *and* history, where form is necessarily not the same as history (even if we agree with Caroline Levine that all the world is made of forms). Sandra Macpherson's appeal for "a little formalism that would turn one away from history without shame or apology" is an appeal for a return to form as just shape. Here, form's separateness from history needs the protection of the properly formalist critic against the pressures of a New Formalism that "ransoms form with history."[12] Macpherson suggests not only that it is possible to isolate form from history but that it is formalism's highest calling. Her formalism may be a strong one, involving natural objects as well as poems, but it ultimately reinforces a doctrine that is broadly accepted in the discipline.

Form's separateness from history is so familiar a definition that it hardly seems to count as one—or perhaps the problem is that negative definitions can feel like partial definitions. So let me propose a more positive and, I think, more precise definition of form. It is not exactly that form is separate from history. It is that literary form has meant, since early in the twentieth century, the *effort* to put literary history aside, the effort to make literary history seem exterior to literature so that literature can appear to us as just shape. The historicizing impulse and the consequent need to dehistoricize, with effort, are fundamental to our disciplinary conception of literary form (in this respect, *form* remains distinct from *genre*).[13] Dehistoricizing efforts were made explicitly and repeatedly in some key moments of discipline formation, at the origins of close reading; these were reactions against the earlier historical view of form. And the dehistoricizing effort happens anew every time we attend to form per se, as part of the method of close reading. Understanding "form" as the name for this kind of analytic effort, the exteriorizing and pushing away of history, also helps us understand something of literary studies' methodological rhythms: the swings back and forth between formalisms and historicisms, the various polemics for uniting once and for all the polarities of history and form. To bring form and history together is not to bridge a great divide but to confront the real meaning of form for modern literary studies. *Form* already is both form and history: the form we want to see and the literary history we are trying to look away from.

When the New Critics theorized their formalist practice in the mid-twentieth century, they were training their readers in the dehistoricizing effort I have been describing. In *The Well Wrought Urn* (1947), Cleanth Brooks characterized his formalism as an experiment in unhistorical thinking. "If literary history has not been emphasized in the pages that follow," he wrote, "it is not because I discount its importance, or because I have failed to take it into account. It is rather that I have been anxious to see what residuum, if any, is left after we have referred the poem to its cultural matrix."[14] It is an effort, Brooks suggests, to put history and our historicist training aside (indeed, his womb metaphor establishes genetic explanation as almost inevitable), but it is an effort that he believes will bring us closer to the poem itself. As Susan Wolfson has observed, critiques of Brooks's antihistoricism have often ignored the "dialectic *with* historicism" evident in such passages, where Brooks is not really refusing history *tout court* in emphasizing the quality of attention demanded by formalism.[15] While it is true that Brooks's antihistoricism has sometimes been exaggerated, I would add that the dialectic model that Wolfson relies on creates confusion of a different sort. For the dialectic to work, literary history and literary form need to be wrenched apart and made conceptually distinct; literary history needs to become an external context, an outside that the inside, form, either refuses or interacts with. What the language of dialectic distracts from is this prior effort to exteriorize history from form.

In later decades, when the close reading experiment became a habit of the discipline, the separation of history and form that Brooks had rhetorically performed came to seem intuitive. But even contemporary formalist reading, even the New Formalist dialectical kind, always demands that initial gesture: the holding at bay—just barely, with effort—of everything that isn't the form. Only then, when the text has been sufficiently dehistoricized to appear *as* form, is history allowed back in.

A GENETIC FORMALISM

Behind New Critical formalism—the formalism we know best—was another literary formalism that we hardly remember at all. That formalism was a *genetic* one, where literary history was understood to be intrinsic to literary form. As I intend it, genetic formalism is the idea, developed in eighteenth- and nineteenth-century literary historiography, that a form's history determines and explains its aesthetic effects, that its genesis is the key to understanding it as technique. Rhyme was at the center of nineteenth-century genetic-formalist thinking. For Romantic-era literary historians, European rhymed poetry began in medieval Provençal lyric, and so the form of rhyme remains an embodiment of the medieval, romantic feelings it was invented to express. This history of the romantic and its concept of form were enormously influential for the nineteenth-century theory and practice of poetry. Recognizing genetic formalism requires looking past our familiar understandings of form and literary history; it also requires adjustment to our histories of the discipline, especially our story about the rise of formalism.

To what extent is the story wrong? Formalism did displace literary historiography, certainly in the classroom, and at least for a time, and that initial displacement did set the terms for each new displacement that came after. But the New Critics were closer to the literary historiography they were working against than we are; they were trained in it, and they knew it better than we do now. A careful reading of New Critical texts alongside their antecedents reveals that the New Critics were dealing with a more subtle problem than form versus history. They were dealing with the problem of what literary history is for, and how its mode of thinking relates to the interpretation of literary form. The story we tell about formalism in literary studies misses something important about New Criticism and the literary historiography it was apparently replacing: the fact that the old historiography, with its genetic explanations, involved a kind of formalism, too.

One major source for that formalism was J. G. Herder, whose empathic historical method influenced both the return to romantic aesthetics and the general historicist ethos of so much nineteenth-century thought. Across his philosophical writings, Herder explored poetry's ramifying pathways backward into its diverse cultural histories (the process he described as feeling one's way in) in order to arrive at a philosophical account of poetic forms. Deep historical inquiry, he argued, is the basis of aesthetic explanation. His fragmentary "Essay on a History of Lyrical Poetry" (1766) offers a compelling justification for this genetic method.[16] He writes,

> [I]t is not only pleasing but also necessary to search for the origins of matters that one wishes to understand with a measure of completeness. Lacking the origin, we obviously miss a part of the history, and how importantly does the history serve the explanation of the whole, especially the most important part of the history from which, in the end, everything is derived; for, as the tree may be derived from its root, the progress and flowering of an art must be derivable from its source. Just as the seed contains, concealed within itself, the entire plant with all its parts, the source of an art contains within itself the entire nature of its product.[17]

Herder declares that the origin *is* the nature of the art form; history *is* the meaning of the form. Origin hunting is a pleasure, but it is also serious and vital work for the poetic theorist. This rendered the theorist also, necessarily, a historian. And, indeed, Herder's genetic method—which led him into an anthropological study of numerous literary cultures beyond Germany—made him an originator of the generalist literary historiography that I am concerned with in this book. As René Wellek wrote (in a wonderfully Herderian phrase), Herder was "the fountainhead of universal literary history."[18]

I'll return to the literary context in a moment, but first I want to point out how familiar, even natural, Herder's view of art looks from the vantage point of Victorian art theory. In John Ruskin's well-known presentation of gothic architecture in *The Stones of Venice* (1853), for example, the architectural form can be read as an "out-speaking" or "expression of its origin," an aesthetic record of human life and human feeling in the Middle Ages. As Ruskin explains, "Gothic architecture has external forms and internal elements. Its elements are certain mental tendencies of the builders, legibly expressed in it; as fancifulness, love of variety, love of richness, and such others. Its external forms are pointed arches, vaulted roofs, etc." According to Ruskin's theory, the meaning of an architectural feature like the pointed arch is its historical-spiritual content. His injunction to read "the stones" like "stanzas" suggests that a broader, or at least kindred, formalism animates architectural and literary material—and indeed, the analogy of medieval literature to gothic architecture was a frequent theme of nineteenth-century histories of art and poetry.[19] Walter Pater's *The Renaissance* (1873), which treats a range of visual and literary art forms, also evinces a genetic-formalist method. For instance, Pater writes that fifteenth-century sculpture "shares with the paintings of Botticelli and the churches of Brunelleschi that profound expressiveness, that intimate impress of an indwelling soul, which is the peculiar fascination of the art of Italy in that century." Here, the pathos-inflected planes of bas-relief, the "wan" coloring and "minor tones" of a painted Madonna, and the dome of a Tuscan cathedral all speak out their historical origin.[20]

Despite the familiarity of these touchstones of Victorian aesthetics, it has not been easy to extend this mode of thinking to our understanding of Victorian *literary* forms because of the particular distortions of our disciplinary history-to-form narrative. Yet nineteenth-century poetic theory also involved fantasies about the history of form. As I have been suggesting, one of the most powerful historiographic fantasies was about the forms and feelings of modern, or "romantic," literature. In Romantic-era literary historiography—the early comparative and synoptic projects of Thomas Warton, the Schlegel brothers, Germaine de Staël, Simonde de Sismondi, and others—efforts to recover medieval literature from damning neoclassical standards involved new investigations into the development of modern European poetics, especially the genre of romance and the form of rhyme. Provençal lyrics, French romances, Dante's terza rima, Petrarch's sonnets, Chaucer's and Spenser's stanzas and stories, Shakespeare's "organic" rhymes, nineteenth-century Romantic poetry: these constituted a discrete literary tradition. The tradition was "romantic" in that it arose from the postclassical melting pot of Southern European medieval cultures and vernaculars (i.e., the Romance languages). "Romantic" also came to name the repertoire of imaginative and emotional elements associated with romantic literary forms: strangeness and magic, adventure, chivalry, the feelings of romantic love.

Since romantic love ostensibly emerged in tandem with romantic rhyme, the feelings of romantic love—its specifically medieval varieties of desire and longing—were thought to have encoded themselves in the rhyme form. So not only does rhymed poetry have a romantic origin, but it retains that origin as part of its structure and meaning.[21] On this model, rhyme is a translated and *translatable* form: the linguistic contingencies often thought to hamper rhyme's translatability (evident, for instance, in the gap between rhyme-rich Provençal or Italian and rhyme-poor English) are trivial compared with the persistent historical meaning and feeling rhyme carries.

This genetic logic is already operative in August Schlegel's groundbreaking account of "the origin and spirit of the *romantic*" in his *Course of Lectures on Dramatic Art and Literature,* which were delivered in Vienna in 1808 (translated into English by John Black in 1815). In the introductory lecture, Schlegel sketches "the grand division" of romantic and classical poetry in baldly affective and genetic terms: "the poetry of the ancients was the poetry of enjoyment, and ours is that of desire: the former has its foundation in the scene which is present, while the latter hovers betwixt recollection and hope." Schlegel adds that romantic poetry's tone of desiring, even in the present, is the permanent residue of its medieval Christian origin. "Let me not be understood to affirm that every thing flows in one strain of wailing and complaint, and that the voice of melancholy must always be loudly heard . . . but still [romantic poetry] will always, in some shape or other, *bear traces of the source from which it originated*."[22] The strong imprint of Herder's method is visible on this genetic definition of modern, romantic poetry.

Germaine de Staël, who had facilitated Schlegel's lecture series during their time together at Coppet, presented a famous reformulation of his scheme in *Germany* (*De l'Allemagne*, 1813); she also found in Schlegel's poetry of desire, recollection, and hope a concrete suggestion about romantic poetic *form*. Following Schlegel, de Staël defines romantic literature as "that kind of poetry which is derived from the songs of the Troubadours; that which owes its birth to the union of chivalry and Christianity," and her view of the poetics of rhyme aligns with that origin story. She sees rhyme as "a modern discovery" whose operations follow chivalry's affective structure. Rhyme, she writes, "is the image of hope and of memory. One sound makes us desire another, corresponding to it; and when the second is heard, it recalls that which has just escaped us."[23] In other words, rhyme is a structure of erotic desire and loss, and reading romantic rhyme still makes us feel those romantic feelings. This is a point that another of de Staël's associates, J. C. L. Simonde de Sismondi, sharpened further in his ambitious, multivolume history of Mediterranean literature, *Historical View of the Literature of the South of Europe* (*De la littérature du Midi de l'Europe*, 1813; trans. 1823). In discovering rhyme, an invention he thought was borrowed from Arabic poetry, the troubadours discovered the prosodic form of romantic longing.[24] Thus, if rhyme calls up our desire, it is because rhyme was, first of all, an expression of desire. "Rhyme," Sismondi writes, "is an appeal to our memory and to our expectations."[25] Again, the history of the form doubles as a theory of the form.

I want to emphasize once more the strangeness of this line of thinking in relation to twentieth-century protocols for understanding poetry. We have inherited from the New Critics an idea of rhyme as pure form, as a structural rather than historical feature of a poem. In the first edition of Cleanth Brooks and Robert Penn Warren's foundational textbook *Understanding Poetry* (1938), for instance, we find that rhyme "forms" poetry by "bind[ing] lines together into larger units of composition"; that it "set[s] up in the mind of the hearer or reader an anticipation of regular recurrence," even that "there is of course a pleasure intrinsic in rime itself." But these effects of rhyme are not presented as historically meaningful, and Brooks and Warren assert elsewhere that no "specific emotional effect can be tied absolutely to a particular metrical instance."[26] There may be "anticipation" and "pleasure" in a reader's experience of rhyme, but they are not correlated to romantic feeling, and certainly not to an imagined origin of Provençal love. Of course, the New Critics also taught us a skepticism about the interpretive value of origin stories. We now know not to confuse an aesthetic object with a story about how the aesthetic object came to be. The most famous version of this error is W. K. Wimsatt and Monroe Beardsley's "intentional fallacy," a variety of genetic fallacy that assumes biographical or historical data can explain a poem. Poetry teachers still train their students to think less about origins and more about the poem in front of them. It would be a kind of genetic fallacy to claim that rhyme's origins determine its effects. But what if a genetic idea like this enters poetic theory and poetic technique?

While it may or may not be a historical fact that rhyme developed as a language of longing, it remains the case that Victorians widely believed in this history of rhyme (instead of a genetic fallacy, we might call it a *genetic fantasy*), and that historical story often conditioned their theorization, practice, and reception of the form. When, for instance, Arthur Hallam wrote in 1831 that rhyme "contain[s] in itself a constant appeal to Memory and Hope," he was describing what we now think of as rhyme's formal and emotional structure, but he was also invoking those earlier romantic histories, and in the context of a historical essay of his own about the romantic literary tradition and the influence of Arabic, Provençal, and Italian poetics on English literature. And when he praised Alfred Tennyson's first volume for its evocation of "Tuscan song" and its "exquisite modulation of harmonious words and cadences to the swell and fall of the feelings expressed," he was aligning Tennyson with the affective poetics of the romantic tradition.[27] When Coventry Patmore celebrated *In Memoriam* in 1850 for its "complete metrical science and feeling," and when he reminded his readers, there and in his influential "Essay on English Metrical Law" (1857), of the "rule" that "rhyme has been said to appeal to memory and hope," he also had

Romantic historiography's genetic fantasy (and Hallam's Victorian mediation of it) in view.[28]

"INTRINSIC" READING AND THE NEW CRITICAL FALLACIES

So what happened to that variety of formalism after the nineteenth century? In this section, I identify some moments in twentieth-century criticism when we can see genetic formalism losing its explanatory power, as twentieth-century critics worked to develop a more autonomous and objective theory of form. I argue that many of New Criticism's key concepts—the "intrinsic" and "extrinsic" approaches to literature, the "intentional fallacy" and "affective fallacy"—should be understood as strategic responses to the genetic idea of form. The New Critical close-reading method was a means of isolating from one another aspects of literary knowledge that were fused together in genetic formalism: knowledge about the literary past, knowledge about what poetry feels like, knowledge about poetic technique. In promoting the objective analysis of poetic technique, the New Critics meant to circumvent the interpretive difficulties of the genetic explanation, not only its dependence on historical information but also its openness to the feelings of historical forms. It is a mark of the success of the New Critical project that we no longer think of form, history, and feeling as intrinsically connected aspects of literary study—that, in fact, it is quite hard to think them back together. But we need to do that if we want to understand nineteenth-century forms on their own, rather than twentieth-century, terms.

W. K. Wimsatt and Monroe Beardsley's "Intentional Fallacy" essay was a central contribution to the critique of genetic reasoning pursued across the disciplines of philosophy, history, and literature in the twentieth century.[29] But as early as the 1910s, literary critics in Russia were already challenging the genetic fantasy as a faulty model of aesthetic form. According to Boris Eichenbaum's 1926 retrospect on the "Theory of the 'Formal Method,'" the Russian Formalists articulated their new concept of form-as-function in relation to the earlier literary-historical scholarship of their teachers. When the Formalists eventually incorporated literary history into their formalist method, it was a historiography of "evolutionary dynamics" focused on the way forms act on forms through historical time.[30] This historiography was an explicit repudiation of Alexander Veselovsky's nineteenth-century method, which emphasized the social genesis of literary forms.[31] The Formalists viewed Veselovsky's ethnographic literary scholarship (influenced by Herder, de Staël, and other European Romantics) as unscientific, a collection of "historical-genetic hypotheses," rather than a theoretical account of literary form.[32] For Eichenbaum, Viktor Shklovsky, and their Formalist cohort, "an explanation of the genetics of [a literary] phenomenon, even if true, does not clarify the phenomenon as a fact of literature."[33] Eichenbaum allows that the genetic explanation may tell us something about history, but that does not make it a satisfactory theory of form.

For the midcentury American New Critics, the formalist practice of close reading required a similar turn away from the genetic explanations offered by literary historiography. But the New Critics also sought to draw a cleaner line between historical and formal methods (and, sometimes, to make their case on moral grounds). On the American side, the Boswell scholar Frederick Pottle stood for the type of genetic historicism (and its troubling consequence, critical relativism) that the New Critics resisted. In *The Well Wrought Urn*, when Brooks argues for the prerogative of the formalist critic to make normative judgments about literature, it is Pottle's frankly historicist and relativist study *The Idiom of Poetry* (1941) that serves as his foil.[34] Brooks considered a universal and transhistorical "standard of values" to be necessary for the criticism of poetry; Pottle felt that absolutism compromised critical understanding. But in the preface to the second edition of *Idiom*, Pottle insisted that he was "a relativist in aesthetics . . . not a relativist in morals" and that he was "no enemy to formalism."[35] A later essay of Pottle's helpfully describes an avowedly "genetic" literary historiography as it was practiced in the midcentury American academy:

> Our philosophy of literary history was probably strongly influenced by the then reigning "scientific" mode in political history and ultimately by the philosophy of natural science. Our natural way of thinking was genetic, and genetic in terms of what Aristotle calls efficient cause, cause from behind, not of what he called final cause or teleology. Consequently, our thinking was strongly chronological. A given poem B

> was written at a particular time X, after a poem A and before a poem C. It had a cause, its author an historical individual; he was influenced by the thought of his time and the literature he had read. This philosophy favored all kinds of close historical study: linguistic, biographical, history of ideas.[36]

Pottle's description of the historicist frame of mind aligns him with earlier practitioners of genetic scholarship. It also reveals something of the methodological variety that characterized literary studies in the moment of New Criticism. But it is clear that Pottle is writing retrospectively about a superseded "way of thinking," one that came to seem increasingly inadequate to the task of literary criticism.

In their influential *Theory of Literature* (1949), René Wellek and Austin Warren differentiated between "extrinsic" and "intrinsic" approaches to literary study, a schema that made it difficult to imagine a formalism that contains historical thinking within it, or a historicism that was "no enemy to formalism."[37] Extrinsic methods address conditions external to the work of art: biography, psychology, social history, the history of ideas (the objects of Pottle's approach). Intrinsic methods pay attention to the poem per se (sound effects like rhyme and meter, stylistics, patterns of image and metaphor, narrative), as well as classifications of genre and principles of evaluation.[38] Intriguingly, the "Intrinsic" portion of the book ends with a chapter called "Literary History," in which Wellek laments the absence of a truly *literary* history, "an internal history" of literature based on aesthetic rather than genetic criteria. This aspirational idea of literary history (inspired, partly, by the Russian Formalists) is presented as a contrast to the dominant kind of extrinsic scholarship that treats literary-historical background or context.

Wellek and Warren were interested in both intrinsic and extrinsic methods; Wellek, in particular, was extraordinarily learned in the history and theory of literary historiography, including the Russian tradition. But they saw formalism's turn toward the intrinsic as "a healthy reaction" against prevailing historicisms, a recognition that "the study of literature should, first and foremost, concentrate on the actual works of art themselves." At best, they felt, literary history (in its broader sense) offers a useful supplement to the work of art; at worst, it "becomes a 'causal' explanation, professing to account for literature, to explain it, and finally to reduce it to its origins (the 'fallacy of origins')." "Yet it is clear," they continue, "that causal study can never dispose of problems of description, analysis, and evaluation of an object such as a work of literary art." These latter problems are the purview of the intrinsic approach, which eschews the possibility that an idea about literary-historical origins might inhere in the form itself. Such an idea would constitute a fallacy of origins, which Wellek and Warren categorize as a distinctly nineteenth-century historiographic mistake.[39]

"The fallacy of origins" of course calls to mind the most powerful New Critical fallacies of all: the intentional fallacy and the affective fallacy. If Wellek and Warren codified the distinction between intrinsic and extrinsic approaches to literature by organizing their book according to those categories, W. K. Wimsatt made the distinction orthodoxy; he also demonstrated how a critic properly vigilant about the fallacies could produce a new model of rhyme. The fallacies essays, which Wimsatt coauthored with the philosopher Monroe Beardsley and republished in his 1954 book *The Verbal Icon*, are best appreciated alongside another important essay of Wimsatt's in that volume, "One Relation of Rhyme to Reason." Taken together, these three essays represent the full unraveling of the genetic theory of form. That Wimsatt intended the essays to be taken together is clear from the introduction to *The Verbal Icon*, where he writes that the chapters of the book "represent . . . what I believe has been my consistent approach to the literary problem at various levels. . . . I believe the essays approximate a rounded whole."[40] Wimsatt's aim in the volume is an account of the poem unencumbered by either extrinsic information or reader response. His name for this unencumbered poem is "technique." He sees the fallacies as evasions that "have frequently come about through a critic's distaste for problems of technique," through an indifference to "technical features (rhyme or figures)" (xvi–xvii). That is, technique is wholly distinct from questions of history and feeling, and attention to history or feeling is necessarily an avoidance of technique. This is of course a total inversion of the logic of genetic form, where a technical feature like rhyme is nothing if not the repository of historical and affective information.

The fallacy essays, in fact, directly address nineteenth-century attitudes toward poetry. "Intention" signifies many things for Wimsatt and Beardsley, but its most immediate meaning is the intention of the author, for which "the critic must go outside the poem" to biography, psychology, literary history, the history of ideas (4). The desire to know what the author intended derives from a conviction that poems are basically expressive of the author's mind and the author's moment. For Wimsatt and Beardsley, this is an old-fashioned critical attitude. They explain, "It is not so much a historical statement as a definition to say that the intentional fallacy is a romantic one" (6). Modern critics should adhere to "internal" rather than "external" evidence, the "objective way of criticism" rather than the "genetic inquiry" (10, 18).[41] If the intentional fallacy is "a confusion between the poem and its origins, a special case of what is known to philosophers as the Genetic Fallacy," the affective fallacy is "a confusion between the poem and its *results*" (21). But this fallacy also has a nineteenth-century origin, deriving from ideas in "romantic reader psychology" about how poems can move readers (34). When a modern critic is tempted, as I. A. Richards often was and as Cleanth Brooks sometimes was, to focus on a reader's emotional response, he must reframe his question in purely intrinsic, objective, and technical terms, in terms of "the poem itself" (33–34).

What might an objective analysis of technique look like if it admits neither historical nor emotional explanation? We have an answer in Wimsatt's famous essay on rhyme. "One Relation of Rhyme to Reason" remains a uniquely important theory of rhyme in general and Alexander Pope's couplet technique in particular.[42] Wimsatt's purpose in the essay is to argue for rhyme as an intellectual rather than emotional structure. He does this through an analysis of rhyme's "semantic character," or the relationship between the meanings of rhyming words. Explaining that simple and "forthrightly emotional" poetry depends on the harmonizing of both sound and meaning, Wimsatt shows how poetry that is more "sophisticated and intellectualized" will use nonparallel meaning (disjunction, antithesis, chiasmus), so that a congruence of sound is accompanied by a witty incongruence of meaning, for example, "Queen" and "screen" (155). Since Wimsatt considers chiastic rhyme to be "the most brilliant and complex of all the forms of rhyme variation," he considers Pope to be "one of the finest English rhymers" (163). Wimsatt implies that Pope's virtue is his protomodernist difficulty, and that this kind of poetics has replaced a less modern one that includes Chaucer's verse, balladry, and "other primitive types of poetry, where the equalities of verse coincide with the parallels of meaning," and even Tennyson's "sophisticated" but archaic *In Memoriam* (154). Literary history is present here, but it serves contrast rather than genetic explanation: medieval (or medievalist) poetry versus neoclassical poetry, feeling versus thinking.

The most interesting aspect of this essay, then, is the counterargument that keeps asserting itself and demanding refutation. Against Wimsatt's celebration of Pope is the midcentury consensus that Pope is insincere and (surprisingly, for us) technically deficient (163). Against Wimsatt's radical idea that rhyme depends on incongruence is the sense that it depends on harmony above all (154). Against Wimsatt's argument for rhyme's intellectual sophistication is the conviction that rhyme has an almost magically emotional effect—that it works on the reader's feelings in ways that must confound the analytic mind of the objective critic.

This last position powerfully evokes nineteenth-century literary historiography. When it arises in the essay's closing pages, however, it is attributed to Henry Lanz, whose book *The Physical Basis of Rime: An Essay on the Aesthetics of Sound* (1931) was the main English-language study of rhyme at the time of Wimsatt's writing and thus the primary target in his polemic. Wimsatt objects above all to Lanz's indulgence of the Romantic view that rhyme "is one of those irrational satellites that revolve around reason. It is concerned not with the meaning of verse but only with its form, which is emotional" (165). Lanz's book is notable for the liminal position it occupies between the genetic and the objective models of rhyme. It takes extremely seriously the ineffable feelings elicited by rhyme, but through a scientific accounting of the vibrations of vowels and other physical phenomena in human speech and music.[43] The chapter titles of Lanz's book reveal the extent to which he remains a student of nineteenth-century poetics and historiography at the same time as he is moving toward Wimsatt's ideal of critical objectivity: "Theory of Riming Vowels" (full of charts, sound graphs, and musical notation), but also "Concerning the Origin of Rime," "History of Rime Theories," "The Logic of Emotions," and so on. Through Lanz, we can still see the historical and affective fantasies that governed the theory of rhyme before New Criticism made it an intrinsic and ahistorical kind of form.

Wimsatt suggests that his focus on semantic meaning involves the substitution of an intellectual for an emotional idea of rhyme.[44] But it is really a more complex set of displacements. It substitutes the contingent meaning of words for the inherent meaning of a form. It substitutes the technical intelligence of rhyme for rhyme's relationship to intellectual history. It substitutes the fantasy of a purely intrinsic explanation for the genetic explanations that continued to trouble the intrinsic/extrinsic divide. All of which is to say that the emotional idea of rhyme is also an intellectual idea of rhyme; it holds inside of it a theory of literary history, a whole international tradition of thinking about the origins and feelings of literary forms. To the extent that our discipline remembers that tradition, it is as the old historicism that New Critical formalism replaced. But it is also the old formalism that New Critical formalism helped us forget.

LITERARY STUDY AND VICTORIAN POETRY

Why should we care about that old formalism? One reason, which I hope to have made clear, is that modern literary studies, with its perpetual method wars, cannot be understood without it. This is, I suppose, a *genetic* claim about the discipline: that its now obscure origin can tell us something essential about its character. But I don't think it is a fallacious claim. New Critical close reading was designed to free us from the genetic explanations that seemed so natural; this is explicit in New Critical theory. We have retained the method of close reading, but we have lost touch with its initial motive—and, consequently, with the kind of thinking about poetry and history, poetry and feeling, feeling and history that close reading theorized against.

Because Victorian poetry emerged from genetic-formalist thinking, that dissociation has made it a particularly elusive analytic object. In the period of New Criticism, a tension between close reading and Victorian poems was already apparent. Indeed, a subplot of the story I've been telling is about the poetry of Tennyson: how central it was to Victorian poetics and, for the same reasons, how challenging it was for New Critical formalism.[45] Tennyson was there in my discussion of Victorian genetic formalism; his poetry occasioned some of Arthur Hallam's and Coventry Patmore's key theoretical pronouncements on form, history, and feeling. And he was there in my survey of New Criticism, too. In Wimsatt's rhyme essay, *In Memoriam* appears as a special exception to the rule exemplified by Pope's verse: it is a poem that is both emotional *and* sophisticated, both dependent on harmonized rhyme *and* formally successful. Tennyson also motivates Wimsatt and Beardsley's formulation of the affective fallacy. When they accuse Cleanth Brooks of mistaking his own emotional response for "the poem itself," they are pointing to Brooks's self-exposing explication of Tennyson's "Tears, Idle Tears" in *The Well Wrought Urn*. Quoting Brooks's observation that "The last stanza evokes an intense emotional response from the reader," Wimsatt and Beardsley counter that "this statement is not really a part of Brooks' criticism of the poem—rather a witness of his fondness for it" (33).

It's not just that Wimsatt and Beardsley catch Brooks accidentally feeling Tennyson's poetry (though there's a little glee in that, too); it's that Brooks has failed to adequately intellectualize his emotional experience, to relocate it from himself to the poem. You could say that Tennyson reveals a vulnerable spot in the theory of close reading. Brooks's objectivity falters over "Tears, Idle Tears," and even Wimsatt has to acknowledge the threat *In Memoriam* poses to his evaluation of Popean rhyme. Clearly, the affective power of Tennyson's poetry was felt even in the twentieth century, even by his sternest critics, even against their own intellectual commitments.

The challenge Tennyson posed to New Critical interpretation is especially evident in Brooks's shifting treatment of his poetry. Wimsatt and Beardsley depict Brooks as uncritically affected by Tennyson's verse, but in *Modern Poetry and the Tradition* (1939), Brooks had used Tennyson as an instrument for devaluing Victorian poetry in general. Declaring that "Victorian poetry hardly calls for extended comment," he attributed its broad aesthetic failure to two of Tennyson's characteristic faults: his "pompous didacticism" and "incredible sentimentality."[46] The damage to Victorian poetry was done, but in *The Well Wrought Urn*, Brooks retreated a little from his earlier critique of "Victorianism" and its feelings. Having been charged by another critic with a careless conflation of "the passionate with the sentimental" and an "exclusiveness" with regard to literary periods, Brooks now offered the more sympathetic chapter on "Tears, Idle Tears" as rebuttal and half-hearted apology. In his analysis of "Tears, Idle Tears," Brooks suggests at first that Tennyson may have "blundered into" a complex and genuinely moving poem. But he ultimately praises Tennyson's management of ambiguity and paradox, demonstrating how the unity and emotional intensity of his poem are produced by its form.[47]

It's telling that in his search for the source of the poem's affective power, Brooks looked only to its broader "structure" and not to its prosody. Form, in his close reading, is the pattern of metaphors, images, and ironic contrasts that hold the poem together. But "Tears, Idle Tears" is a tour de force of stanza and sound effect, an apparently unrhyming poem that is structured by the rhymes that, astonishingly, are not there:

Tears, idle tears, I know not what they mean,
Tears from the depth of some divine despair
Rise in the heart, and gather to the eyes,
In looking on the happy autumn-fields,
And thinking of the days that are no more.

Fresh as the first beam glittering on a sail,
That brings our friends up from the underworld,
Sad as the last which reddens over one
That sinks with all we love below the verge;
So sad, so fresh, the days that are no more.

Ah, sad and strange as in dark summer dawns
The earliest pipe of half-awaken'd birds
To dying ears, when unto dying eyes
The casement slowly grows a glimmering square;
So sad, so strange, the days that are no more.

Dear as remember'd kisses after death,
And sweet as those by hopeless fancy feign'd
On lips that are for others; deep as love,
Deep as first love, and wild with all regret;
O Death in Life, the days that are no more![48]

The poem's prosodic features—its isomorphic stanzas, its strong lineation and terminal emphases, its echoing refrain, its scattered assonance and consonance (what Arthur Hallam called the "diffused resemblances" of romantic rhyme), its irregular and internal rhymes—collude to make end rhyme an overwhelmingly present absence.

Tennyson reported that the poem was about "the passion of the past, the abiding in the transient."[49] It's more specifically about a sequence of related longings—for seasons past and "days that are no more," for our mourned dead, for our own fading life and the world we leave behind, for the beloved who doesn't love us back, for a "first love" that is permanently over—and Tennyson uses its verse form to make all those varieties of longing felt. The poem seems to be built out of unfinished rhymes: diffused half-rhymes, but also a sequence of terminal rhyme halves that never find their matches. As so many critics have suggested, rhyme isn't really missing. It is *missed*.[50]

How exactly does Tennyson create such effects? And why doesn't Brooks comment on this aspect of the poem's form? Why does he say that "the last stanza evokes an intense emotional response from the reader," without offering a theory of the stanza's work as a stanza? Part of the answer is that rhyme was being pried away from its romantic connotations—its genetic associations with history, desire, recollection, and hope. If, as Brooks and Warren wrote in *Understanding Poetry*, no "specific emotional effect can be tied absolutely to a particular metrical instance," then rhyme (or its spectral presence) can't create an emotional atmosphere, or conjure a historical feeling, or move a reader to tears.[51] But that doesn't mean that Brooks was completely insensitive to the emotional quality of Tennyson's sound effects; neither T. S. Eliot nor W. K. Wimsatt was. It seems more likely that he didn't have an adequate account of them. As Graham Hough observed in a 1951 essay responding to Brooks, "It is easy to feel these [sonic] effects, but to me they remain quite unanalyzable."[52] Genetic formalism's feeling-of-history—"the passion of the past" as a literary-historical idea, as a phenomenon of form—had become *just feeling*. And what rushed into the void left by the genetic theory of form were the New Critical dangers of subjectivism, impressionism, and mere appreciation. Tennyson's poem frames the problem well: the tears come, but we "know not what they mean."

Our collective forgetting of genetic formalism has oversimplified our disciplinary history, and it has limited our sense of methodological possibility. It has also been a loss for the study of Victorian poetry, which remains an oddly marginal field. Our familiar literary histories still tend to position Victorian poetry as the maudlin and naive precursor to modernism; poetry survey courses still give short shrift to

Victorian poems; Victorian studies, for the majority of literary scholars, still really means the study of the Victorian novel.[53] I propose that the minor status of Victorian poetry in the discipline is closely connected to our twentieth-century definition of formalism. Victorian poetry often appears to us as sentimental, archaic, over-rhyming, overwrought. Even if we love Victorian poetry, we don't know how to read its feelings rigorously. For so long, formalist rigor and historicist rigor seemed to be the opposite of reading for feeling, so the formalist or historicist reader was left with poetic feelings that embarrassingly exceeded the available critical methods.[54] Genetic formalism explains the mismatch between Victorian poetry and twentieth-century methods; when New Criticism worked to undo genetic formalism, it also made Victorian poems harder to know. Even if we can still feel them, we don't know what it is we are feeling. What we are feeling, this book argues, is a lost knowledge about poetic form.

The chapters that follow show how a renewed acquaintance with that knowledge can change the way we read Victorian poems—and the way we talk about the poetic effects that seem to glitter just beyond the verge of criticism.

⊙ 2 ⊙

Arthur Hallam and the Origins of Rhyme

The last chapter defined genetic formalism through the antihistoricist and antiaffective polemics of New Criticism, in order to show retrospectively what it had been before it was dissolved under the pressure of twentieth-century formalism. This chapter moves in the opposite direction, demonstrating how Victorian genetic formalism developed out of a Romantic genre of literary-historical scholarship called "general literary history." While chapter 1 emphasized the historical nature of nineteenth-century formalism, this chapter draws out the formalism inherent in nineteenth-century literary-historical thought, especially the thought made possible by an international perspective on the history of literature. The figure at the heart of this chapter is Tennyson's close friend, collaborator, and muse Arthur Hallam, whose writings turned the genetic thinking of literary historiography into a foundation for Victorian poetic theory. In Hallam's scholarly understanding of poetry, in his vision of the transnational history of forms, in his passionate belief in the Arabic and Italian origins of English literature, and in his affective theory of rhyme, I see the immediate source of the Victorian genetic formalism whose impact on poetry I explore in the next part of the book.

Until now, I have been arguing that rhyme's meaning changed as New Criticism began, on one hand, to identify form as an ahistorical, objective concept and, on the other, to define literary history as external to literary form. I suggested that the genetic idea of rhyme so important to Victorian poetics became difficult to think about—or even remember—after form and history were made into antithetical objects of critical attention. But New Criticism wasn't the only cause of genetic formalism's decline, even if it definitively turned the page on the genetic theory of rhyme. It was also the case that literary historiography itself changed, both over the nineteenth century and as it entered the modern academy. Academic specialization (in period fields, in national literatures, in more modestly comparative methods) narrowed the scope of literary historiography and altered the kinds of questions that could be asked about poetic form. Put simply, questions about the origin and development of forms are big questions, and they require a similarly expansive conception of literary history.

General literary history (also called "universal" or "synoptic" literary history, or sometimes "world literature") offered that expansive conception of the literary past. It was a genre that emerged in the late eighteenth century, blazed brightly for several decades, and then burned out. An intellectual antecedent of both modern literary history writing and the discipline of comparative literature, general literary history aimed for a broad, though not necessarily universal, view of literary development over historical time and across national and linguistic boundaries.[1] Most ambitiously, it treated "all literature," ancient and modern; or, more moderately, just the literature of Europe or the literature of the Mediterranean or the European literature of the last three centuries. The tradition was itself international and multilingual, including public lecture series and popular multivolume books in Italian, Spanish, German, French, and English.

For all its limitations, general literary history had special capacities. As René Wellek and Austin Warren observed in defense of that extinct genre, its "super-national" purview had acknowledged a fundamental historical reality: the history of forms, themes, genres, techniques, metrics, and even literary movements "is obviously an international history." By contrast, nation- and period-bound literary histories can only be partial histories of literary phenomena. Wellek and Warren traced the genre back to "the founders of literary history in the nineteenth century: such men as the Schlegels, Bouterwek, Sismondi, and Hallam," and they saw the promise of its revival in the work of their own contemporaries, Ernst Robert Curtius and Erich Auerbach.[2] They also saw general literary history as the ultimate horizon of literary-historical scholarship. "Literary history as a synthesis," they wrote, "literary history on a super-national scale, will have to be written again.... [I]n this conception lies the future of historical literary studies."[3]

Although the international history of forms was one reason why

Wellek and Warren valued general literary history, their intrinsic/extrinsic binary effectively isolated formalist interpretive practices from what they called "historical literary studies." And this binary has held for some more recent aspirants to Wellek and Warren's ideal. Franco Moretti, for instance, theorizes his idea of "distant reading" as antonym to the method of close reading (even as he avows both "sociological formalism" and comparative morphology as approaches to world literature).[4] However, the nineteenth-century version of general literary history had rich intellectual ties to practices of formal interpretation, precisely *because* its bird's-eye view and narrative style lent themselves to genetic stories about forms. This isn't to say that general literary history was primarily a history of forms; it wasn't. Rather, stories of literary forms ran alongside accounts of the political and economic history of nations, the formation of vernacular languages, biographies of authors, critical descriptions of literary masterpieces, and philosophical reflections on the historical forces of progress or decline. But for nineteenth-century readers interested in the craft of poetry, those genetic stories suggested a powerful theory of form and its uses.

Arthur Hallam was one such reader. In this chapter and the next, I show how his intimate familiarity with general literary history—through his own study and through the scholarly community of his historian father, Henry Hallam—helped him invent Victorian poetry as a distinct aesthetic category. I follow a critical consensus in regarding Hallam as one of the first and most significant theorists of Victorian poetics and his friend Alfred Tennyson's *Poems, Chiefly Lyrical* (1830) as an origin point for Victorian poetry itself. But here I further specify why that was so. I argue that Hallam's critical prose and Tennyson's early poems represent translations of the genetic claims of literary history into new principles for making and interpreting poetic forms—in other words, for a Victorian historiographic poetics.

A key to that poetics is Arthur Hallam's famously enigmatic statement on rhyme: "Rhyme has been said to contain in itself a constant appeal to Memory and Hope." Although Hallam's statement has become an axiom of formalist close reading in the field, in its original context—an essay on Italian and English literature—it described a set of *historical* phenomena: the migration of rhyme from Arabic to Provençal poetry and the cultivation of rhyme's expressive properties by the troubadours. Hallam borrowed his idea from Romantic literary history writing, most directly from Jean Charles Léonard Simonde de Sismondi's *Historical View of the Literature of the South of Europe* (1813). This intellectual background matters, both for our understanding of Victorian poetics and for our ways of approaching questions of form. It affirms that in the nineteenth-century imagination, rhyme's effects were tied to its origins: no form without history. Victorian rhyme theory involved a genetic fantasy about the origin of European poetry, and it arose from the "extrinsic" material of general literary historiography. Following Hallam's sentence back to its sources thus compels us to better historicize our own concept of form.

It also compels us to think more elastically about the linguistic and cultural boundaries of Victorian literature itself, even if that means straining against the conventions of specialization. Victorian writers (many of whom knew more languages than the scholars who now study them) had a more intricate understanding of English literature than our own. They read and wrote about the international histories of forms, and they used those histories to reimagine the possibilities of English poetry. Shaped as we are by the disciplinary divide between English literature and comparative literature, we can miss the ways comparative and generalist thinking shaped English literature before those disciplines formed.[5] Hallam's theory of rhyme points toward a concept of English poetry as already, and inherently, international. It suggests that Victorian poets had a larger literary world in view not just when they read or translated non-English verse, but as soon as they set out to think with, and think in, rhyme.

The view of literature that Hallam presents in his literary-historical writing is generalist and international, but it is not global. Hallam is interested in a specific line of transnational development that moves from Arabic to European vernacular literature. While elucidating English poetry is his motivation, English is not a privileged telos. Rather, Hallam is trying to undo an English fantasy of linguistic and cultural purity by returning to so-called origins. Showing that English literature is partly made from Italian literature, and Italian literature is partly made from Provençal literature, and Provençal literature is partly made from Arabic literature, he argues that national literatures are compounds, not elements. Rhyme is one proof that the forms and feelings of English literature were never only English.

This chapter begins by looking very closely at Hallam's genetic idea of literary form, and especially his account of the origin of rhyme. It then locates Arthur Hallam's criticism in a Romantic intellectual milieu that includes Hegel, Henry Hallam, and Sismondi. My aim in this chapter is to show, broadly, how literary history was transformed into poetic theory in the nineteenth century; and, more particularly, how a controversial origin story from general literary historiography became an affective and genetic theory of rhyme. In part 2 of this book, I recover the significance of that genetic theory for Victorian poetic practice.

ARTHUR HALLAM'S CRITICISM

Aside from his statement on rhyme, Arthur Hallam's reputation rests on two major contributions to Victorian literature: the review of Tennyson's early poems, entitled "On Some of the Characteristics of Modern Poetry, and on the Lyrical Poems of Alfred Tennyson" (1831), which brilliantly interpreted their artistry to a reading public that might not otherwise have taken notice; and, of course, his more iconic but less active role as the lost muse of *In Memoriam* (1850). The importance of Hallam's review is almost unquestioned, both in Tennyson studies and in the larger field of Victorian studies; we tend to agree that it helped create the taste by which Tennyson, and much of the poetry of his period, would be appreciated.[6] The review's primary argument is that Tennyson is a modern "Poet of Sensation" whose heightened sensory perceptions, intensity of feeling, technical innovation, and "worship of beauty" mark him as a genius and also condemn him to the disapproval of an undiscerning public.[7] Although Hallam claims not to be "play[ing] the part of a fashionable lady who deludes her refractory mate into doing what she chooses by pretending to wish the exact contrary," his appeal to "feeling hearts and imaginative tempers" conjures a cohort of sympathetic readers whose appreciation of Tennyson's poetry makes them exceptional people "of Sensation," too (198).

Hallam's review has long been understood as a theoretical counterpart to Tennyson's poetry—an analysis of, and an influence on, his early poetics—as well as a cult text for the aestheticist movement later in the century.[8] The essay was originally published in *The Englishman's*

Magazine and then, in abridged form, in Henry Hallam's edition of *Remains in Verse and Prose of Arthur Henry Hallam* (1834), which was reprinted several times throughout the nineteenth century and itself reviewed in some major literary periodicals.[9] In the 1890s, W. B. Yeats described the review as "one of the most profound criticisms in the English language"; and Richard Le Gallienne argued in his own 1893 edition of Hallam's work that it was "one of the early examples in England of that aesthetic criticism which is now so generally accepted amongst us."[10] In a 1951 essay widely cited by Tennyson scholars, Marshall McLuhan characterized the review as "a manifesto as decisive in the issues it raises as Wordsworth's Preface to *Lyrical Ballads* or Mr. Eliot's 'Tradition and the Individual Talent'"—a verdict that Eileen Tess Johnston echoed in 1981.[11] And in the important revaluations of Victorian poetics by Carol Christ and Isobel Armstrong, the review stands as a major work of Victorian criticism whose "analyses resonate throughout the century" and into modernism.[12] In short, it is difficult to read or write about Tennyson's work without confronting this foundational text.

The case has been far otherwise for Hallam's literary-historical essay, "Oration, on the Influence of Italian Works of Imagination on the Same Class of Compositions in England." The "Oration" is less obviously tethered to Tennyson's career, and although Hallam's prose is enormously important within Tennyson's orbit, much of what lies outside that orbit has been forgotten. This includes several philosophical and critical essays—on sympathy, on Cicero, on Christianity, on Professor Gabriele Rossetti's Dante scholarship—and over a hundred poems, many of which were intended for joint publication with Tennyson's 1830 poetry before Hallam's father's veto. Though the "Oration" is barely remembered now, it was known to Victorian readers, particularly in the wake of *In Memoriam*, when Hallam had become an object of myth and vicarious desire.[13]

It is a mistake to see the Tennyson review as theoretically independent of the "Oration." In addition to offering its own compelling story about the movement of literary forms—particularly from the Islamic Middle East into Europe—the "Oration" illuminates the aesthetic criteria Hallam brings to his judgment of Tennyson's poetry, which turn out to be criteria derived from the genetic and transnational narratives of Romantic literary historiography. In disclosing the rigorously historicist quality of Hallam's thought, the "Oration" has the power to deepen our understanding of a formative moment for Victorian literature.

COMPOUND LANGUAGE, COMPOSITE LITERATURE: ARTHUR HALLAM'S "ORATION"

Arthur Hallam's "Oration"—like so much literary historiography in the period—began as an oral performance. It was delivered at Trinity College Chapel in December 1831 to an end-of-term audience that included his father and Alfred Tennyson, as part of the reward for having won the previous year's college declamation contest.[14] The "Oration" was then published as an essay by W. Metcalfe in 1832 before being reprinted, along with the Tennyson review, in Henry Hallam's *Remains*. The subject Arthur Hallam chose for the prize lecture combined, in T. H. Vail Motter's words, "his chief intellectual and spiritual interests: a philosophy of love and beauty, Italian and English literature, and the 'vital light' of a 'true spiritual Christianity.'"[15] Hallam appeared to have mixed feelings about the essay he produced, dismissing it as a "hasty compositio[n]" and a "little performanc[e]" in his letters.[16]

Although the "Oration" was an undergraduate effort, it was also an assertive contribution to the international enterprise of general literary historiography, which had been a largely Continental tradition. The most recent—and best known—work in the genre was Sismondi's history of Southern European literature. Sismondi's French-language study had been widely noticed in the English press (Hazlitt wrote an influential review of it); it was also translated into English by Thomas Roscoe in 1823 for a large popular readership.[17] While Samuel Taylor Coleridge lectured on European literature in 1818 and Thomas Carlyle would do so in 1838, there had been no major work of general literary history written in English.[18] Arthur Hallam's father's massive contribution to general literary history wasn't yet finished; it appeared, to great acclaim, a few years after Arthur's death.

One task of the "Oration," then, was to argue for the methodological and ethical value of a "super-national" perspective on literary language and literary form.[19] A second task was to demonstrate the assimilative structure of English literature in particular. And a third, subtler, task was to perform the assimilative style of general literary historiography. In those histories, as I've said, poetic forms are seen to develop over time and across national borders; the histories followed a similar model of making. Historians would borrow, translate, repeat, and modify the work of their colleagues and forebears, sharing in the production of a grand transnational, translinguistic historiographic opus.[20] In his own synthetic treatment of literary history, Hallam embodies this tradition.

The "Oration" followed Hallam's review of *Poems, Chiefly Lyrical* by only five months, and it clearly reads as a continuation and expansion of that earlier argument. Hallam had ended his Tennyson review with a move outward from the poet himself to a more general point about the assimilative nature of the English language. In his final "word of praise," Hallam commends Tennyson for his use of "thorough and sterling English," by which he means Tennyson's use in his poetry of the full spectrum of English words, not just those with Saxon roots but Latinate words, too. This appreciation leads Hallam to the remark, likely adapted from Hugh Blair, that "ours is necessarily a compound language; as such alone it can flourish and increase; nor will the author of the poems we have extracted be likely to barter for a barren appearance of symmetrical structure that fertility of expression and variety of harmony which 'the speech that Shakespeare spoke' derived from the sources of southern phraseology" (198).[21] Beginning from the idea that "pure English" is always an oxymoron, Hallam concludes by suggesting that the greatest English literature is that which most willingly embraces the diversity of its linguistic heritage, which involves Southern European as well as Northern European influences—and that the future of the English language depends upon a continued relationship to languages and literatures outside of itself. Hallam's comparison of the relatively unknown Tennyson with Shakespeare, whom he himself would describe in the "Oration" as "the most universal mind that ever existed" (229), is surely a risky note to end on.[22] But it is also a clever way to account for some of the idiosyncrasies of Tennyson's verbal style that might otherwise be attributed to his juvenility. Instead of an amateur, Tennyson is represented as already a master, since he understands—as his critics might not, but as Shakespeare did—the real nature and potential of the English language.

With the "Oration," Hallam shifts from a literary-critical to a historical and theoretical mode; with no specific reference to Tennyson this time, he retrieves the thread he dropped in the review and proceeds to tease out its broader implications for the study of literature. Here, Hallam launches his polemic against national literary histories. He argues that a super-national vision of literature requires hard work, an effort to override our natural preference for both easy answers and self-aggrandizing narratives. "There is in the human mind a remarkable habit," he begins, "which leads it to prefer in most cases the simple to the composite, and to despise a power acquired by combination in comparison with one original, and produced from unmixed elements." He continues,

> Doubtless some good motives have had a share in forming this habit, but I suspect pride is answerable for nine tenths of the formation; especially when anything immediately belonging to ourselves is the circumstance for which our curiosity requires an origin. Wherever we trace a continued series of ascending causes, we can hardly escape the conviction of our insignificance and entire dependence: but if by any accident the chain is broken, if we see darkness beyond a particular link, we find it easy, and think it fine, to flatter ourselves into a belief of having found a beginning, and the nearer we bring it down to ourselves the better satisfied we remain. (213)

The desire for origins, Hallam observes, is a natural human desire, but it can also be an obstacle to the study of national literature. Literary historians "less honest than patriotic" seek to prove "the aboriginal distinctness of their national literature, and its complete independence of the provision of any other languages" (213–14). This, despite a broad consensus that "the spirit of commercial enterprise has leveled the barriers of countries, and triumphed over the immensity of ocean." With language that recalls the economic view of *Weltliteratur* proposed by Goethe, Marx, and many critics today, Hallam insists that literature has been shaped by an international "commerce of mind" (214).[23]

This is not really a polemic against origin stories. It is a polemic against fragmentary histories that begin and end with the nation. Hallam proposes a different historical method: an examination of "the component parts of any national literature ... to ascertain, by correct analysis, the number and relative proportion of its elements; to decide, by the application of history, from what juncture in social progress each particular complexion of sentiment had its origin" (214). Thus, Hallam's concept of the literary-historical origin is more like a "juncture." What looks like an absolute beginning from the perspective of national literary history is instead a link to other literary cultures. Hallam argues that the recognition of this fact requires no great degree of scholarship; any reader with "a liberal education" can verify it (214). Once again, Shakespeare serves as his positive example. In sixteen representative lines of the poet's work, Hallam finds proof of the richness and diversity of English. Paradoxically, in its etymological variety (including words with Romance, Teutonic, Greek, and Latin roots), "the whole [passage] is a beautiful specimen of pure English, and falls with complete, easy, uniform effect on the ear and mind" (215). The "purity" and aesthetic charm of English therefore derive from an essential diversity.

Despite its prominence in the title, then, the idea of direct influence has a relatively minor place in Hallam's argument. He imagines a more profound kind of assimilation process, a "universal and always progressive movement" whose dominant metaphor is chemical—even alchemical (214).[24] Modern cultures are forged, Hallam says, in a "sublime . . . process by which the few original elements of society are dashed and mingled with one another, severing forever and coalescing within a crucible of incessant operation, and producing at each successive point new combinations, which again, as simple substances, are made subservient to the prospective direction of the Great observant Mind" (214). This variety is markedly the condition of "romantic" literature, whose four constituent elements are Christian, Teutonic (from the North), Roman (from the South), and "Oriental" or "Arabian" (from the East) (218). The geographical coordinates have temperamental corollaries too, and as history proceeds, the elements combine to produce the variegated personalities of each national identity. Hallam's stereotypes are the familiar climatological clichés popularized by Montesquieu and Germaine de Staël: "the fervid meditations of the East"; the "rapid reason of the West, the stormy Northern temper" and "the voluptuous languors of the Meridian" (214). The "romantic spirit" that animates medieval European literature is made up of all four.[25]

So, although the ostensible aim of the "Oration" is to explore the relationship between Italian and English literatures, Hallam's essay is much more ambitious than the title suggests. From his first sentences,

Hallam dispenses with the concept of fixed national identity. "English" and "Italian" cease to be stable terms interacting with one another, and the principle of combination takes precedence. Just as English is a hybrid language and Italian is an amalgam of older languages (it was "the last and most complete among the several tongues that arose out of the confusion of Northern barbarians with their captives of the conquered Empire" [216]), Italian literature is a compound thing. Its superiority does not rest on the originality of its writers, even if Hallam celebrates Dante as an unparalleled genius. Dante is a genius partly because of the ways in which he *isn't* original. More valuable than originality is the kind of perfection that medieval Italian literature achieved by "taking into itself, into its own young and creative vigor, the whole height, breadth, and depth of human knowledge, as it then stood" (223).[26] One of the most important bequests of Italian to English literature, along with its Christian spirit, is this assimilative sensibility.

Indeed, for Hallam, the best English poets have embodied the Italian principle. In the same way that Dante and Petrarch drew on their classical and medieval antecedents—Plato and Virgil, and the troubadour poets Sordel and Arnaud de Marveil—to create a Christian love poetry "which dwells 'like a star apart'" (224), Chaucer and the Elizabethan poets learned from Dante and Petrarch. They adopted not only their poetic forms—"in their canzonets, madrigals, devises, sonnets and epithalamiums"—but also the "mode of sentiment" and the "melodious repose in which are held together all the emotions [they] delineate" (228–29). After Shakespeare, Hallam describes a progressive "extinction of the Italian influence" and its replacement (due to Dryden) with the "death-dance of Parisian foppery and wickedness" (230n23). But though the essay traces a general decline in the literature of the previous two hundred years, it doesn't close with the disappointing present. Instead, its historical narrative reaches into the future for a utopian poet who might revive the romantic, assimilative spirit of Dante's Christian Europe. Thus, Hallam's literary history is descriptive, but it is also prescriptive. If a contemporary poet immerses himself in the poetic culture of medieval Europe (and if Europe itself rediscovers its spirituality), he may be able to produce a correspondent poetry. Hallam ends his essay with the hope for an "English mind that has drunk deep at the sources of Southern inspiration, and especially that is imbibed with the spirit of the mighty Florentine" (234).[27]

Strangely enough, this ending sends us back to the review of Tennyson's poetry, for which the "Oration" now seems to be a belated preparation—a prequel as well as a sequel. Hallam has, after all, already aligned Tennyson with Dante and Petrarch, who "produce two-thirds of their effect by *sound*." And he has already identified Tennyson with the precise model of poetic influence that the "Oration" so meticulously expounds. Of Tennyson's poem "Oriana," Hallam had written, "We know no more happy seizure of the antique spirit in the whole compass of our literature.... The author is well aware that the art of one generation cannot *become* that of another by any will or skill; but the artist may transfer the spirit of the past, making it a temporary form for his own spirit, and so effect, by idealizing power, a new and legitimate combination" (194). As Dante did before him, Tennyson has absorbed the lessons of literary history into his own original poetic practice. The "Oration" suggests that Tennyson's appropriation of Dante's specific poetic style, his Tuscan sound effects, is in fact secondary to Tennyson's creative emulation of the historicist and assimilative aesthetic that Dante himself exemplified.[28]

THE ORIGINS OF RHYME

Hallam's theory of rhyme is one component of this larger assimilative theory of influence. Like English literature more broadly, English rhyme is the record of a long, transnational process, the repository of the "mode[s] of sentiment" of the various cultures it has passed through on the way to the English present. So rhyme is a formal device for Hallam, but it is much more than that: it represents the emergence of modern Europe and its romantic spirit; it proves the multicultural nature of English poetry; it is a record and instrument of historical feeling.[29] Rhyme is also the occasion for Hallam to bring Arabic poetry more fully into his story of literature and to engage with the possibility of Western literature's indebtedness to the East.

The story Hallam tells about medieval Europe appears at first to be a familiar one, moving from the literary vacuum of the "period of utter darkness" at the beginning of the millennium through to the Italian Renaissance.[30] The turning point in this story is the coalescence of

Mediterranean vernaculars—what he calls the Romane *patois*—into literary languages and the sudden emergence of lyric poetry in medieval Provence and the Italian republics. Hallam describes these events in vividly metaphorical terms:

> [T]hose forms of speech [were] soon to arise from their illiterate and base condition, to express in voices of thunder and music the wants and tendencies of a new civilization, and to animate with everlasting vigor the intellect of mankind. . . . [A]fter five centuries of preparatory ignorance, the flame burst from beneath the ashes, never again to be overcome. . . . The [Provençal language, or Langue d'Oc] especially began to offer the phenomenon of a new literature, dependent for nothing on monastic erudition, but fresh from the workings of untaught nature, impressed with the stamp of existing manners, and reacting upon them by exciting the imagination and directing the feelings of the people. A thousand poets sprang up, as at an enchanter's call. (217)[31]

In positioning Southern France as the cradle of modern literature and Provençal poetry as the spontaneous expression of modern personhood ("the wants and tendencies of a new civilization"), Hallam rehearses a commonplace of European historiography.[32] "New" is the watchword of this episode of literary history: new languages are born, and with them a new civilization and "a new literature" that seems to come out of nowhere and owe nothing to the civilizations that preceded it.

But this new element, Hallam is quick to show, is really just a spectacular new compound. Even the features that look newest of all, like the theme of chivalry in the new literature, are the product of Hallam's cultural "crucible" and derive from a synthesis of Christian Mariolatry, Gothic domesticity, and, above all, the passionate "Arabic imagination," where "most probably the first pattern of that amorous mysticism" of romantic love appeared (219). Islamic sensibilities and art forms were introduced into Europe through the period of sustained cultural exchange that began with the Islamic golden age of the Abbassides (also known as the Abbasid Caliphate, around the eighth century) and continued with the Crusades. Through a combination of "itinerant Eastern reciters," cross-cultural encounters in Muslim Spain, and European crusaders returning from the East, Europe was infused with the attitudes, styles, and forms of Islamic culture (220). Some of the permanent results were "softened prejudices, enlarged imaginations, and a more ardent love of letters" (221).

Departing from a prevalent Eurocentric myth, Hallam attributes chivalry, romantic love, and even the imaginative and literary cast of mind to a civilization outside of Europe. And his argument goes further: it isn't just the themes and tenor of this literature that are borrowed from the Islamic world but also "the outward forms of literary composition": major narrative genres like the fable and the novel, poetic forms of rhymed verse, and elaborate figurative conceits (Thomas Warton is an important, and acknowledged, source for this history of romantic fiction). Hallam's treatment of literary form thus tracks much of so-called Western literature back to Eastern sources. But the most significant contribution of Eastern to Western culture, in his view, is rhyme, the "transmission" of which "from the Levant" "decided the whole bent of modern poetry" (221–22). Hallam's definition of rhyme is both broad and precise. He isn't referring only to the sonic pairing of two words at the ends of lines but to a whole prosodic system organized around assonantal resemblance and stanzaic patterning. In the phonic character of rhyme, Hallam hears a long historical itinerary from Arabic to Provençal to Italian poetry:

> I mean the use, at least the extensive and varied use, of Rhyme. This appears to be the creation of Southern climates: for the Southern languages abound in vowels, and rhyme is the resonance of vowels, while the Northern overflow with consonants and naturally fall into alliteration. . . . No poetry, however, in the world was so founded on rhyme as the Arabian; and some of its most complicated [rhyme patterns] were transferred without alteration to the Langue d'Oc, previous to their obtaining immortality in the hands of Dante and Petrarca. (222)[33]

Hallam is espousing here the "Arabist" or "Hispano-Arabic" theory of rhyme, which had been argued for and against intermittently since the sixteenth century.[34] In the early nineteenth century, it was popularized anew by Sismondi, whose *Historical View of the Literature of the South of Europe* related Hallam's genetic story of romantic literature over the course of four scholarly volumes. Sismondi, along with August Schlegel, was a member of Germaine de Staël's Coppet salon, and his work in general literary history advanced the Romantic revaluation of medieval and Romance-language poetry. Like Hallam's essay, Sismondi's book offered a historical hypothesis for how modern European literature developed a character that was so distinct from—and not inferior to—classical literature.

In borrowing Sismondi's Arabist theory of rhyme, Hallam takes on, but also modifies, a complicated mixture of Romantic historicisms and orientalisms. On one hand, Hallam attaches high aesthetic value to medieval Arabic culture, contrasting it with the European Dark Ages and crediting it with the aesthetic revitalization of Europe (in contrast to many contemporaries who denied such a possibility). On the other hand, that same chronology positions Arabic literature as the developmental past of European literature, making of the "Orient" the site of European fantasy and self-knowledge that Edward Said theorized in his 1978 *Orientalism*—and affirming Dipesh Chakrabarty's proposition that Europe has been "the sovereign, theoretical subject of all histories."[35] In Joseph Phelan's reformulation of Said and other scholars of empire, such an "archaizing tendency" also enabled "the powerful illusion of a non-progressive and unvarying East," which was one ideological condition of imperial expansion over the nineteenth and early twentieth centuries.[36]

And yet, in the terms of the Herderian historicism whose influence I have been considering, origins are not superseded; they persist as an essential and *present* part of the art form. So it's not quite right to say that Hallam's is a straightforwardly progressive theory. When English poetry rhymes, on Hallam's model, it is enacting its ongoing debt to Arabic literature. Thus, in a counterpoint to Annmarie Drury's observations about the "incorporative impulse" of Victorian poetry—whereby poet-translators treated Arabic and other non-English poetries as resources for the renewal of English—Hallam's claim is decidedly genetic: modern English poetry does not need to discover Arabic poetry as a source of inspiration, because Arabic poetics was incorporated from the start.[37]

Like so many documents of Romantic orientalism, Hallam's approach to Arabic literature involves both positive and negative caricatures of the East. He describes the customs of the seraglio as "pernicious to society" and also "not incapable of charming the imagination" (220). And there is no doubt that Hallam's theory of rhyme is charged with a naive attraction to the exoticism of medieval Arab culture (his critical treatment of Tennyson's "Recollections of the Arabian Nights" elaborates on the erotic and nostalgic charms of Arabic fiction). But Hallam's frank admiration for Arabic literature as a contributing feature of English literature was not a mainstream position. His writing was a relatively late addition to the Arabist theory of rhyme, which by the 1830s had lost much of its authority. By the end of the century, as María Rosa Menocal remarks, it had become "virtually taboo." Menocal, who spent her academic career as a medievalist restoring credibility to the Arabist theory, hypothesizes that two later nineteenth-century developments contributed to its obsolescence: imperial Europe's intensifying effort to figure Arab people as inferior and in need of subjugation; and the consolidation of Romance studies as a self-enclosed academic field. Late twentieth-century Romance studies and medieval studies, she argued in 1987, were still unable to imagine such influences on European literature, partly (and ironically) because of the conceptual power of Said's East-West dichotomy. Yet Menocal insisted that it was a more persuasive theory of influence than those currently accepted.[38]

Menocal's scholarship drew on Roger Boase's meticulous reconstruction of the Arabist theory over several centuries of thought in his *Origin and Meaning of Courtly Love* (1977). Boase, like Menocal, considered the Arabist theory to have an undeniable logic. He writes, "There are, on the whole, strong grounds for supporting this theory, even if some of the arguments used are false. The cultural supremacy of the Islamic world in the period immediately preceding the rise of the troubadour lyric is indisputable, and the importance of Arabic scholarship as a medium for the transmission of Greek classical texts is widely acknowledged."[39] Roberto Dainotto expressed a similar view in his 2006 essay on the Arabist theory of rhyme: "It seems frankly implausible to me that three centuries of Islam in Europe, and of Arabic—or better, Semitic—sciences developed between Sicily and Al-Andalus, would have been of no consequence for European versification."[40] Dainotto's detailed work on the subject—in his book *Europe, In Theory* (2007) and a set of related articles—has substantially filled out the intellectual prehistory of the Arabist theory and parsed its political meanings, especially for the historiography of Europe. Although Hallam does not feature in any of their studies, the work of all these scholars offers crucial context for his position.

If Hallam's contribution arrived toward the end of the Arabist theory's long moment, that doesn't mean that the theory entirely disappeared; as subsequent chapters of this book show, the broader genetic thinking inherent in the Arabist theory of rhyme—and the basic conviction that rhyme's origin and development mattered for poetic theory—outlasted the particulars of any historical claim. Indeed, another aspect of Hallam's rhyme theory, equally important to later poets, was its larger conception of literary history. Hallam wasn't only concerned with the geographical origin of rhyme. He was also interested in rhyme's periodizing force, its status as—in Germaine de Staël's words—"a modern discovery."[41] De Staël, who (with August Schlegel) famously divided classic from romantic literatures, was not a proponent of the Arabist theory. Nonetheless, she understood European literature as a story about the before and after of rhyme.

Drawing on the thought of de Staël and her Coppet group, and likely Coleridge, too, Hallam declares that rhyme marks the insuperable difference between classic and romantic literature, and between the ancient and modern person. In a long and dense footnote to his description of the transmission of rhyme from the East to the West, he characterizes rhyme as an instrument of feeling that was perfected by the moderns for the moderns. It is a technology more sophisticated and more finely calibrated than poetic meter:

> Rhyme has been said to contain in itself a constant appeal to Memory and Hope. This is true of all verse, of all harmonized sound; but it is certainly made more palpable by the recurrence of termination. The dullest senses can perceive an identity in that, and be pleased with it; but the partial identity, latent in more diffused resemblances, requires, in order to be appreciated, a soul susceptible of musical impression. The ancients disdained a mode of pleasure, in appearance so little elevated, so ill adapted for effects of art, but they knew not, and with their metrical harmonies, perfectly suited, as these were, to their habitual moods of feeling, they were not likely to know the real capacities of this apparently simple and vulgar combination. (222n10)

At the beginning of the footnote, Hallam sets up a hierarchy of sound effects. Meter makes the smallest demands on our faculties of "Memory and Hope"; it counts as "harmonized sound," but its patterns are rhythmic rather than musical. Next is rhyme proper (either end rhyme or some other version of full rhyme), what Hallam calls the "recurrence of termination."[42] End rhyme, in its most basic form, is not a strictly modern invention. As Hallam knew, there were some isolated instances of rhymed couplets—used at the service of meter—even in classical Latin poetry.[43] Although end rhyme introduces a sound texture more varied than metrical feet, it isn't in itself the utmost that rhyme can be. More subtle than symmetrical end rhymes are the kind of sound patterns that Hallam earlier described as "the extensive and varied use of Rhyme"—everything on the spectrum of assonance, from the melodious play of vowels across a line to the interlacement of a multirhyme stanza. These are the "diffused resemblances" that the ancients, in their insensitivity, were unable to appreciate. They wrote their poetry in meter, Hallam suggests, because the austere classical sensibility was unfit for rhyme.

By invoking (and updating) the old quarrel of the ancients and the moderns, and by representing the moderns and their rhyme as triumphant, Hallam articulates a strongly Romantic attitude toward the history of poetry. In so doing, he contests Milton's neoclassical judgment on rhyme, which had remained a powerful critical norm.[44] To explain his choice of blank verse for his epic poem, Milton too contrasted ancient and modern poetics, but in this case to the credit of the ancients: "The measure is English heroic verse without rhyme, as that of Homer in Greek, and of Virgil in Latin, rhyme being no necessary adjunct or true ornament of poem or good verse, in longer works especially, but the invention of a barbarous age, to set off wretched matter and lame meter."[45] Milton's view of rhyme follows Thomas Campion's; it is the "vulgar and easy kind of poesy" resulting from Latin's "pollution" with "Barbarian" influences and from "barbarized Italy."[46] Both Campion and Milton take the orthodox view of the medieval period as an uncivilized and unpoetic interval between antiquity and the Renaissance. We can see that the historical processes that yielded the Romance languages and romantic literature are simply valued differently by Campion and Milton, on one hand, and Sismondi, de Staël, and Hallam, on the other. One literary historian's "pollution" is another's sublime combination. Against this background of historical rhyme theory, Hallam's Middle Ages—the fertile period that produced for the first time a "soul susceptible of musical impression" and a poetic music to match—appears all the more dazzling.

Because his purview is general literary history and not just English literary history, Hallam is able to unsettle two orthodoxies: the one that privileges classical over modern poetics, and the one that privileges the English (and, more broadly, the European) tradition over the other literary cultures of the world. In terms of chronology, rhyme represents a break; in terms of culture, rhyme represents a bridge. As I've been suggesting, Hallam wasn't the only literary historian to think about prosody in these terms, but he helped transform a live historiographic debate about the origin of rhyme into a usable theory of how rhyme works.

"MEMORY AND HOPE": HISTORY, FORM, FEELING

"Rhyme has been said to contain in itself a constant appeal to Memory and Hope." Even though this sentence is hidden away in a footnote of the barely read "Oration," it has since Hallam's death become one of the utterances most closely identified with his myth. The sentence is usually abstracted from its context and turned into an evocative kind of shorthand—for Hallam's tragic genius; or for Tennyson's characteristic style; or for the emotional capacities of poetry; or for the paradoxical work of elegy, the poetic genre whose most recognizable nineteenth-century face is Hallam himself. The mystique of the sentence is only heightened by the fact that it appears already to be a quotation when Hallam uses it—"Rhyme *has been said* to contain in itself a constant appeal to Memory and Hope"—yet he gives no indication of its provenance. If there is a source for the quotation, it hasn't mattered much; its profundity, critics have suggested, belongs to Hallam alone. Coventry Patmore cited the sentence twice, in an 1850 review of *In Memoriam* and in his 1857 "Essay on English Metrical Law"; both essays take it seriously as the basis for a theory of prosody.[47] In the twentieth century, Christopher Ricks made poignant use of Hallam's observation at the conclusion of his own biographical study of Tennyson, connecting it to Tennyson's life and death and to his late poem "Crossing the Bar" (1889): "It is a perfect epitome of Tennyson's essential movement," he writes, "a progress outward which is yet a circling home."[48] After Ricks, Hallam's sentence returned to the task of explicating the dynamics of the ABBA *In Memoriam* stanza (it's an uncanny fact of critical history that Arthur Hallam keeps teaching us how to read his own elegy). Such is the aim of Seamus Perry's lovely remark that the stanza is "one of the great formal responses to the occasion of elegy, recognizing the obligation to move on, while honestly registering a compulsion to retrogress. . . . If each *In Memoriam* stanza begins with hope, it soon relapses into sad memory."[49]

Why has the "Memory and Hope" formulation been so useful for understanding how rhyme works in Victorian poetry and beyond? Part of the answer might be that it helps us describe a quality of prosody that we feel but find difficult to name. We can mark out a rhyme scheme, but that notation still fails somehow to account for the way a rhyme tugs on us as we read and hear it. Hallam's sentence holds out a satisfyingly layered idea of rhyme: it acknowledges something literally true about its operations—that it works across (and helps produce) the past-present-future axis of poetic time as we experience it; but it also gestures at rhyme's less quantifiable, more ineffable effects. It promises something that poetic theory is still looking for: an affective theory of rhyme. As J. Paul Hunter has suggested, our theoretical vocabulary for this aspect of rhyme remains limited. In "Seven Reasons for Rhyme," he devotes his seventh "reason" to a function that he describes as "abstract and frankly speculative . . . as yet, in fact, almost languageless. . . . It involves creating a prevailing tone or mood through sound." Hunter's own "tentative" speculation isolates vowels as the agents of rhyme's most elusive effects, because although vowels "have of themselves no necessary relationship to meaning as such [they] do in fact set up tonal associations that come close to, almost anticipate, a meaning function."[50] In Hunter's suggestions, we find some key components of Hallam's concept of rhyme: the characterization of rhyme as "the resonance of vowels," and the identification of vowels with emotional content. Unlike Hunter, however, Hallam *names* rhyme's two primary affective dimensions: Memory and Hope.

Of course, restored to the context of Hallam's literary history, "Memory" and "Hope" have associations beyond poetry's temporality on the page or in the ear, the way we remember and wait for recurring rhyme sounds. These terms also index the much larger forms of historicity and modernity that Hallam's concept of rhyme encompasses. In his view, rhyme is not just a literary effect *with* a history, but a signifier for the processes of literary history: the disjunctions and continuities, the renovations and innovations that give rise to modernity. The terms

"Memory" and "Hope" integrate these historical and affective connotations, suggesting that poetic forms might always arrive bearing the scars of where they have been.

It's worth remembering, too, that Hallam doesn't take credit for the expression that posterity insistently attributes to him. To read the sentence closely is to register not only the keywords "Rhyme," "Memory," and "Hope," but the connective tissue holding those terms together. In noting that rhyme "has been said" to work in a particular way, Hallam doesn't just direct us to the history of rhyme, but to the history of histories of rhyme—that is, to the larger Romantic milieu that helps explain the "Oration."

The remainder of this chapter develops a fuller picture of Romantic literary historiography, constellating Hallam's rhyme theory with the historicisms of Hegel, Henry Hallam (Arthur's father), and Sismondi. All three of these thinkers investigate the origin of rhyme, and all three entertain broadly "derivationist" views: they consider the possibility that rhyme had a definite historical and geographical origin rather than simply being a universal and transhistorical human impulse.[51] Hegel's and Henry Hallam's histories of rhyme, in departing from the Arabist theory, show what was at stake in the origin debate. Moreover, they present a useful contrast to Arthur Hallam's strongly positive valuation of romantic rhyme. Sismondi's literary history (which Hegel may have read and which Henry Hallam certainly read) was more than just Arthur Hallam's source for the Arabist theory. It was also a lesson—conveyed through the story of one troubadour poet's desire—about the productive entanglements of history, feeling, and form.

HEGEL'S ROMANTIC RHYME

While general literary history has mostly been forgotten, and with it, the controversy over the origin of rhyme, the impress of that genre and that controversy remains visible in one of the most enduring Romantic texts. G. W. F. Hegel's *Aesthetics,* with its masterful synthesis of eighteenth-century and Romantic art theory and historiography, approaches the subject of rhyme genetically, and in doing so reveals another side of the rhyme debate around the time of Hallam's "Oration."[52]

The *Aesthetics* presents what looks at first like a similar vision of rhyme to Arthur Hallam's, with a similar complex of form, historicity, and feeling. The historical transition from quantitative meter to rhyme-based and accentual-syllabic prosody corresponds with Hegel's overarching theory of the shift from classical to romantic art forms. Meter becomes an insufficient external representation of poetry's "inner message" as Christianity emerges and as "the artistic imagination" becomes "more inward and spiritual." Romantic (i.e., postclassical) poetry "tries to find in sound the material most correspondent to this subjective life"—and "romantic rhyme" with its "soul-laden note of feeling" is the inevitable result. Like Hallam, Hegel is eloquent about the pleasure we take from rhyme—although he considers assonance and internal rhyme, Hallam's "diffused resemblances," inferior to the "complete accord" of perfect end rhyme.[53] The more complex a pattern of end rhymes is, the more likely it is to produce pleasure in the reader. In terms that anticipate Hallam's "constant appeal to Memory and Hope" and call to mind another meaning of "romantic rhyme," Hegel accounts for the way we experience the time between rhyme words:

> [Rhymes] are united, or separated, or brought into the most complex relations whether close or more distant. Consequently, it is as if the rhymes now find one another immediately, now fly from one another and yet look for one another, with the result that in this way the ear's attentive expectation is now satisfied without more ado, now teased, deceived, or kept in suspense owing to the longer delay between the rhymes, but always contented again by the regular ordering and return of the same sounds. (1030)

But even if rhyme brings the pleasures of desire, deferral, and satisfaction, Hegel still insists that its sound is "coarser" and more "thumping" than "the delicate movements of rhythmical harmony," and that it "does not need so finely cultivated an ear as Greek versification necessitates" (1028).

Hegel's view of rhyme is consequently more ambivalent than Hallam's. Although rhyme in its spirituality transcends the "stuffiness" of meter, meter nonetheless belongs to a prelapsarian period of linguistic plenitude. Only with the "corruption" of absolute "natural" quantities that resulted from the barbarian invasions did the need for another prosodic system arise. Hegel's tone is elegiac as he describes rhyme as a bittersweet recompense, "the one possible compensation offered for this loss" (1027). So when he echoes Goethe's question—"Do the wide folds (of classical metres) suit us as they did antiquity?" (1031)—he is making a rather different point from Hallam. Hallam's ancients were misguided in disdaining the joys of rhyme and preferring quantitative meter instead. They assumed rhyme was a blunt instrument and therefore missed its most delicate and melodious operations. In Hegel, there is even less choosing. The ancients couldn't have chosen rhyme even if they could hear it properly, just as the moderns cannot revert to pure quantitative meter.

This apparently small distinction points to a significant difference of opinion between Hegel and Hallam. In a further subsection within the nested subsections of "Versification" and "Rhyme," Hegel, too, deals explicitly with "the origin of rhyme"—which he sees as a primarily Western phenomenon. The source of rhyme is to be found in "the rhythmical system itself"; it appears in embryonic form in a classical language—Latin—when it turns to Christian hymnody, and it develops through the innovation of Leonine verse (1025).[54] If a non-Latin origin is required, Hegel offers an alternative: the Germanic languages. Even though "the truly harmonious sound of rhyme in its complete development is absent" in Scandinavian poetry, the example of the alliterative *Edda* shows a versification approaching rhyme (1026). Hegel rejects outright the Arabist theory that Arthur Hallam propounds:

> On the other hand, of course the origin of this new principle of versification has been sought amongst the Arabs, but, for one thing, the culture of their great poets falls in a period later than the occurrence of rhyme in the Christian West, while the range of pre-Mohammedan art had no effective influence on the West; for another thing, there is inherent in Arabic poetry from its first beginnings an echo of the romantic principle, so that the knights of the West at the time of the Crusades were quick enough to find in Arabic poetry a mood that echoed their own. Consequently, just as the spiritual ground from which poetry arose in the Mohammedan East was akin to that from which it arose in the Christian West (although it was external to it and independent of it), so we may conjecture that a new sort of versification originally arose independently in both. (1025)

Hegel disputes an Eastern source for rhyme on several grounds. If quasi-romantic rhyming is apparent in Arabic poetry, it is an "echo" of European poetry, rather than an influence on it; if Europeans did in fact borrow from Arabic versification, it is only because it "echoed" forms and feelings that were already theirs; if, finally, rhyme *has* to have originated in the East, it must have been a simultaneous and coincidental—an "external" and "independent"—development alongside Western rhyme.

Why does Hegel pay so much attention to a history of rhyme that he doesn't accept? In Simon Jarvis's reading of this part of the *Aesthetics*, Hegel entertains such origin stories only in order to prove the intrinsic historical correlation between rhyme and modern (Christian, European) subjectivity. These competing narratives "are offered and then set aside in favour of an explanation which will carry the right sense of necessity.... Since its origins are *necessary*, rather than external, we may view rhyme, even, as one aspect of the conditions of possibility of that interiority—and this because, as becomes clear, it can in a certain sense be said that the *subject* rhymes, for Hegel." At the same time, "rhyme is part of what allows a subjectivity thus conceived to sustain itself."[55] So Hegel's romantic rhyme, with its "soul-laden note of feeling," both produces and answers to the modern subject's new spiritual needs. Isobel Armstrong's own response to Jarvis's essay takes a second look at what she calls "Hegel's epistemological myth," further exploring the implications of the historical rupture between "the time of rhythm" and "the time of rhyme." Armstrong argues, in particular, that the different uses of the caesura in metrical versus rhymed versification—its transition from a concrete unit of time to "an abstract, empty pause"—denote in Hegel "a catastrophic break in history." This "caesural thinking" does not simply describe the historical difference between an unalienated and alienated time; it is itself a modern, alienated mode of thinking. Variations on Hegel's caesural thinking can be found in Shelley, Marx, Freud, and Benjamin, she concludes, where "Meaning is made in and by the gap [and the] empty space is the marker of modernity."[56]

Hegel (and Jarvis and Armstrong) clarify precisely what Arthur Hallam *isn't* doing. While Hallam's history of rhyme also postulates a break between the ancients and the moderns, he doesn't conceive of that break as a traumatic rupture; on the contrary, it signals a softening and enlarging of sensibilities, a refinement of taste. Rhyme does not spring spontaneously from older forms of Western poetics but develops in early medieval Arabia and the Levant and then travels into Europe, deciding, as he says, "the whole bent of modern poetry." The external source that Hegel so strenuously rejects is the basis of Hallam's idea of European literature, which becomes modern as it moves through diverse cultural spaces, accumulating influences.

HENRY HALLAM AND THE HISTORY OF LITERATURE

Another prominent dissenter from the Arabist theory—one much closer to Arthur Hallam and more directly associated with the project of general literary history—was Arthur's father, Henry. Henry Hallam attended Arthur's Cambridge oration as his proud parent, but he also happened to be one of the greatest living authorities on the literature of medieval Europe. In 1818, at the age of forty, he had published *View of the State of Europe during the Middle Ages,* which immediately established him as a major nineteenth-century historian.[57] He was also likely in the early stages of his own ambitious work of literary history, *Introduction to the Literature of Europe in the Fifteenth, Sixteenth, and Seventeenth Centuries* (1837–39; I discuss this text more fully in chap. 4). Both multivolume studies give serious attention to medieval European literature. Even in the apparently less literary-historical *Middle Ages,* Henry Hallam devotes several sections to the development of Romance-language poetry and its culmination in the career of Dante, whose *Divine Comedy* he treats at length.

Henry Hallam's vast knowledge of European history was undoubtedly a source for Arthur's own historiography. Although Henry didn't quite share Arthur's passionate attachment to Dante—Henry would later call the poet his son's "favourite" and "the master mover of his spirit"—they did share a sense of Dante's enormous historical importance.[58] "His appearance," Henry Hallam writes vividly in *Middle Ages,*

> made an epoch in the intellectual history of modern nations, and banished the discouraging suspicion which long ages of lethargy tended to excite, that nature had exhausted her fertility in the great poets of Greece and Rome. It was as if, at some of the ancient games, a stranger had appeared upon the plain, and thrown his quoit among the marks of former casts which tradition had ascribed to the demigods.[59]

As this passage implies, Henry held a lower opinion of the troubadour poets who preceded Dante's arrival on the field. Where Arthur characterizes their advent as "a thousand poets [springing] up, as at an enchanter's call" (A. Hallam, *Writings*, 217), Henry's comparison is less enthusiastic: they suddenly appear "like a swarm of summer insects ... in the southern provinces of France" (3.541). (In *Literature of Europe*, this simile would soften a little to "the gay insects of spring.")[60] Henry finds their poetry tedious and superficial, but at the same time he credits them with inventing modern versification and laying the foundation for Dante's prosodic achievement. In words that seem to anticipate Arthur's description of rhyme in both the "Oration" and "Characteristics," Henry observes that "their poetry was entirely of that class which is allied to music, and excites the fancy or feelings rather by the power of sound than any stimulancy of imagery and passion" (*Middle Ages*, 3.544).

Although Henry Hallam's *Literature of Europe* is preoccupied mainly with the literature of the Renaissance, it begins with a chapter titled "On the General State of Literature in the Middle Ages to the End of the Fourteenth Century," which covers very similar terrain to Arthur's "Oration." This is where Henry Hallam directly confronts the question of rhyme's origin, and where the two Hallams more forcefully disagree. Like Hegel, Henry dismisses the possibility of an Arab origin, but he presents a different rationale for a Latin one:

> I have dwelt, perhaps tediously, on this subject, because vague notions of a derivation of modern metrical arrangements, even in the languages of Latin origin, from the Arabs or Scandinavians, have sometimes gained credit. It has been imagined also, that the peculiar characteristic of the new poetry, rhyme, was borrowed from the Saracens of Spain. But the Latin language abounds so much in consonances, that those who have been accustomed to write verses in it well know the difficulty of avoiding them, as much as an ear formed on classical models demands; and as this gingle [*sic*] is certainly pleasing in itself, it is not wonderful that the less fastidious vulgar should adopt it in their rhythmical songs. It has been proved by Muratori, Gray, and Turner, beyond the possibility of doubt that rhymed Latin verse was in use from the end of the fourth century. (1.41–42)

In Henry Hallam's account, rhyme evolved directly out of consonance—the repetition of consonant sounds at the ends of words—instead of assonance; he is foregrounding a different part of the rhyming syllable's anatomy, and, in this instance, its less "musical" component. Partly because Hallam is a meticulous historian, and partly because his histories are composed as books rather than lectures, he assiduously documents his sources. The "vague notions" of rhyme originating with "the Saracens of Spain" he attributes primarily to the error and misguided nationalism of Spanish Jesuit historian Juan Andrés: "Andrés, with a partiality to the Saracens of Spain, whom, by an odd blunder, he takes for his countrymen, manifested in almost every page, does not fail to urge this. It had been said long before by Huet, and others who lived before these subjects had been thoroughly investigated.... He has been copied by Ginguené and Sismondi" (1.41–42n).

Here, Henry Hallam handily sketches out two axes of the derivationist rhyme debate as it stood in the 1830s, with the Latinists on one side and the Arabists on the other. In his telling, the Arabist theory reaches back to the seventeenth-century literary historian Pierre Huet, is elaborated by Juan Andrés in his *Dell'origine, progressi e stato attuale d'ogni letteratura* (1782–99), and is then "copied" by two members of the Coppet group, Pierre-Louis Ginguené (1811) and Sismondi (1813). In 1818, the same year as Henry Hallam's *Middle Ages* was published, August Schlegel issued a rebuttal to the Arabist theory in *Observations sur la langue et la littérature provençales*. Rejecting the positions of Ginguené and Sismondi, who simply "reproduced" the "doctrine" of Andrés, Schlegel emphasizes the unlikeliness of an Arab origin: "The sectarians of Muhammad had not the slightest influence on anything that constitutes the original genius of the Middle Ages.... The taste for rhyme is in nature and rests on a musical principle. We find elements of these consonances more or less in all languages."[61] Like Henry Hallam and Hegel, Schlegel dismisses the theory that Arthur accepts as "an undoubted fact" (219).

Henry Hallam was, of course, uniquely positioned to evaluate the merits of Arthur's literary historiography. When Arthur was still alive, Henry didn't hesitate to express his opinion that the "Oration" was weaker than some of Arthur's other work—but he was proud enough to send copies of Arthur's compositions to his friends, with a mild disclaimer about "the cloudy state of new wine, which will not disguise from a connoisseur's taste a racy flavour and a strong body" and the reminder that "he is not quite twenty-one." At the same time, Henry writes, "I am not perhaps quite misled as a father in thinking his performances a little out of the common."[62] After Arthur's death, Henry would offer a more serious assessment of the "Oration." In his touching preface to the *Remains,* he attempts an even-handed evaluation, one that further explicates both the "new wine" and the "out of the common" qualities of Arthur's intellectual efforts:

> Though the bent of Arthur's mind by no means inclined him to strict research into facts, he was full as much conversant with the great features of ancient and modern History, as from the course of his other studies and the habits of his life, it was possible to expect. He reckoned them, as great minds always do, the ground-works of moral and political philosophy, and took no pains to acquire any knowledge of this sort, from which a principle could not be derived or illustrated.... In the history of literary, and especially of philosophical and religious opinions, he was deeply versed, as much so as it is possible to apply that term at his age.[63]

Henry's characterization of Arthur's historiographic method makes a distinction between his own professional approach—"strict research into facts"—and a more intuitive kind of erudition. Instead of historical details, Arthur is concerned with "the great features of ancient and modern History." We can recognize this quality in Arthur's broad-stroke delineation of ancient and modern prosodic systems, and the consequent conclusions he draws about the modern "soul susceptible of musical impression." But even if Arthur's style is looser and more imaginative than his father's, it would be difficult to overstate Henry Hallam's importance to his son's thinking, writing, and research. Not only was Arthur working, with the "Oration," in his father's signature genre—European history—but he was also clearly drawing on materials in various languages that he had special access to as the son of a professional scholar. As I have suggested, one of the most important sources that Arthur Hallam used for the "Oration" was one that he never named, Sismondi's *Historical View of the Literature of the South of Europe.*

SISMONDI'S MEMORY AND HOPE

J. C. L. Simonde de Sismondi has no real profile in Victorian studies. He is now better remembered as an economist whose political theories influenced Hegel and Marx. But in the nineteenth century, his historiography was extremely well known. In addition to his literary history, he wrote a sixteen-volume history of the Italian Republics and a history of France that ran to dozens of volumes. *The History of the Italian Republics in the Middle Ages* (1807–18) taught many prominent nineteenth-century writers (among them, Byron, the Shelleys, Carlyle, and George Eliot) how to think about Italian history and art, and it was a major influence on the Italophilic and medievalist tendencies in Victorian culture. Ruskin was reading it when he toured Italy in 1845, studying it at breakfast, using it as a guidebook to Italian cities, and ultimately deriving from it his genetic theory of architecture.[64]

Sismondi's *Historical View of the Literature of the South of Europe* (1813, based on a lecture series delivered in Geneva in 1811) was also extremely popular in the period. Like de Staël's work, it was concerned with the link between literature and social institutions. As a result, it was *literary history* in two ways: it was a study of the way social and economic history produced literature (history viewed in relation to the literature it made), and it was a study of literary sequence and causality (a history of literature itself). The book was generalist, insofar as it treated Southern European literature as a totality, but it also explored individual literary cultures in detail. Embedded in Sismondi's historical narrative were specimens and descriptions of a variety of verse patterns from Arabic, Persian, Provençal, Italian, Spanish, and Portuguese poetry. This was a common enough practice in literary history writing and had obvious pedagogical benefits, but it also distinguished Sismondi's work from the general literary history of his predecessor, Juan Andrés.[65] Despite the "wonderful erudition" of Andrés's *Dell'origine*, it suffered, according to Sismondi, from a paucity of examples; as a result, "he has not succeeded in giving a clear idea of the writers and works of which he has collected the names, nor does he enable his readers to form their own opinions."[66] Sismondi's books, on the other hand, introduced a large audience, learned and lay, to a diverse archive of literary forms with which they might not otherwise be acquainted.

In relation to Andrés's work especially, Sismondi's historiography looks more synthetic than original. As both Dainotto and Guido Ettore Mazzeo (Andrés's biographer) have pointed out, Sismondi takes whole paragraphs directly from Andrés. Mazzeo determined that Sismondi was a plagiarist as a result, but Dainotto sees Sismondi's history as a "total rewriting of Andrés's theory."[67] This more nuanced assessment actually comes closer to Romantic notions of history writing. Henry

Hallam, who admits that Sismondi "copies" Andrés, makes room in the introduction to his own literary history for a range of historiographic styles, from the bibliographically transparent and exhaustive to the more opaque. "Without censuring those who suppress the immediate source of their quotations," he writes, "I may justly say that in nothing I have given to the public has it been practiced by myself" (*Literature of Europe*, 1.xiv).

For his part, Sismondi shares Henry Hallam's belief in a plurality of historiographic methods and regards his own opaque style as the enabling condition of his project. He makes his position clear in a lengthy meditation on the problem of originality in scholarship:

> In the execution of a design so extensive, and so much beyond the capacity of a single individual, I shall not have the presumption to affect originality. I shall eagerly avail myself of the labours of the critics and literary historians; and I shall, occasionally, be under the necessity of borrowing from them their opinions on works which I have not myself read, and which I can do no more than point out to the attention of my readers.... [In a long footnote, he continues,] I here beg to acknowledge generally my obligations to all these critics, because in a work from necessity of so condensed a character, and composed to be read as lectures, I have frequently availed myself of their labours, and sometimes even of their thoughts, without citing them. If I had wished, as in an historical work, to produce my authorities for every fact and opinion, it would have been necessary to have added notes to almost every line, and to have suspended, in a fatiguing manner, the delivery of the lecture, or the attention of the audience. In critical history it would be ridiculous to attempt never to repeat what has been said before; and to endeavour to separate, in every sentence, what belongs to ourselves from what is the property of others, would be little better than vanity and affectation. (1.12–14)

Sismondi obviates allegations of plagiarism by referring to the inherently collaborative nature of critical historiography. Not only are claims to historiographic originality unsavory, he argues, they are founded on a fallacy. The genre of history writing depends on the progressive, collective labor of a sequence of historians, while the pleasure of reading histories and listening to historical lectures depends on a light bibliographic touch. The most enjoyable histories, he suggests, are those that do not belabor their all-too-obvious debts. Whether or not Sismondi was obscuring his sources in the printed books, his manuscript lecture notes include marginal references to Andrés, with volume and page numbers scrupulously recorded.[68]

Henry Hallam's approach is different from Sismondi's; he frequently acknowledges his own scholarly obligations to his multitudinous sources, including Sismondi. But he nonetheless writes admiringly of Sismondi's work, applauding the accessibility of its "flowing and graceful style": it succeeds, he avers, "in all that it seeks to give,—a pleasing and popular, yet not superficial or unsatisfactory, account of the best authors in the southern languages" (*Literature of Europe*, ix).

While Henry Hallam acknowledges his own debt to Sismondi, Arthur Hallam does not. And there is very little documentation—anywhere—of Sismondi's influence on Arthur Hallam. Martin Blocksidge's biography of Arthur Hallam only notes that he stayed with Sismondi, a family friend, twice while traveling through Switzerland in 1822.[69] But we know from Hallam's letters to his father and others that in the spring of 1827 he was engrossed in reading Sismondi's *Italian Republics*, which had just been translated into English.[70] And *Historical View of the Literature of the South of Europe* was surely in the family library, given Henry Hallam's extensive citations.

Many of the moments in the "Oration" when Arthur Hallam's rhetoric is most stylish and most polemical seem to be drawn directly from Sismondi's work—and in these borrowings we perceive both the historical material *and* the assimilative historiographic ethos of Sismondi. For example, Hallam's insistence on the fictional status of chivalry—"In truth," he writes, "feudality and chivalry correspond as real and ideal"—is a surprisingly self-assured claim for such a young historian (218). It appears founded, though, on Sismondi's famous discussion of the same subject, where the more seasoned historian cautions,

> We must not confound chivalry with the feudal system. The feudal system may be called the *real life* of the period of which we are treating, possessing its advantages and inconveniences, its virtues and its vices. Chivalry, on the contrary, is the *ideal* world, such as it existed in the imaginations of the Romance writers. (1.87, emphasis mine)

When Hallam's discussion of European chivalric poetry turns to its Eastern origins, the same source is closely followed. Arguing that "in the forms of Arabic imagination appeared most probably the first pattern of the *amorous mysticism* [of the troubadours] I have been describing," Hallam echoes (with a gentler inflection) Sismondi's words: "This delicacy of sentiment amongst the Troubadours, and this mysticism of love, have a more intimate connexion with the poetry of the Arabians and the manners of the East than we should suspect, when we remember the ferocious jealousy of the Musulmans, and the cruel consequences of their system of polygamy" (A. Hallam, 219; Sismondi, 1.93).[71] There are also many striking similarities between Hallam's and Sismondi's accounts of the transmission of the chivalric aesthetic from the East to the West. The descriptions of the seraglio as both "a temple and a prison" and the relationship of that environment to the chivalric sensibility in Provençal verse take the same verbal and syntactic shape in both Hallam's and Sismondi's histories (A. Hallam, 220; Sismondi, 1.94). While Hallam does not follow Sismondi's argument to its bitter end—a lurid description of modern Morocco as a "deser[t] of burning sand, which the human tyrant disputes with the beast of prey"; of modern Iraq as "a heap of ruins"; of all Arab territories as self-destructively overcome by "ignorance, slavery, terror, and death" (1.75–76)—he clearly takes inspiration from Sismondi's discussion of the amatory cultures of Arabia and Provence.[72]

The most intriguing example of Sismondi's influence is Hallam's comment on rhyme, which reproduces almost verbatim Sismondi's words on the same subject: "La rime est un appel au souvenir et à l'espérance."[73] Hallam's phrasing, "Rhyme has been said to contain in itself a constant appeal to Memory and Hope," acknowledges a precedent for this idea, but he never discloses the source. When Patmore quotes Hallam in 1857, he seems to be unfamiliar with the derivation of both this quotation and another insight that he attributes to Hallam but that also appears in Sismondi: that Southern European languages, because they are vowel heavy, lend themselves to rhyme, while the consonants of Northern languages are conducive to alliteration.[74] Patmore's praise of Hallam is extravagant and rests on these two passages from the "Oration." He calls him "a young writer who, had he lived a few years longer, would probably have been famous without the monument of the most beautiful elegiac poem of modern times."[75] In the critical edition of Patmore's essay, the source of the "Memory and Hope" quotation remains obscure. By way of clarification, the editor's annotation only suggests, "Sidney . . . Webbe . . . and Daniel all had recognized in rhyme an aid to memory."[76] Unaware of Hallam's engagement with Sismondi's Continental historiography, Patmore's editor only considers English antecedents for Hallam's thought—and, consequently, the most instrumental connection between rhyme and memory: rhyme is a mnemonic device.

For Sismondi, however, rhyme is a visceral, sensory, and emotional experience. It brings together two pleasurably painful kinds of desire—a yearning for the past and a yearning for the future. It becomes a mystical and musical conduit of passionate feeling between poet and reader. This is a troubadour achievement, Sismondi tells us. Those poets, adapting the virtuosic monorhymes of Arabic lyrics, "varied their rhymes in a thousand different ways. They crossed and intertwined their verses, so that the return of the rhyme was preserved throughout the whole stanza; and they relied on their harmonious language, and on the well exercised ears of their readers, for making the expectation of the rhyme, and its return after many verses, equally productive of pleasure. In this manner, they have always appeared to me to have been completely masters of rhyme, and to have treated it as their own peculiar property" (1.107–8). Here is the passage that proved so generative for Hallam:

> *Rhyme is an appeal to our memory and to our expectations* ["l'espérance"].[77] It awakens the sensations we have already experienced, and it makes us wish for new ones. It increases the importance of sound, and gives, if I may so express myself, a colour to the words. In our modern poetry, the importance of the syllables is not measured solely by their duration, but by the associations they afford; and vowels, by turns, slightly, perceptibly, or emphatically marked, are no longer unnoticed, when the rhyme announces their approach and determines their position. What would become of the Provençal poetry, if we perused it only to discover the sentiment ["la pensée," the thought], such as it would appear in languid prose? It was not the ideas alone which gave delight, when the Troubadour adapted his beautiful language to the melodious tones of his harp; when, inspired by valour, he uttered his bold, nervous, and resounding rhymes; or, in tender and voluptuous strains, expressed the vehemence of his love. The rules of his art ["la prosodie"], even more than the words in which he expressed

> himself, were in accordance with his feelings. The rapid and recurring accentuation, which marked every second syllable in his iambic verses, seemed to correspond with the pulsations of his heart, and the very measure of the language answered to the movements of his own soul. It was by this *exquisite sensibility to musical impressions,* and by this delicate organization, that the Troubadours became the inventors of an art, which they themselves were unable to explain. They discovered the means of communicating, by this novel harmony, those emotions of the soul, which all poets have endeavoured to produce, but which they are now able to effect, only by following the steps of these inventors of our poetical measures. (1.116–18; emphasis mine)

This passage teases out much that remains implicit in Hallam's allusion to Sismondi. "Memory" and "Hope" gain a physiological concretion—they correspond to former sensations and ones that are wished for—but they also gain historical texture. More strongly even than in the "Oration," prosodic music (composed of rhyme and its corollary, accentual-syllabic meter) is allied to the ineffable experiences of romantic love and courtly longing that achieved a kind of expression in Provençal poetry. Indeed, so linked are prosody and feeling—through the troubadour's "exquisite sensibility to musical impressions"—that future uses of troubadour form can reproduce something like troubadour feeling. Here is a fuller picture of Hallam's modern, rhyming subject, with "a soul susceptible of musical impression" (222).

Significantly, in Sismondi's mythology Provence isn't credited with the origin of rhyme, or with the origin of courtly love; the Islamic Middle East is. Nor is Provence the place where rhymed poetry was polished: that's medieval and Renaissance Italy. But Provence is the crucial middle step. Provence is responsible for two related features of European prosody that have had a lasting impact. The first is the discovery of affective form—that is, the way prosody can be used to convey *exquisitely* the feelings that elude direct description. The second Provençal innovation, which is the natural extension of affective prosody, is the wild proliferation of "poetical measures" to reflect the almost infinite range of feelings in need of expression. From this historical perspective, Provençal rhyme looks back to its medieval Arabic origins, and it looks forward to its romantic future.

THE *AMOUR DE LOIN* OF RHYMI

One anecdote in Sismondi's narrative vividly dramatize bist theory and hints at how a genetic *story* about literary history can become a usable *theory* of literary form. It's the legend of Geoffrey (Jaufré) Rudel, the twelfth-century troubadour whose experience of "distant love" appeared to allegorize the formal properties of rhyme. This anecdote, a favorite of nineteenth-century poets and critics, suggests a way to read and write rhyme historiographically.[78]

As Sismondi tells the story in his chapter on the poetry of Provence, Rudel has heard reports of a beautiful and virtuous Countess of Tripoli and fallen in love with her sight unseen. The lovelorn Rudel sets out on a boat to find his countess but gets sick on the journey. She learns that a poet is dying of love for her, and she meets him aboard the ship, where they have a touching encounter before he is "silenced by the convulsions of death." In Sismondi's faintly rhyming formulation, Rudel "was buried at Tripoli, beneath a tomb of porphyry, which the countess raised to his memory, with an Arabic inscription" (1.105).[79] Other accounts elaborate on the countess's grief: she becomes a nun and spends the rest of her life devoted to Rudel's memory. This story is about love in solitude and over long distance. For Rudel the love is prospective and for the countess it is retrospective, but in both cases the moment of their meeting is just a blip in a longer story of longing. The story had been told before, but in Sismondi's historiography it takes on special narrative significance. Rudel is not just one of the first troubadours, and he is not just the personification of *amour de loin*—"distant love"—a prototype and extreme variant of courtly love. He is also a crucial figure in the transnational history of rhyme, a poet who turns Arabic verse forms into Provençal lyric.

Sismondi introduces Rudel as his narrative pivots from Arabic to Provençal prosody. He writes, "In Arabic poetry … the second verse of each couplet terminates with the same word, and this repetition has been, likewise, adopted by the Provençals. A remarkable example of it may be found in some verses of Geoffrey de Rudel," and then he tells Rudel's story and presents a poem that resembles the Arabic couplet form (the *ghazal*) he has just described.[80] Here is Thomas Roscoe's translation of Sismondi's Rudel poem, which appeared alongside versions in Provençal and French. Note the play of monorhyme against repetition, with every other line landing insistently on the word "afar" [*luench/loin*].

> Angry and sad shall be my way,
>   If I behold not her afar,
> And yet I know not when that day
>   Shall rise, for still she dwells afar.
> God! Who hast formed this fair array
>   Of worlds, and placed my love afar,
> Strengthen my heart with hope, I pray,
>   Of seeing her I love afar.
> Oh, Lord! Believe my faithful lay,
>   For well I love her though afar,
> Though but one blessing may repay
>   The thousand griefs I feel afar.
> No other love shall shed its ray
>   On me, if not this love afar,
> A brighter one, where'er I stray
>   I shall not see, or near, or far. (1.104–6)

On the page, the repeating word "afar" (or "loin" or "luench") seems to denote the spatial and temporal distance that the other rhymes reach across. The poem doesn't just describe *amour de loin*: it convinces us that rhyme intrinsically is *amour de loin*—a kind of long-distance longing.

The poem appears to corroborate Sismondi's historical argument about the transmission of rhyme through the Mediterranean, and it helps make his case for the elegiac and erotic properties of rhyme. It demonstrates, through the poem's material verse structure, both the international genealogy and the poetics he is promoting.[81] When Sismondi comes to his general observations about rhyme, he makes its formalization of troubadour love explicit. The troubadours, adapting the rhymes of Arabic poetry into a variety of stanzaic forms, found "the secret and mysterious associations" between modern prosody and the emotions. When the troubadour "uttered his bold, nervous, and resounding rhymes; or in tender and voluptuous strains, expressed the vehemence of his love," he was discovering that "rhyme is an appeal to our memory and to our expectations" (1.116–17).

Which brings us back to the aphoristic sentence of Arthur Hallam's that took on the status of a theory in the nineteenth century: "Rhyme has been said to contain in itself a constant appeal to Memory and Hope." On the face of it, Hallam's statement addresses rhyme's formal and affective qualities only. It tells us that the distance between two rhyme words is a space of desire: the first word bends toward the second—longs for it, even—and the second word, when we reach it, remembers the first (and its longing), maybe with a retrospective longing of its own. As readers we participate in this desire, so that when we read rhymes, the hoping and remembering and longing are also ours. This is an account of rhyme on the page and in the body and mind; it seems resolutely ahistorical. But of course, it isn't. What rhyme *contains in itself* is stories about the history of rhyme: Rudel's hope and the Countess of Tripoli's memory; Provence's worship of Arabic poetry; the way the troubadours tuned Arabic rhyme to their loving and longing feelings; the way the Italian and English poets tuned their own prosody to the troubadour's song. Hallam's romantic theory of rhyme, borrowed from Sismondi, is a scholarly fantasy about rhyme's many translations—the transnational, translinguistic, transhistorical journey by which modern rhyme arrived. For Sismondi, Arthur Hallam, and their contemporaries, that literary history is the burden rhyme carries.

PART II

Historiographic Forms

◎ 3 ◎

Alfred Tennyson's Lyric Stanza

Sismondi's genetic theory of rhyme plainly influenced Arthur Hallam's literary-historical writing and the poetic theory embedded there; as we'll see, it also gave Hallam a critical vocabulary for approaching Tennyson's poetry. But this book is pursuing a bigger argument: that literary histories like Sismondi's made Victorian poetry what it was. Literary-historical ideas are legible in the *shape* of Victorian poems, in their lines and rhymes and stanzas. What has become merely, opaquely "form" was once transparently (or at least translucently) historical. And what has become merely, inscrutably "feeling" was once the more obvious effect of historiographic form. Reading for historiographic form can change our experience and evaluation of a Victorian poem. As I hinted in my discussion of "Tears, Idle Tears," it can also illuminate and make newly analyzable an experience of a poem that we already have. It can reveal that a reading experience we recognize as aesthetic may also be an unrecognized encounter with literary-historical ideas.

Let's reconsider Tennyson's *In Memoriam* with this possibility in mind. Hallam's Sismondian description of rhyme has been cited often to explain the strangely sad form of the ABBA *In Memoriam* stanza, the melancholy feeling of its progressive and regressive rhymes. But without the literary-historical aspect of Hallam's "Memory and Hope" formula, we can't really account for the precision of Tennyson's technique. Sismondi's genetic theory lets us see that the emotional force of Tennyson's stanza derives from an *amour-de-loin* understanding of rhyme: an effort to draw attention to the spatial and temporal coordinates of stanzaic form—understood also as emotional coordinates—that accord with his elegiac theme.

In Memoriam is a consummately romantic poem: a love poem

patterned on the love poems of the romantic tradition that fascinated Hallam, and not only insofar as its rhyme scheme resembles a Petrarchan quatrain.[1] Like the lyrics of Petrarch, Dante, and Rudel, Tennyson's elegy is about impossible love, the erotic amplification of long-distance desire, and the blurring of desire and grief. Notice, for instance, how these lines meditate on the pain and pleasure of loving across a distance:

> O days and hours, your work is this
> To hold me from my proper place,
> A little while from his embrace,
> For fuller gain of after bliss:
>
> That out of distance might ensue
> Desire of nearness doubly sweet;
> And unto meeting when we meet,
> Delight a hundredfold accrue.[2]

The *amour de loin* that *In Memoriam* describes involves distances of time (past, present, and future; memory and hope) and space (earth and heaven). Toward the end of *In Memoriam,* we arrive at the consolatory idea that the separations brought about by Hallam's death yield a sort of erotic union:

> Dear friend, far off, my lost desire,
> So far, so near in woe and weal;
> O loved the most, when most I feel
> There is a lower and a higher;
>
> Known and unknown; human, divine;
> Sweet human hand and lips and eye;
> Dear heavenly friend that canst not die,
> Mine, mine, for ever, ever mine;
>
> Strange friend, past, present, and to be;
> Loved deeplier, darklier understood;
> Behold, I dream a dream of good,
> And mingle all the world with thee. (129.1–12)

These lines are structured by a series of paradoxes that help us interpret the poem's form. Hallam is both nearby and "far off," both human and divine, both lost and possessed, both estranged and omnipresent. In a poem preoccupied with the elegiac "use [of] measured language" (5.6), the lines inevitably suggest the paradoxical work of rhyme as well: its separating and unifying functions; its action in durational poetic time ("past, present, and to be") and across vertical stanzaic space ("a lower and a higher"). Because the poem invests the gap between past and present, lower and higher with the emotional content of grief and desire, the rhymes acquire that content, too. And the sequence of terminal sounds sensitizes us to rhyme's effects, progressively calibrating our ear. As we move through each quatrain, we are made to experience the differences among not rhyming (AB), adjacent rhyming (BB), and rhyming over a distance (A–A). The *In Memoriam* stanza seems to ask: Can you feel that (AB)? No? Can you feel it now (BB)? What about *now* (A–A)? And we do. The A–A long-distance rhyme thrums with longing (and perhaps a kind of prosodic "after-bliss").

Something like this mimetic interpretation is available to the modern reader; what has not been available is the rich historiographic mythology that informs the formal mimesis. With the benefit of that intellectual context, we see that Tennyson's ABBA stanza form actually theorizes romantic rhyme as such. Like the historiographic prose of Sismondi and Hallam, it makes a genetic argument about the feelings contained in rhyme. The *In Memoriam* stanza represents all rhyme—but especially the distance rhyming of the romantic stanza—as a matter of *amour de loin*, a memory of Rudel's medieval desire.

In Memoriam may seem an unlikely heir to Sismondi's history. It isn't a poem about Jaufré Rudel. It isn't even overtly about literary history, beyond its generic ties to elegy and sonnet. But *In Memoriam* is an important case partly *because* the historiographic element is not transparent. The poem has come down to us as a paragon of Victorian feeling and one of the century's most distinctive formal achievements. I suggest that the prosodic feeling of the *In Memoriam* stanza—felt in the nineteenth century and still feelable now—is the product of Tennyson's long experiment with historiographic form.

This chapter locates the beginning of that experiment in the reciprocal relationship between Tennyson's early poetry and Arthur Hallam's interpretation of it. While chapter 2 focused on Hallam's contribution to general literary history, I also alluded to a broader engagement with literary historiography in his and Tennyson's work. I proposed that

Hallam's better-known and slightly earlier review of Tennyson's poems should be regarded as historiographic literary criticism, insofar as it models the transformation of literary-historical theories into tools for close reading. And I suggested that Tennyson's early poetry can be read for historiographic form as craft.

This chapter takes those claims further. I begin by examining the importance of the stanza in Tennyson's practice, and the poet's evolving thinking about the representational and expressive potential of that form. I then show how Hallam's "Characteristics" essay theorizes the process of turning literary history into poetry, using Sismondi's literary-historical categories to describe and evaluate Tennyson's compositional method in *Poems, Chiefly Lyrical* (1830). The Sismondian figure of the "Poet of Sensation" especially helps Hallam explain Tennyson's inventive approach to "lyrical" poetry and stanzaic form. The latter part of the chapter turns to two poems that for Hallam exemplify Tennyson's sensation poetics, "Recollections of the Arabian Nights" and "The Ballad of Oriana"; and I identify the ways in which those poems materially engage with Hallam's and Sismondi's ideas about the roots of the modern lyric stanza. With "Arabian Nights" and "Oriana," Tennyson manipulates the form of the stanza to create poetic effects that are recognizable as historiographic. In the case of "Arabian Nights," Tennyson's virtuoso stanzas evoke orientalist fantasies about rhyme's original relationship to creativity. In "Oriana," Tennyson turns his historiographic formalism toward the romantic pathos of "Memory and Hope." Both these poems find Tennyson dreaming, with Hallam, the medievalist dream of a perfectly responsive form. I suggest, finally, that Tennyson's verse forms—with their ongoing commitments to the principles of novelty, specificity, and expressiveness—retain the historiographic investments of these early poems, even as the historical content seems to fall away.

STANZAIC MEANING, STANZAIC FEELING

Tennyson's poetic forms have been read as mimetic and expressive since the nineteenth century. This has been particularly true of *In Memoriam*: from its publication onward, readers have noticed a felicitous correspondence between the poem's rhyme structure (ABBA) and the poet's elegiac intention. "How exquisitely adapted the music of the poem is to its burden," wrote George Henry Lewes in the *Leader* in 1850, "the stanza chosen, with its mingling rhymes, and its slow, yet not imposing march, seems to us the very perfection of stanza for the purpose"; and Charles Kingsley, writing in *Fraser's Magazine* the same year, described the stanza as "so exquisitely chosen, that while the major rhyme in the second and third lines of each stanza gives the solidity and self-restraint required by such deep themes, the mournful minor rhyme of each first and fourth line leads the ear to expect something beyond, and enables the poet's thoughts to wander sadly on, from stanza to stanza. . . ."[3] In recent years, critics have been just as eager to hear significant feeling in *In Memoriam*'s form—and frequently, as I have been suggesting, with an ear to the "Memory and Hope" dynamics that Arthur Hallam described.

It strikes me as important that Tennyson thought he invented the *In Memoriam* stanza when he began to use it in the 1830s.[4] This means that he was writing in a stanza form that was both "so exquisitely chosen" and, in his mind, new. In its deviation from previous elegiac forms—from classical elegiacs, from Milton's pastoral elegy, from Thomas Gray's ABAB elegiac stanza—it looks like an attempt to reimagine the formal needs of elegy, a very different enterprise from selecting a stanza form ready-made and already freighted with generic and literary-historical associations. In this sense, Tennyson's *In Memoriam* stanza is something like Dante's invention of terza rima for the *Divine Comedy*: an effort to make stanzaic meaning from scratch.[5]

And yet, that is an oversimplification of what Tennyson likely believed he was doing and, from the Victorian perspective, what Dante had done. For expressive potential to be found in the organization of a stanza, that potential would have to be understood to be latent in a stanza's component parts (rather than simply a product of generic convention). In other words, the combination of fit and novelty only works if stanzaic architecture is believed to be generally, as well as specifically, eloquent. An early theorization of stanzaic eloquence can be found in Dante's *De vulgari eloquentia* (1304) and *Vita nuova* (1293), both of which are preoccupied with parsing the language of stanzaic form.[6] In *De vulgari eloquentia*—an examination of Provençal poetry and a manual for composition, as much as a defense of vernacular poetics

Dante describes the *canzone*'s stanza as a "spacious edifice, mansion, or receptacle ... a unified structure of lines and syllables bound by a certain musical setting and the harmonious disposition of its parts," or a "poetic fabric" that can "rejoice in being woven." The component parts of a stanza are called "feet," "head," and "tail."[7] This mix of metaphors—from architecture, music, textiles, anatomy—does not quite culminate in instructions for generating particular meanings or effects, but it does present the stanza as a set of elements whose combinatorial possibilities are neither fixed nor arbitrary.[8] The stanza is a built thing and the poet is, as Dante says of the troubadour Arnaut Daniel, a *fabbro*: a craftsman. In the *Vita nuova,* the prose interludes are concerned with minute formal exegeses of the sonnets and canzoni (e.g., "This sonnet has three parts. In the first ..."),[9] or with meditations on the numerological significance that moves between the poet-speaker's world and text, especially regarding the number nine.

What is less explicit in Dante's own work but explicit everywhere in nineteenth-century Dante criticism is the idea that the form of his poetry was a language in itself, and not just a vehicle for (or even an allegorical mirroring of) his poetry's thematic content. For Arthur Hallam, H. F. Cary's benchmark blank verse translation of the *Divine Comedy* failed to translate the poem, because it missed this crucial register: "[S]o important an integral part of every great poem is its musical structure, that an admirer of Dante, however much he is compelled to admire Mr. Cary's excellent work, must feel the infinite difference produced by that single alteration."[10] For Thomas Carlyle, too, terza rima was a language appropriate to the material of the poem not because it resembled it but because it was identical with it. The rhyme language—again, "musical," "architectural"—*is* the poem and is inseparable from its passionate feeling.[11] That Dante's theory and practice of the stanza were of keen interest to Tennyson is evident from a letter Hallam sent to him soliciting "a good deal of knowledge from you concerning metres which may be serviceable, as well for my philosophy in the notes as for my actual handiwork in the text."[12] Tennyson's reply has been lost along with all the other letters he wrote to Hallam, but Hallam's request for help with his *Vita nuova* translation indicates that he considered Tennyson to be as invested as he was in the material and philosophical dimensions of stanzaic form.[13]

Indeed, Tennyson's poetic output reveals a career spent in the workshop of the stanza. In the delicate warp and weft of "The Lady of Shalott" (1833, 1842), in the prosodic mood swings of *Maud* (1855), Tennyson keeps striving for "the very perfection of stanza for the purpose."[14] Even in the blank verse landscapes of *The Princess* (1847) and *Idylls of the King* (1859–85), he makes room for rhymed stanzas; and even his last poems appear to be fresh experiments in stanzaic form. The valedictory "God and the Universe" (1892), with its two quiet stanzas of rhyming tercets, rings with Dantean music.[15] At the same time, it has its own distinctive architecture—long lines of seventeen syllables—and its own expressive force, bringing both the minimal and the vast into the same stanzaic compass:

> Will my tiny spark of being wholly vanish in your deeps and
> heights?
> Must my day be dark by reason, O ye Heavens, of your boundless
> nights,
> Rush of Suns, and roll of systems, and your fiery clash of
> meteorites?
>
> Spirit, nearing yon dark portal at the limit of thy human state,
> Fear not thou the hidden purpose of that Power which alone is
> great,
> Not the myriad world, His shadow, nor the silent Opener of the
> Gate. (*Poems*, 1–6)

This brief lyric, written the year Tennyson died, shows an unexhausted interest in the eloquence of stanzaic form, and an unending quest for new poetic languages. Such commitments won Tennyson the praise of T. S. Eliot. In a retrospective summary of Tennyson's career, Eliot observed that "His variety of metrical accomplishment is astonishing"; he "extended very widely the range of active metrical forms in English." Even in the earliest poems, writes Eliot, Tennyson "was doing something new . . . something not derived from any of his predecessors." And in the midcareer *In Memoriam* and *Maud*, Eliot finds Tennyson exhibiting "the greatest lyrical resourcefulness that a poet has ever shown." To Eliot, "Tears, Idle Tears" is proof that Tennyson is "the great master of metric as well as of melancholia" and that no "poet in English has ever had a finer ear for vowel sound, as well as a subtler feeling for some moods of anguish."[16]

Tennyson's interest in building new poetic forms was closely allied to Hallam's interest in the affective element of rhyme, its "constant appeal to Memory and Hope." The newness Eliot noticed in Tennyson's early verse forms was a product of his and Hallam's literary-historical thinking, and the "lyrical resourcefulness" Eliot noticed in *In Memoriam*, *Maud*, and "Tears, Idle Tears"—the exquisite adjustment of form and sound to feeling—was a natural extension of that historiographic thought.

POEMS, CHIEFLY LYRICAL

Reading through Tennyson's first solo volume of poetry, *Poems, Chiefly Lyrical*, can be a disorienting experience. Superficially, it has almost no cohesion, racing over a dizzying number of poetic forms, both traditional and new. Each of the fifty-six poems seems to test a fresh combination of rhythms, rhymes, and line lengths, as if the young poet is feeling around for something that works—or trying to prove, in the manner of an embroidery sampler, that he can make any stitch work.

At worst, Tennyson's early critics saw this formal variety as the ineptitude of an amateur. John Stuart Mill, for instance, complained that he "often seems to take his metres almost at random"; and Samuel Taylor Coleridge, although he commended the "beauty" of Tennyson's first productions, was distressed to find that "I can scarcely scan his verses."[17] The solution that Coleridge proposed was a rigorous program of metrical training that emphasized consistency above all:

> What I would, with many wishes for success, prescribe to Tennyson,—indeed without it he can never be a poet in act,—is to write for the next two or three years in none but one or two well-known and strictly defined metres, such as the heroic couplet, the octave stanza, or the octo-syllabic measure of the Allegro and Penseroso. He would, probably, thus get imbued with a sensation, if not a sense, of metre, without knowing it, just as Eton boys get to write such good Latin verses by conning Ovid and Tibullus.[18]

Coleridge assumes that meter is a skill that Tennyson has not yet acquired. The undisciplined versifier, he suggests, should imitate examples of metrical regularity until he internalizes and is able to reproduce their rhythms, almost despite himself. What the poet of *Christabel* seems strangely to miss is the technical discipline with which Tennyson has approached his craft. Although his lyrics resist accentual-syllabic regularity, they do so—as the self-consciously experimental *Christabel* does—in a theoretically consistent way.

The coherence of Tennyson's first book is difficult to perceive if we think of his prosody, as many of his critics have, primarily in terms of the metrical line. But despite his later iambic achievements—from the metronomic tetrameters of *In Memoriam* to the supple pentameters of *The Princess* and *Idylls of the King*—*Poems, Chiefly Lyrical* is quite systematically unmetrical.[19] That is, the majority of its poems are governed less by meter than by rhyme. Most lyrics display audaciously challenging stanzaic patterns—whether that means a complex entanglement of multiple rhymes or the increasingly improbable repetition of a single rhyme sound. Tennyson later expressed embarrassment at many of these youthful experiments and declined to reprint some poems that had particularly intricate metrical and rhythmic patterns, but it's clear at this point in his career that the stanza, rather than the line or the metrical foot, is his primary unit of composition.

One discerning critic, of course, immediately recognized this. In his review of *Poems, Chiefly Lyrical*, Arthur Hallam lists fourth among "five distinctive excellencies" of Tennyson's style "the variety of his lyrical measures, and exquisite modulation of harmonious words and cadences to the swell and fall of the feelings expressed" (192). Hallam was making two related points about Tennyson's use of form. First, the eclecticism that feels scattershot to Coleridge and Mill is a virtue. Second, and more than that, it is a sign of absolute prosodic control; Hallam suggests that Tennyson is unusually attentive to the relationship between form and feeling (as Eliot will later say, "Tennyson's surface, his technical accomplishment, is intimate with his depths"), and that attention necessarily results in a multiplicity of finely calibrated—and differentiated—lyrical forms.[20]

Undergirding Hallam's praise is a well-developed, if unfamiliar, definition of lyric that both poet and critic seemed to share. For Hallam and the young Tennyson, lyric was an *idea about form*; it was defined not so much by the slippery abstractions of temporality and subjectivity—the post-Romantic commonplaces, and recurrent problems, of lyric studies—as by formal virtuosity and formal expressivity.[21] Instead of the classical voice of Sappho or Pindar, or the Romantic voice of Wordsworth, its models are the sensitive rhyme schemes and innovative stanzaic designs of medieval romantic poetry, as those were described and interpreted by scholars of literary history. This medievalist, historiographic idea of lyric informs both Hallam's account of the "Poet of Sensation" and Tennyson's stanzaic music.

SISMONDI AND THE POETRY OF SENSATION

Hallam's review of *Poems, Chiefly Lyrical,* "On Some of the Characteristics of Modern Poetry, and on the Lyrical Poems of Alfred Tennyson" (1831), is best known for framing Tennyson as a "Poet of Sensation" in the vein of Keats and Shelley, rather than a Wordsworthian "Poet of Reflection." The poet of sensation, according to Hallam, is an exceptional person, more alive to sensory experiences than his fellow men, and more able to translate those experiences into poetry than the majority of even his fellow poets. Shelley and Keats, for example, were "[s]usceptible of the slightest impulse from external nature, their fine organs trembled into emotion at colors, and sounds, and movements, unperceived or unregarded by duller temperaments. Rich and clear were their perceptions of visible forms; full and deep their feelings of music" (186). Tennyson, says Hallam, shares the sensitivity of Shelley and Keats—like them, "He sees all the forms of nature with the 'eruditus oculus,' and his ear has a fairy fineness"—but he surpasses both, because he avoids their greatest ideological and stylistic weaknesses. Ultimately, Hallam insists that in Tennyson, "[t]he features of original genius are clearly and strongly marked . . . we recognize the spirit of his age, but not the individual form of this or that writer. His thoughts bear no more resemblance to Byron or Scott, Shelley or Coleridge, than to Homer or Calderón, Firdúsí or Calidasa" (191). In this strikingly international list of nonresemblances, Hallam is making a perverse sort of claim: Tennyson is *unlike* everyone else, just like those giants of world literature whom he in no way resembles. Throughout the review, Hallam treads this fine line between identifying Tennyson with his best precursors—whether in English or in Greek, Spanish, Persian, or Sanskrit—and always distinguishing him from them. This is the central paradox of the poet of sensation: he is both generic and completely new.

One of the most influential readings of "Characteristics" is Isobel Armstrong's in *Victorian Poetry*.[22] Her book put Hallam at the center of the field, using his charismatic personality and the text of his review to introduce her case for the political and aesthetic sophistication of Victorian poetry. In Hallam's account of the "'two-fold' consciousness" of the poet of sensation, Armstrong sees an early articulation of the "double poem," which she takes to be the defining form of Victorian poetry.[23] Demonstrating the essay's ties to contemporary comparative philology, historiography, theology, mythography, and philosophy, and its various debts to Kant, Herder, Schiller, Grimm, and Bopp, she views it as a composite work whose conclusions are nonetheless "dangerously" original. Though Hallam's key terms "sensation" and "reflection" bear a strong resemblance to Schiller's "naive" and "sentimental," Armstrong finds that they don't quite correspond to either Schiller or Kant. She writes,

> In taking over, via Schiller, the Kantian aesthetic of disinterested free play and making an intransigent distinction between sensation and reflection Hallam never fully defined what he intended by these terms. Emotion, feeling, sensuous experience, sense data, intuition, are all rather different but all possible significations of "sensation." Unlike Kant, for whom "reflection" might be glossed as epistemological ideas (in the third critique at least) and "sensation" as the unique representations of the data of experience by consciousness, Hallam was not exact and left unquestioned a dichotomy between thought and sensation which was filtered through Schiller into categories which actually construct the division they describe.[24]

Without disputing Armstrong's claims for the importance of German idealism to the Cambridge group, I would characterize the review as a reformulation more than a synthesis. Hallam likely found in Sismondi's work many of his central concepts ready-made. As Sismondi himself was drawing on contemporary philological and philosophical thought (especially Herder's, Schiller's, and de Staël's), his work already contained the synthesis of ideas and discourses that Armstrong describes. Sismondi's literary historiography is a study of language and literature, a theory of aesthetics, and a philosophy of history all at once.

The opening pages of *Historical View of the Literature of the South of*

Europe, which present the unifying thesis of Sismondi's survey, seem to have provided Hallam with the concepts he used to approach Tennyson's poems. In Sismondi, Hallam would have encountered the poet of sensation and the poet of reflection; in Sismondi, he would have found the diagnosis of modern melancholy and what he calls the "return of the mind upon itself," with its turning away from "community of interest."[25] What is remarkable about Hallam's essay is less the invention or adoption of such terms than their canny repurposing.

In Sismondi's books, sensation and reflection are historical categories, with periods of spontaneous feeling yielding to periods of reflection in the development of literary cultures (Sismondi's French terms are *sentiment* and *réflexion*; Roscoe's English translations are "feeling" and "reflection"). It is not so much that sensation belongs to one particular historical epoch versus another—ancient versus modern, for example, as is broadly (though not absolutely) the case for Schiller—but that sensation and reflection are two successive periods within a particular national literary history. The early Greeks and the troubadours both shared the sensitive and creative energy that Hallam assigns to Tennyson: "Feeling with them takes the lead of judgment, and may conduct them to the highest results," Sismondi writes, "Such was Greece in her infancy; such, perhaps, were the European nations, in their first developement, during the middle ages; and such are all nations which by their native energy rise out of barbarism, and which have not suffered the spirit of imitation to extinguish their natural vigour" (1.3).

Concrete examples strengthen the polemical force of this distinction. By incorporating a wide range of primary materials—specimens of Arabic, Persian, Provençal, Italian, Spanish, and Portuguese poems—Sismondi can make his historicist case for revaluing the verse forms and styles of early Romance poetry, which French neoclassical taste has devalued. "[A]s I have proposed," he writes, "rather to make the reader acquainted with the masterpieces of foreign languages, than to pass a judgment upon them according to arbitrary rules . . . I have had recourse to the originals as often as it was in my power . . . and it is my intention rather to extract and give translations . . . than to detail the doubtful opinions of critics" (1.12–13). Sismondi wanted his French readers to judge historical romantic literature on its own terms, rather than holding it up to alien standards of taste. Though he translates his extracts into modern French—and Roscoe further translates them into English verse in the 1823 edition—Sismondi is attentive to the challenge of working across languages. In his closing paragraphs, he implores his readers to spend a few months studying Spanish and Italian, so that they might better hear the music in these poems (4.571).

One might think that Sismondi's examples would be useful models for the working poet; they gather, all into one place and to an unprecedented degree, so much stanzaic variety. And framing all of these forms are discussions of the prosodic systems that govern the poetry in each language, sometimes even with scansion marks. But Sismondi's introduction makes clear the difference between masterpieces and models. He argues that poets at the origins of literary cultures do not rely on models; they invent the systems that they use. When a culture first begins to express itself in its own literary language—when it has not yet begun to reach for the rules derived from other cultures and other languages—its poets are prosodic innovators. However, Sismondi cautions, the spirit of imitation inevitably creeps in. "Reflection," he says, "soon succeeds to this vehement effervescence.... The mind feeds upon its own enthusiastic feelings, which withdraw themselves from the observations of others" and "the energy of the mind is seen to react continually upon itself" (1.6, 5). Sismondi offers several instances of this decline: the Romans eventually copied the Greeks, the Arabs began to worship Aristotle, the Italians in the sixteenth century and the French in the seventeenth began to imitate the ancients, and then the Germans, Polish, and Russians began to imitate the French. For Sismondi, the reflective turn tells in prosody. Reflective poets "encumber themselves with the fetters of a refined versification" and resort mechanically to "the return of rhymes which restrict their thoughts" (1.5). So rather than presenting his poetic extracts as models to be copied, they often stand as poignant reminders of what was possible before European literatures became reflective.

As a result, the chapters that treat the origins of modern lyric poetry emphasize the ideal of formal innovation, using their extracts and descriptions to demonstrate what poetic forms can look and feel like when they are not being imitative. The two poetic cultures that developed rhyme—medieval Arabic and Provençal—both wrote poetry that was "entirely lyric" (1.60); both poetries were characterized by deep feeling, especially "the passion of love" (1.94); both cultures highly valued the production of new forms of poetic expression. Arabic and Persian poets like "Al-Monotabbi of Cufa" [*sic*] and Ferduzi, rejecting the "cold" poetry of the Greeks, invented "bold metaphors," "extravagant allegories," and "excessive hyperboles" (1.59). As Keats, that other poet of sensation might say, they loaded every rift with ore: "They burdened their compositions with riches, under the idea that nothing which was beautiful could be superfluous. They were not contented with one comparison, but heaped them one upon another, not to assist the reader in catching their ideas, but to excite his admiration of their colouring" (1.60).[26] On the authority of the orientalist William Jones, Sismondi points to the same spirit of artful "extravagance" in Arabic and Persian versification, which apparently married formal constraint with prosodic pyrotechnics, as when "the same rhyme, or rather the same terminating vowel is repeated in every other line for several pages" or when the poet "regularly pursued in his rhymes all the letters of the alphabet" (1.61–62).[27] In Provençal poetry, as we've seen, Sismondi found the troubadours expanding the affective range of this prosodic system, "var[ying] their rhymes in a thousand different ways" to express the varied and ineffable "emotions of the soul" (1.107, 1.118).[28] Though the troubadours adopted the subtle mechanism of rhyme from the Arabians, they are nonetheless "the inventors of our poetical measures," because they developed the European rhymed stanza, with its infinite variability (1.118). Medieval Arabic and Provençal poetry both appear as examples, on the world-historical scale, of what Hallam will term sensation poetics.

"Characteristics" is a work of criticism that metabolizes literary historiography, turning Sismondi's historical theories into a way of reading, and writing, contemporary poetry. It makes of Sismondi's historicism a kind of formalism—though that risks being a clumsy characterization of both writers' work, which always seems to move smoothly between the macro and the micro, the world-historical scene and the prosodic detail on the page. In Arthur Hallam's review, Sismondi's historical categories are dehistoricized to the extent that poets of sensation and poets of reflection can coexist in the same culture and moment, as Keats and Wordsworth do (this is ultimately how Schiller understands the naive and sentimental, too—and, by extension, his own relationship to his contemporary, Goethe). Yet Hallam's account of sensation and reflection isn't without historical resonance. Echoes of Sismondi's argument can be heard throughout the review, as when

Hallam remarks that "the age in which we live comes late in our national progress. That first raciness and juvenile vigor of literature ... is gone, never to return. Since that day we have undergone a period of degradation" (189). And elsewhere: "Hence the melancholy which so evidently characterises the spirit of modern poetry; hence that return of the mind upon itself" (190). The framework, then, of Sismondi's historiography provides a context for representing Tennyson as almost impossibly gifted—as a genius out of time.

When Hallam finally comes to the criticism of Tennyson's poems, Sismondi is everywhere. Like Sismondi's vigorous poets, Tennyson "imitates nobody" (191). Many of the "distinctive excellencies" of Tennyson's style are in fact values associated with Sismondi's medieval lyric poets—not just the "exquisite modulation" of meters but also "his luxuriance of imagination, and at the same time his control over it" (191). Indeed, the poems that Hallam chooses to close read (which he orders sequentially according to his Arabist chronology of rhyme) are striking experiments in stanzaic and figurative imagining.[29] The two that he treats first and at the greatest length are "Recollections of the Arabian Nights" and "The Ballad of Oriana"—two poems that, as Hallam frames them, borrow the formal methods of medieval romantic poetry. They evoke historical sensation poetics without copying—indeed, *by not copying*—any particular historical form.

At first glance, these poems couldn't be more different from one another. "Recollections of the Arabian Nights" is an orientalist fantasy apparently inspired by two tales in Antoine Galland's 1704–17 French translation of the *Arabian Nights*.[30] The narrative is a child's dream vision of a boat ride down the Tigris river in "the golden prime / Of good Haroun Alraschid"—the historical period that Sismondi associates with the efflorescence of medieval Arabic poetry.[31] Each of the fourteen stanzas brings the entranced child deeper into an increasingly luxurious landscape, until he finds himself face to face with a beautiful Persian princess and, finally, King Haroun Alraschid himself. "The Ballad of Oriana," based on a Scottish border ballad, tells the tragic story of woman who is killed when she accidentally intercepts an arrow shot by her lover. The poem is a first-person account of the lover's grief and regret. Formally, "Oriana" is distinguished by an intensely repetitive and recursive ballad stanza. Although these poems look and sound nothing alike, together they measure out the extraordinary scope of Tennyson's early lyric craftsmanship. "Oriana" is a bold display of prosodic redundancy, testing the limits of a single rhyme sound, whereas the special accomplishment of "Arabian Nights" is its diversity of rhyme scheme within a consistent stanzaic frame.

The poems also appear to engage with two completely different generic and literary-historical traditions: on one hand, medieval Arabic fiction and its appropriation by European orientalism; on the other hand, early modern British balladry and its antiquarian revival. If "The Ballad of Oriana" seems to gesture toward the domestic origins of English poetry in English and Scottish song, "Recollections of the Arabian Nights" dramatizes an encounter with literary otherness. As Hallam reads them, however, the two poems are part of a unified aesthetic project and address themselves to a coherent historiographic theory. In Hallam's Sismondian reading of Tennyson, literary history appears less as a collection of discrete sources and models (e.g., the tale, the ballad; Galland, Scott) than as one continuous story about the origins of literary forms.

Hallam's historiographic literary criticism doesn't account for every feature of *Poems, Chiefly Lyrical.* But it does help us see the historical aspect of Tennyson's early formalism—and especially how his stanzas can cite ideas about literary history without reproducing specific literary-historical precedents, like the *ghazal* or the *ruba'i,* or some familiar version of a ballad stanza.[32] Neither poem uses a recognizable historical verse form, but—and partly because of this—their stanzas can be viewed as historiographic forms. These poems interest me because their formal engagement with literary history is both extremely concrete and extremely abstract. Tennyson uses rhyme patterns and stanzaic shapes and sounds to think, with Hallam, about originality as a historical phenomenon, about a tradition of poetic newness that reaches back into the distant past.

"RECOLLECTIONS OF THE ARABIAN NIGHTS"

"Recollections of the Arabian Nights" was not Tennyson's first poetic fantasy of the Orient. Many of the poems he wrote before *Poems, Chiefly Lyrical* treated Eastern themes, often inspired by his reading of

William Jones, whose collected works were at Tennyson's childhood home in Somersby.[33] Nor was it his last. As Joseph Phelan has argued, Tennyson's relationship to the East developed and hardened over the course of his career, moving from his dreamy "infatuation with the *Arabian Nights*" to the "crudely racial language" of later poems like "Locksley Hall Sixty Years After" (1886).[34] But among the early poems of that type, "Arabian Nights" is the most prosodically ambitious.

Along with its heavy-handed historical fiction and conventional repertoire of orientalist tropes, "Arabian Nights" exhibits a surprisingly sophisticated approach to historical form. The poem has fourteen stanzas whose proportions are tightly controlled. All of the stanzas are made up of eleven rhyming lines, and each of them culminates in a refrain that repeats itself, with only the smallest of variations on the same formula ("For it was in the golden prime / Of good Haroun Alraschid!"). Here is the first stanza:

> When the breeze of a joyful dawn blew free
> In the silken sail of infancy,
> The tide of time flowed back with me
>   The forwardflowing tide of time;
> And many a sheeny summermorn,
> Adown the Tigris I was borne,
> By Bagdat's shrines of fretted gold,
> Highwallèd gardens green and old;
> True Mussulman was I and sworn,
> For it was in the golden prime
>   Of good Haroun Alraschid.[35]

Within the uniform stanzaic frame, Tennyson's rhymes appear inconsistent almost to the point of randomness, but his ability to sustain the impression of arbitrary rhyming across the sequence of stanzas results in a virtuosic display of combinatorial possibilities. The challenge Tennyson has set himself with this poem is formidable: devising a fresh interpretation of an eleven-line rhyme pattern for nearly every stanza. It is a problem of probability as much as poetics. Because of its extraordinary exertions to avoid repeating rhyme schemes, "Arabian Nights" allows us to see prosodic variety as design rather than accident.[36]

As Hallam remarks, variety is the guiding aesthetic rule of "Arabian Nights." He attributes his experience of the poem's "freshness" to Tennyson's inventive picture-making. "Originality of observation," he enthuses, "seems to cost nothing to our author's liberal genius; he lavishes images of exquisite accuracy and elaborate splendour, as a common writer throws about metaphorical truisms, and exhausted tropes."[37] And Hallam is right: every stanza delivers new and gorgeous images of "citronshadows" (2.4), "diamond rillets musical" (5.4), "varycoloured shells" (6.2), "[t]all orient shrubs, and obelisks / Graven with emblems of the time" (10.8–9), the Persian girl with "argentlidded eyes" and "many a dark delicious curl" (13.3, 7).[38] Herbert Tucker notes the lush, synesthetic quality of many of these descriptions, "as if in Haroun's pleasure dome the senses are temporarily divided ... for the sheer pleasure of reunion"[39]—but we also observe in Tennyson's extravagant figuration the unapologetic heaping upon one another of "bold metaphors," a performance in poetry of "the idea that nothing which [is] beautiful could be superfluous."[40]

In this dream vision the visual world naturally takes precedence, and the profusion of nonvisual sensations tend to work in service of the visual to intensify its effect. The variety that proliferates in "Arabian Nights" is of a distinctly visual nature, with disparate images coalescing into densely geometrical motifs. More striking even than the synesthetic mingling of eye and ear is the blurring Tennyson achieves between natural and artificial kinds of beauty and order. There's little formal difference, for example, between the artisanal fretwork on "Bagdat's shrines of fretted gold" and the way patterns of light and darkness decorate the larger environment: on the "shadowchequered lawn" (10.3); in the latticework shadows of "the long alley's latticed shade" (11.2); in the dappling sun that embellishes the "level lake with diamondplots / Of saffron light" (8.8–9). There is also a kind of visual rhyme between the "spangled floors" of the pavilion and "the starstrown calm" of the reflective river (11.6; 4.3). And between the floral needlework of the "broidered sophas" and of King Haroun's golden cloth—"Engarlanded and diapered / With inwrought flowers" (2.8; 14.5–6)—and the following figurative description of a flowering field:

> The sloping of the moonlit sward
> Was damaskwork, and deep inlay
> Of breaded blosms unmown, which crept
> Adown to where the waters slept. (3.5–8)[41]

In some images, the handicrafts are concrete, and objects like flowers and stars are the ornamental representations that give them beauty; in other images, flowers and stars are part of the natural world and the handicraft is a metaphor for their pleasing organizational design. But the frequent slippages between one kind of patterning and another make these distinctions hard to keep track of and finally irrelevant. Ultimately, all of "Arabian Nights" feels like one continuous and richly decorated tapestry.[42]

In their obvious craftedness, Tennyson's variegated stanzas join in this unifying artisanal design. The intricacy of the "Arabian Nights" stanza draws attention to two related but distinct aspects of stanzaic form: the shape of the poem on the page—what John Hollander termed "graphic prosody" or "the poem in the eye"—and the rhyme pattern that seems to generate the shape (an appeal to both the eye and the ear).[43] In many poems these aspects are almost indistinguishable, so that the outer architecture of the stanza and its internal music appear mutually constitutive. In "Arabian Nights," these two aspects of stanzaic form are pried apart. The visible stanza constitutes one kind of design, while each rhyme pattern constitutes another: a design within a design. Tennyson's procedure highlights the aesthetic and synesthetic experiences of stanzaic reading—and the hard work a poet performs to both enable and mystify those experiences.

Against its ornamented mise-en-scène, the acute formalism of the "Arabian Nights" stanza becomes legible as another feature of the poem's orientalist and medievalist aesthetics, insofar as it participates in the poem's historical fantasy about the golden age of Islamic art and craft—its fantasy about a whole world wrought over with exquisite arabesques.[44] One way to visualize Tennyson's complex rhyme work in "Arabian Nights" is to mark out the "bands" between corresponding rhymes, a notation system used by George Puttenham in his *Art of English Poesy* (1589) to illustrate the range of rhymed stanza forms available in English.[45] Here, Puttenham's system renders visible the detailed prosodic "damaskwork, and deep inlay" of the "Arabian Nights" stanza (fig. 1). To the extent that these stanzas articulate the poem's aesthetic fantasy in their rhyme patterns, they might be described as mimetic: another instance of Tennyson using form to say more, or better, the particular thing he wants his poem to say. As I've been emphasizing, though, this is not a matter of finding in the archive of literary history a

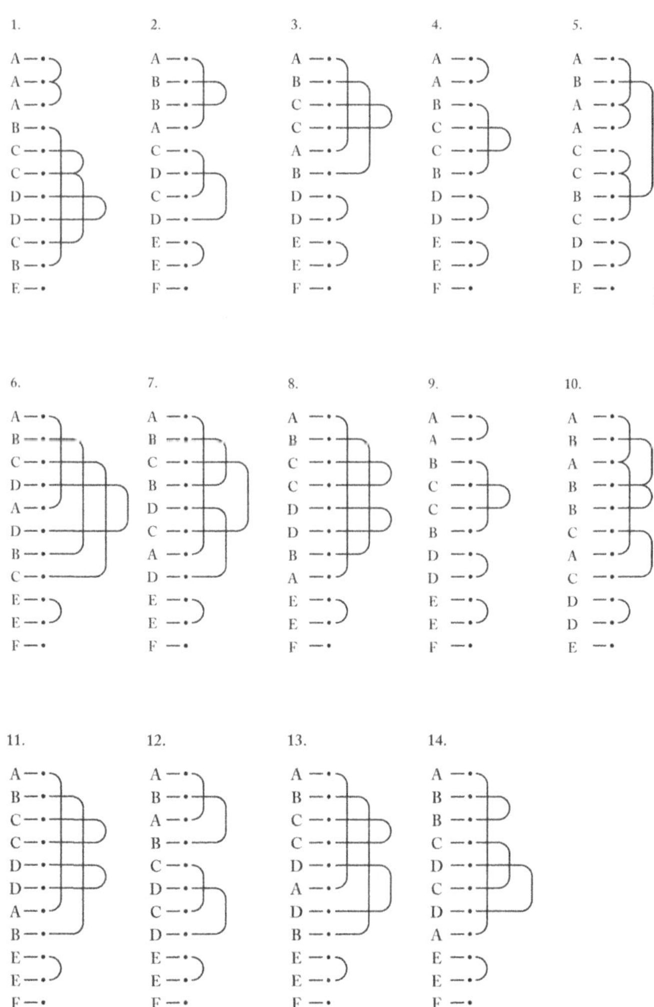

FIGURE 1. Rhyme schemes of Tennyson's "Recollections of the Arabian Nights" (1830).

verse form that particularly matches the narrative or historical material of the poem. In fact, from the perspective of historical fidelity, the "Arabian Nights" stanza is an anachronism. It doesn't look like Jones's and Sismondi's Arabic forms, with their elaborate systems of monorhyme or their pursuit, in rhyme, of "all the letters of the alphabet." It looks more like Sismondi's descriptions of the Provençal and Italian *canzone*, with its refrains and its interlaced stanzas and its acrobatic sestinas and its rhymes "varied . . . in a thousand different ways."[46] It looks less like a medieval Arabic poem, as that form was understood by European literary historians, than like the impact of medieval Arabic poetics on early European poetry: the effect of one culture of sensation poets learning from, but not exactly imitating, another. In other words, it is more a historiographic than a historical form. This poem represents literary history as a dream—or the *recollection* of a dream—in which, impossibly, "the tide of time flow[s] back with me, / The forward-flowing tide of time" (1.3–4). As each stanza circles back to its refrain, the poem reminds itself that "the golden prime" names a kind of desire—for perfection, for beginnings—rather than a historical time or place.

"THE BALLAD OF ORIANA"

While "Arabian Nights" is preoccupied with the seductive inaccessibility of origins, "The Ballad of Oriana" is—by Hallam's lights—evidence that prosody archives the literary-historical trace. In "The Ballad of Oriana," Hallam finds the poetic technique of Italian lyric operative in ballad form, and this prompts him to elaborate the affective component of genetic formalism: the idea that old forms carry the old feelings they were invented to express. The focus of Hallam's analysis is specifically the feeling of Tuscan poetics. But like the stanza of "Arabian Nights," the stanza of "The Ballad of Oriana" also tells a larger romantic story about stanzaic form.

Hallam reads "The Ballad of Oriana" as an exemplary use of literary history. The title of the poem indicates that Tennyson is working within the ballad tradition, but Hallam maintains that this ballad is radically different from other "Modern Ballads" in its careful negotiation of the relationship between new and old. Tennyson's great achievement, according to Hallam, lies in his ability to differentiate between an imitative use of literary conventions and a creative application of literary-historical lessons:

> We know no more happy seizure of the antique spirit in the whole compass of our literature; yet there is no foolish self-desertion, no attempt at obliterating the present, but everywhere a full discrimination of how much ought to be yielded and how much retained. The

> author is well aware that the art of one generation cannot *become* that of another by any will or skill; but the artist may transfer the spirit of the past, making it a temporary form for his own spirit, and so effect, by idealizing power, a new and legitimate combination. If we were asked to name among the real antiques that which bears greatest resemblance to this gem, we should refer to the ballad of *Fair Helen of Kirkconnel Lea* in the *Minstrelsy of the Scottish Border*. It is a resemblance of mood, not of execution. They are both highly wrought lyrical expressions of pathos; and it is very remarkable with what intuitive art every expression and cadence in *Fair Helen* is accorded to the main feeling. (194)

Instead of naming the concrete narrative or generic materials that Tennyson borrows from the ballad tradition—and they are many: the trope of tragic love, for instance, or the form of the refrain—Hallam emphasizes the "spirit" of the old ballads that Tennyson has managed to distill into a new "form" that partakes of both the past and the present.[47] As a poet of sensation, it is important that Tennyson's procedure owes as much to his poetic feeling as it does to his poetic skill. "The Ballad of Oriana" is "highly wrought" in two different but involved ways. It is a masterfully executed artwork, and it is also an expression of passionate emotion. Through the same "intuitive art" that governs the "Fair Helen" ballad, Tennyson creates an original poem that operates in the same way that "Fair Helen" does: by establishing a correspondence between the poem's formal and affective registers.[48]

But Hallam insists that Tennyson's ballad goes further even than "Fair Helen" does in this kind of correspondence, and that it derives inspiration from a deeper literary source than Scottish balladry: the lyric poetry of medieval Italy. Hallam suggests that lyric poetry is in fact defined by an idea of expressive form:

> The characters that distinguish the language of our *lyrical* from that of our *epic* ballads have never yet been examined with the accuracy they deserve. But, beyond question, the class of poems which in point of harmonious combination *Oriana* most resembles, is the Italian. Just thus the meditative tenderness of Dante and Petrarch is embodied in the clear, searching notes of Tuscan song. These mighty masters produce two-thirds of their effect by *sound*. Not that they sacrifice sense to sound, but that sound conveys their meaning where words would not. (194)

Whereas "Fair Helen" uses "every expression and cadence" to shore up its atmospheric effects, Tuscan poetry works with smaller prosodic units: "notes" and "tones." It uses a "harmonious combination" of individual sounds, and these combined sounds are expressive in ways that phrases, words, and larger rhythmic patterns are not.[49] Echoing Sismondi's description of troubadour rhyme, Hallam remarks that "there are innumerable shades of fine emotion in the human heart . . . which are too subtle and too rapid to admit of corresponding phrases. . . . Yet they exist . . . and in music they find a medium through which they pass from heart to heart. The tone becomes the sign of the feeling; and they reciprocally suggest each other" (195). This is the musical and emotional language of form that Hallam and Carlyle heard in Dante's terza rima and that Sismondi traced to the troudabour lyric stanza. Hallam does not name outright the poetic effect that he is describing (as assonance or rhyme); he stays at the level of abstraction and more or less sustains the conceit of music. But if we follow his argument about the differences between "The Ballad of Oriana" and "Fair Helen" further than he does, we can see how vowel tones and their rhymes might accumulate into feelings.

The clearest connection between the two poems is the story, which turns on a tragic accident that leaves the heroine dead. In "Fair Helen," Helen intercepts a shot meant for her lover and fired by his rival, and the lover's consequent retaliation is gruesome: "I hacked him in pieces sma'," he tells us. In "The Ballad of Oriana," the pathos is pitched higher still, as Oriana is shot by the lover himself when his target steps aside and leaves her in his arrow's path. This is a crucial revision, since it means that the lover is doubly burdened—with the loss of his beloved as well as with the unbearable knowledge that he is himself responsible for her death. When he exclaims, "Oh cursed hand! oh cursed blow! / Oriana!" it is a cry of self-reproach for a starkly unredeemable loss. When Helen's lover utters almost the same words, the effect is quite different: his affirmation of vengeance also pays tribute to a sacrifice that is not without its martyrly beauty:

> Curst be the heart that thought the thought,
> And curst the hand that fired the shot,
> When in my arms burd Helen dropt,
>   And died to succour me![50]

Just as Tennyson borrows the tragic outline of the ballad's narrative only to magnify its tragic possibilities, he approaches the ballad's form in the spirit of hyperbole. Scott's "Fair Helen" stanza is made up of a monorhymed triplet and a fourth line whose rhyme remains consistent throughout the poem. In the ballad's first stanza, the narrative quality of this fourth-line refrain is immediately apparent.

> I wish I were where Helen lies,
> Night and day on me she cries;
> O that I were where Helen lies,
> On fair Kirkconnell Lee![51]

In five of the ten stanzas, the fourth line acts as a refrain, establishing and circling back to the one central location of all the narrative's key events—Helen's death, the murder of her murderer, the place of her burial and grave, the place where the lover wishes to be buried in turn—"On fair Kirkconnell Lee." In the remaining five stanzas, however, the fourth line only rhymes with this refrain (most frequently on the word "me") and doesn't restate it.

Tennyson references these elements of rhyme and refrain but presses them to extraordinary new lengths. Instead of using a rhyming triplet and a final refrain, his poem's stanza monorhymes five times and obsessively rings its refrain—simply the word "Oriana"—a remarkable four times, between almost every narrative line. In the first stanza of Tennyson's poem, the affective consequences of this sonic thickening are impossible to miss.

> My heart is wasted with my woe,
> Oriana.
> There is no rest for me below,
> Oriana.
> When the long dun wolds are ribbed with snow,
> And loud the Norland whirlwinds blow,
> Oriana,
> Alone I wander to and fro,
> Oriana.[52]

Tennyson's first line sounds a lot like the ballad's first line; it has the same tone of desolation, the same iambic tetrameter rhythm, and it begins accumulating a similar sequence of *w* sounds—compare "My heart is **w**asted **w**ith my **w**oe" to "I **w**ish I **w**ere **w**here Helen lies." But very quickly a pattern of open-mouthed vowels (here, long Os) emerges as dominant: *w**o**e, **O**riana, n**o**, bel**o**w, **O**riana, sn**o**w, **O**riana, N**o**rland, bl**o**w, al**o**ne, fr**o**, **O**riana.* The pain that the poem describes becomes an audible—almost a visible—howl.[53]

The most notable difference between Tennyson's prosody and the ballad that inspired him, then, is the density of vowel sounds and the consequent intensification of the affective element—in Hallam's terms, the Italianization of the ballad material. So where the speaker of "Fair Helen" simply *describes* the experience of being haunted by the lost woman—

> Night and day on me she cries;
> Out of my bed she bids me rise,
>   Says, "Haste, and come to me!"[54]

—"The Ballad of Oriana" makes haunting an effect of form. The lover's subjective experience is not, as it is in "Fair Helen," hygienically sealed in the poem's diegesis; it has seeped outward to the shape and sound of the poem. The persistent refrain "Oriana" performs the lover's stymied efforts at coming to terms with his loss in a series of increasingly urgent vocatives:

> Oh! breaking heart that will not break,
>   Oriana,
> Oh! pale, pale face so sweet and meek,
>   Oriana,
> Thou smilest, but thou dost not speak,
> And then the tears run down my cheek,
>   Oriana:
> What wantest thou? whom dost thou seek,
>   Oriana? (8.1–9)

This refrain (the burden) invokes ballad conventions but also—in its excesses—defamiliarizes them. For Hallam, the excessiveness is the point; after entertaining the idea that "the name occurs once too often in every stanza," he concludes that "the proportion of the melodious cadences to the pathetic parts of the narration could not be diminished without materially affecting the rich lyrical impression of the ballad" (195). And it is true that "Oriana" behaves strangely for a refrain. Unlike the phrase "On fair Kirkconnell Lee," the repetition of the name here does almost no contextualizing work. Once Tennyson has established that Oriana is the sole object of the lover's thoughts, the word can only be an index of the lover's unrelenting grief—his singularly heavy burden. Rhetorically, it is pure apostrophe: the Petrarchan lyric address as ballad refrain. Sonically, it is as close to pure assonance as a multisyllabic word can come: the Petrarchan feminine rhyme on overdrive. As Anna Barton compellingly puts it, "Oriana" is "so pervasive that the arrow can hit no other target"; in the repetition of the heroine's name, the stanza offers a formal analogue for the fatal intercession of Oriana's body "atween" the lover and the arrow meant for him.[55]

By reducing the ballad refrain to just one word, and by expanding the field of action of that one word to the entire stanza, Tennyson blurs the distinction between refrain and rhyme. If refrain creates continuity across stanzas, "Oriana" is a refrain, because all the stanzas share the recurrence of that word. But the sequence of "Oriana"s also constitutes an internal structure within each stanza, one that plays against its system of monorhymes to become something both less and more than monorhyme: a scheme of identical rhymes. Identical rhyme is less of a rhyme than monorhyme, because it doesn't fulfill what we think of as the basic requirement of rhyme: the combination of repetition and difference that is apparent in the shift from, say, "cheek" to "seek."[56] But for the same reason, identical rhyme is a stronger and more perfect rhyme than monorhyme, achieving the objectives of monorhyme more completely than monorhyme can. The feeling of melancholic inertia that the monorhymes already produce in "The Ballad of Oriana" is exacerbated by a contrapuntal rhyme scheme that *won't* evolve with each new iteration in its sequence. Here, rhyme's appeal to memory becomes traumatic; in Hallam's Sismondian terms, the poem suffers from too much memory, and too little hope. Tennyson has isolated the most expressive elements of the medieval Tuscan stanza, and he has made them the primary material of his poem. In doing so, he calls attention to the quiet persistence of Romance-language poetics—its techniques, its effects—in all modern European stanzaic forms.

But Tennyson is also reminding us of the debt European poetry owes to Arabic poetics. If the "Arabian Nights" stanza suggested a historiographically focalized view of stanzaic form—Arabic literature seen retrospectively through the scrim of Provençal rhyme—the effect in "The Ballad of Oriana" is more layered and more auditory: an English ballad heard in the key of a Tuscan sonnet heard in the key of an Arabic *ghazal*. The ballad's monorhymes and refrain, in addition to citing the unusually monorhymed ballad stanza of "Fair Helen," and in addition to multiplying the expressive Italianate vowels, recall the repetitive structure of Sismondi's Rudel poem, which itself recalls the rhyme-and-refrain pattern of the Arabic and Persian *ghazal* as Sismondi describes it. Sismondi had used that rhyme-and-refrain pattern to prove the genetic relationship between Provençal and Arabic lyric. Tennyson adapts it into English by way of Italian, restoring the history of the English and Scottish ballad to a longer and more international history of rhyme.

It is easy to see why Hallam chooses "The Ballad of Oriana" as a case study for Tennyson's poetic method in *Poems, Chiefly Lyrical*. It beautifully condenses his history of rhyme. But more importantly, it exemplifies his theory of sensation poetry. Tennyson's form is not imitative; it seems to be brand-new and, like the "Arabian Nights" stanza (and the *In Memoriam* stanza and the "Tears, Idle Tears" stanza), developed precisely for its occasion. One could hardly imagine the same stanza being so appropriate to any other poem, or imagine the same poem with a different stanza. And Hallam insists that this particular fit of form to affective content—of "tone" to "feeling"—makes the poem *lyrical*. That is, the extravagant quantity of sad and sonorous "Oriana"s produces "the rich lyrical impression of the ballad."

Hallam's definition of "lyrical" thus involves a form that is full of feeling, but the feeling in "The Ballad of Oriana" is of a special kind. It isn't exactly Tennyson's feeling—or if it is, it is Tennyson's feeling for feeling and for affective form, rather than an expression of his own subjective experience. This idea of lyric is romantic and expressive, but not in the ways that are usually meant when "the Romantic lyric" is invoked. It is romantic in a historiographic sense: it derives from ideas like those of Sismondi, about what modern poetic forms were invented to do when romantic literatures were first coming into being. And it is expressive insofar as it reaches for an always subtler and more perfect correspondence between the poem's feeling and its form.

Tennyson continued to develop and refine the romantic lyric stanza long after Hallam's death. In fact, Hallam's death prompted some of his most sophisticated efforts in that direction. The depersonalized, formalized feeling of "Oriana" goes some way toward clarifying the "lyrical" quality of more autobiographical poems like "Tears, Idle Tears" and *In Memoriam,* without recourse to expressivist theory. If romantic feeling is already *in* the forms of rhyme and assonance and already an ideal of the lyric stanza, then the poet's task is to cultivate those emotive possibilities: to meticulously arrange the prosodic components in such a way that lets them speak—or, as Ruskin might say, "out-speak"—the historical feelings they carry.[57] The stanza form of *In Memoriam,* as I have suggested, seems conscious of itself as a structure of desire and grief. It seems to speak about, as much as through, the *amour de loin* and memory-and-hope of rhyme. The stanza form of "Tears, Idle Tears" accomplishes an even more impressive feat: it evokes rhyme's romantic longing at the same time as it makes rhyme itself a lost object of desire. Through its assonances, its almost rhymes, and its missed rhymes, the "Tears, Idle Tears" stanza yearns hopelessly and hopefully toward the condition of rhyme. T. S. Eliot and Graham Hough heard these sounds in "Tears, Idle Tears," and they intuitively felt them to be the location of the poem's feelings. But they didn't register the historiographic theories of rhyme and lyric motivating Tennyson's stanza craft. Eliot said that Tennyson was "the great master of metric as well as of melancholia." What Eliot didn't say is that, for Tennyson, the melancholy was part of the prosody, and it had been since the origin of rhyme.

◎ 4 ◎

Elizabeth Barrett Browning's Unblank Verse

Tennyson's "Tears, Idle Tears" proves that an unrhymed stanza isn't necessarily the opposite of a rhymed one. Stanzaic form can amplify or mute rhyme, it can diffuse rhyme into assonance and consonance, it can move rhyme from the end of the line to its middle, but it never really dispenses with rhyme. What about the more extreme case of blank verse? Could "unrhymed" blank verse also be understood as a rhymed form? To pose the question in another way, consider two passages of poetry by Elizabeth Barrett Browning (EBB), one published in 1850 and the other in 1856:

> . . . 'Nay' is worse
> From God than from all others, O my **friend**!
> Men could not part us with their worldly jars,
> Nor the seas change us, nor the tempests bend:
> Our hands would touch for all the mountain-bars,—
> And, heaven being rolled between us at the **end**,
> We should but vow the faster for the stars.[1]

> Of writing many books there is no **end**;
> And I who have written much in prose and verse
> For others' uses, will write now for mine,—
> Will write my story for my better self
> As when you paint your portrait for a **friend**,
> Who keeps it in a drawer and looks at it
> Long after he has ceased to love you, just
> To hold together what he was and is.[2]

The first passage is the closing sestet of the second sonnet of *Sonnets from the Portuguese*, and we can recognize immediately the Petrarchan sequence of end rhymes that bind the sestet together: "friend," "jars," "bend," "bars," "end," "stars." The second one is the opening octave of *Aurora Leigh*. The rhyme scheme is much looser, but it is apparent nonetheless. The strongest rhyme is a repetition from the sonnet, and it is a rhyme that shows up all over EBB's corpus: *end* and *friend*. This rhyme helps define the octave as an octave, at the same time as it subdivides the octave into a pair of quatrains. That is, the symmetrical positioning of the rhyme words at the ends of lines 1 and 5 seems to mark out the verse as a well-appointed (if minimalist) stanzaic room. And, once we realize that we're in such a room, we start to notice its more modest decorations, like the half-rhyme of "it" and "is" along the right-hand margin. If we keep looking and listening, resemblances are everywhere. The assonance of "end" and "friend" reverberates in "better," "self," "when," and "together." Within individual lines, there are other alliterative and assonantal echoes: "story for," "paint your portrait for," "he has ceased." Like the sonnet sestet, this stanza is limned by end rhyme, but it is also held together by a dense constellation of more subtle sound effects—the "diffused resemblances" of Arthur Hallam's romantic rhyme.

Why does it feel perverse to describe the opening lines of *Aurora Leigh* as a rhymed stanza rather than a verse paragraph? Perhaps because *Aurora Leigh* is EBB's masterpiece of blank verse, and literary history seems to tell us that blank verse is a triumphantly rhymeless form: it was adopted by Milton in 1667 as a reproach to the "barbarous" medieval culture that produced rhyme, and after Milton it evolved toward increasingly open forms. Milton's negative definition—"English heroic verse without rhyme"—has persisted through centuries of use.[3] In 1705, Joseph Addison described the form as verse "where there is no rhyme."[4] The 1785 edition of Samuel Johnson's dictionary defined it as verse "without rhyme; where the rhyme is *blanched*, or missed," and the Victorian forerunner of the *Oxford English Dictionary* concurred.[5] Blank verse is still basically understood as "unrhymed."[6] This opposition affects readings of many Victorian poets who wrote in both blank verse and stanzaic forms. Certainly, EBB's Petrarchan sonnets are seen to represent her engagement with medieval rhymed lyric, whereas her blank verse *Aurora Leigh* apparently belongs to another canon altogether: an epic lineage reaching back through Milton, Virgil, and Homer.

Yet categories of rhyme and rhymelessness are an awkward fit for the poetry of Elizabeth Barrett Browning, who was notorious for rhymes that did not rhyme enough.[7] *Sonnets from the Portuguese* is full of off-rhymes (*move/strove, ways/grace*), while *Aurora Leigh* employs the range of rhyme effects I enumerated above—from unusually dense patterns of internal rhyme, alliteration, assonance, and consonance to perfect end rhymes that turn verse paragraphs into stanzas. An early reviewer, struggling to identify the melody of *Aurora Leigh*, observed that it "has not the measured cathedral flow of the Miltonic blank verse": "It catches the sound of the oak wrestling in the storm, but it listens to the song-bird also."[8] There are compelling formal reasons, then, to suppose a continuous prosodic project across EBB's varied body of work. Rather than two poles of rhyme and not-rhyme, her poetry suggests a spectrum of rhyme gradations.

There are historical reasons, too. EBB's poetry owes much to her encounters with literary history; her extensive study of classical and modern literature is well documented both in the criticism and in her own letters. But she was also deeply invested in the nineteenth-century discourse of literary historiography, those competing narratives that dramatized and interpreted the historical relations of authors and forms. Live debates in literary historiography—about the origin and development of rhyme, the periodization of poetic history, the nature of aesthetic forms—powerfully shaped EBB's prosody, particularly her evolving understanding of the affinities between blank and rhymed verse. Evidence of EBB's direct, scholarly participation in these debates can be found in two barely explored places: the annotated margins of her copy of Henry Hallam's *Introduction to the Literature of Europe in the Fifteenth, Sixteenth, and Seventeenth Centuries* (1837–39) and a literary-historical essay called "The Book of the Poets," which she published anonymously in 1842. I trace her marginal annotations beyond the pages of *Literature of Europe*, showing how her charged responses to Hallam's history registered in her own work, both her historiographic prose and her historiographic prosody.

This chapter makes two main claims about EBB. The first is, quite simply, that the literary histories that she read and wrote explain much of the formal strangeness of her poetry. Her manipulations of blank verse and rhyme derive from a serious engagement with contemporaneous literary-historical scholarship, and revisiting that neglected scholarship promises a fuller picture of her life and work. The second is that EBB's poetry itself articulates her Romantic vision of literary history. She treats poetic form as a uniquely powerful language for making—and settling—historiographic arguments. As an essayist she merely contradicts Hallam, but as a poet she can prove him wrong. In making these claims, I am developing this book's larger one about the vital bonds between formalism and historicism in the nineteenth century. For EBB, as for so many Victorian poets, literary history was a poetic theory, and prosody was a way to write history.

TWO LITERARY HISTORIANS

Henry Hallam, whom I have discussed in relation to his son Arthur, was a Victorian intellectual celebrity. He was already one of England's preeminent historians when the dizzyingly wide-ranging *Literature of Europe* made him its preeminent historian of literature and the acknowledged pioneer of comparative literature in English. Nearly seventy years later George Saintsbury could still proclaim that "to the English student of literary history and of literary criticism, Henry Hallam must always be a name *clarum et venerabile*."[9] Hallam's name has since faded, as has his style of totalizing historiography, now seen as methodologically unsophisticated when it is remembered at all.[10] Yet his long and wide view of literary history was enormously generative for EBB. In his poetic origin stories and transnational lineages, she found the material she needed to think expansively about poetic form.

Indeed, EBB's study of literary history initiated a fertile period in her poetic career. In the early 1840s she began to translate Petrarch and to produce a voluminous body of sonnets. By 1844–45 she was also beginning to draft *Aurora Leigh*.[11] All the while, she was working hard at imperfecting rhyme, at loosening the fit of the end rhymes that structured stanzas. Her 1844 collection was criticized for its "paucity of rhyme," its "inadmissible" half-rhymes (such as *islands/silence, desert/unmeasured*), and its rhyme-tending lines that were found to be "entirely rhymeless."[12] EBB's retort to such criticism is famous: "A great deal of attention, … far more than it wd. take to rhyme with conventional accuracy, … have I given to the subject of rhymes,—& have determined in cold blood, to hazard some experiments." These experiments were founded, she maintained, on "much thoughtful study of the Elizabethan writers" and on the authority of Mediterranean poetics.[13]

EBB's assertion that the broad sweep of literary history helped her innovate rhyme is borne out in her own literary-historical writings. While "The Book of the Poets" is not exactly a lost text, it has not been sufficiently mined for insight into her poetics. It is sometimes referenced in EBB scholarship, but it has mostly served critics as a store of information about her opinions of individual poets rather than as an integral work of literary historiography and criticism.[14] But that is exactly what it was. When it was commissioned to be a sequence of articles running in the *Athenaeum* in the summer of 1842, EBB's assignment was twofold: to pretend to write a review of a new anthology of poetry—*Book of the Poets: Chaucer to Beattie* (Scott, Webster & Geary, 1842)—but actually to write a survey of English poetic history.[15] By her own report, she found it "awkward" to "marry the two offices of reviewer and poetical historian," feeling much more invested in the historiographic part of the project.[16] With impressive rhetorical skill, she therefore finesses the phrase "the book of the poets" away from the denotation of a particular unexceptional volume and toward a more general conception of literary history and canonicity, to which the title of her own essay quickly comes to refer.

At this point EBB settles into the more satisfying role of "poetical historian." Instead of assessing the contents of an ephemeral anthology, she is commanding the widest possible view of English literature. "Our poetry has an heroic genealogy," she declares, before tracing its origins south, north, and ultimately, east: through Armorica (now Brittany and surrounding territories), to Spain, to the Arabian Peninsula; and through Germany, to Scandinavia, to Georgia and Persia.[17] By the time poetry develops in England as English poetry, a hybrid of the northern and southern strains, it is humming with the voices of half a dozen other cultures. Its specific prosodic attributes, its "intonation" and "cadence," represent both the residue of lost or distant poetries and the freshness of a new combination.

EBB is rehearsing here the great creation myth of eighteenth-century literary historiography, Thomas Warton's Arabian-Nordic theory of poetry.[18] It is an account of the origins of what Warton calls "romantic fiction," a "species . . . entirely unknown to the writers of Greece and Rome."[19] In a dissertation appended to his *History of English Poetry*

(1774–81), Warton attributed the qualities of chivalric romance—evident in eleventh-century tales of Arthur and Charlemagne and in the sixteenth-century poems of Spenser—to the complex, multicontinental process of accretion and synthesis that EBB also describes (as we saw, Warton's theory was a source for Arthur Hallam, too). This narrative was part of a larger historiographic design that favored imagination over reason, and medieval and Renaissance invention over neoclassical sophistication.[20] Warton's origin story was powerful and in the ensuing decades helped consolidate Romantic aesthetics, but it was not uncontroversial. In 1837 Henry Hallam had argued against it: "I cannot believe that so baseless a fabric [as the Armorican hypothesis] will endure much longer."[21] So EBB's use of this familiar historiographic theme at just this juncture is strategic: in addition to marking the move from reviewer to historian, it presents a challenge to Hallam's renowned neoclassicism.[22] In such moments—indeed, in the larger essay—Hallam is EBB's chief interlocutor.[23] Hallam's work was both a gift and a spur: it offered her a comprehensive view of European poetry and an aesthetic program against which to clarify her own.

EBB names Hallam only once in "The Book of the Poets," near the end. It is a moment of uncharacteristic candor. In general, she is decorously indirect about her adversaries—she has argued with "certain critics," "a chief critic," "those 'base, common, and popular' critical voices ... in and out of various 'arts of poetry'"—but she pulls no punches here (4.446, 453, 467). "We will do anything but agree with Mr. Hallam," she writes, "who, in his excellent and learned work on the Literature of Europe, has passed some singular judgments upon the poets.... [But the] crying truth is louder than Mr. Hallam, and cries, in spite of Fame" (4.468). Although she acknowledges Hallam's formidable research, she strongly disagrees with his critical opinions, which are both "singular" and somehow orthodox. On one side of a divide stand Hallam and "Fame," and on the other side stand EBB and "truth." In the contest that EBB imagines, Hallam and "Fame" are terribly loud; it is her challenge to be louder still.

The loudness that EBB attributed to Hallam was not entirely imagined. When she was writing "The Book of the Poets," his *Literature of Europe* was still new, and very well respected. In the periodical press, reviewers were more apt to express awe than to register complaint. As one American reviewer soberly put it, "Any critic who can discover imperfections or errors in the work, is fully entitled to exercise his art upon it, for his labors are worthy of some reward, and as he is likely to receive no other, he may claim it in the privilege of fault-finding. We have no idea of criticising the work."[24] A reviewer at the *London Quarterly Review* praised the volumes as "systematic, comprehensive, and trustworthy" and Hallam as a critic of "masculine good sense."[25]

Hallam's project did have impressive scope. It extended from the medieval period to 1700 and covered the entire continent of Europe. Its definition of literature was also broad, including poetry and imaginative prose as well as theological literature; speculative, moral, and political philosophy; aesthetic criticism; jurisprudence; mathematics and science. There had been previous attempts to approach literary history from one angle or another—biography, genre, nation—but few general literary histories had been ventured on this scale. More comparative and broad than Warton's English history; more integrated than the collective universal history project of Johann Gottfried Eichhorn, Friedrich Bouterwek, and others (1796, 1799, 1805–11); more wide-ranging than Sismondi's history of Mediterranean literature (1813) or Girolamo Tiraboschi's and Pierre-Louis Ginguené's Italian literary histories (1772–82, 1811–16); Hallam's *Literature of Europe* was unprecedented.[26]

So when EBB announces in "The Book of the Poets" that "we will do anything but agree with Mr. Hallam," she is pitting her little essay against one of the most ambitious intellectual projects of the nineteenth century. In doing so, she makes enormous claims for the essay's generic aspirations. By daring to disagree with Hallam, EBB confirms that she is not simply writing a review. She is writing an account of literary history that constitutes itself in relation to, and in its difference from, the authoritative historiography that the "trustworthy" Hallam personifies. Her antagonism toward such authority may have stemmed from her feeling of exclusion from it.[27] No woman's name appeared in Hallam's catalog of antecedents (even if he did defer to the late Germaine de Staël in his discussion of Shakespeare). EBB certainly had reason to suspect that Hallam would disapprove of her work should he ever discover its authorship. In an 1842 letter written just after "The Book of the Poets" was published, she recalls a particularly stinging passage on Beaumont and Fletcher in which "Mr. Hallam observes in his learned work upon the Literature of Europe that 'no woman of common respectability' wd. read either. So we will hold our respectability to be *un*common—like our reading."[28] EBB's revenge for this slight in "The Book of the Poets" is a masterful analysis of Beaumont and Fletcher's "centauresque" style (4.465)—proving not just that she could read them, but that she could read them exceedingly well.

EBB IN THE MARGINS

The marginalia make EBB's complex relationship to Hallam graphic. Her copies of *Literature of Europe,* now held at the Armstrong Browning Library at Baylor University, are the 1837–39 first editions of each volume. The many correlations between her marked-up books and "The Book of the Poets" suggest that her most studious engagement with Hallam's work occurred in the first half of 1842, as she was preparing to write her own essay.[29] In the crowded margins of the Hallam volumes, EBB's historical and critical arguments emerge as arguments with her predecessor, as EBB talking back—often very loudly—to Hallam himself. The volumes are riddled with underlining, x's, insertions, queries, and corrections in EBB's hand. She seems to consider herself a better reader of poetry, a better translator, and a better judge of poetic merit than Hallam, and is happy to exercise what his American reviewer called "the privilege of fault-finding." In the first volume, she offers a grammatical line edit on page 314 and fixes Latin translations on pages 323 and 394. She finds continuity errors ("Why ?—see the author's own view p-489" [1.492]). She makes factual corrections on subjects ranging from the Protestant Reformation to the emergence of accentual-syllabic meter to the proper referent in a John Suckling poem. She makes note of Hallam's expression of doubt "as to the Armorican origin of romantic fictions," as well as of his conviction that rhyme can be traced to the consonants of the Latin language rather than to the vowels of the Saracens of Spain (1.47, 40–42).

The moments of strongest disagreement involve Hallam's evaluations of poets and their styles, which EBB finds either infuriatingly lukewarm or wrong. This is particularly true of the English Renaissance poets: EBB's marginalia build a case for the special poetic attainments of that cohort. To Hallam's remarks about George Gascoigne's "strength and sense," she appends "& poetry," and underlines his too moderate phrase "respectable place among the Elizabethan versifiers";

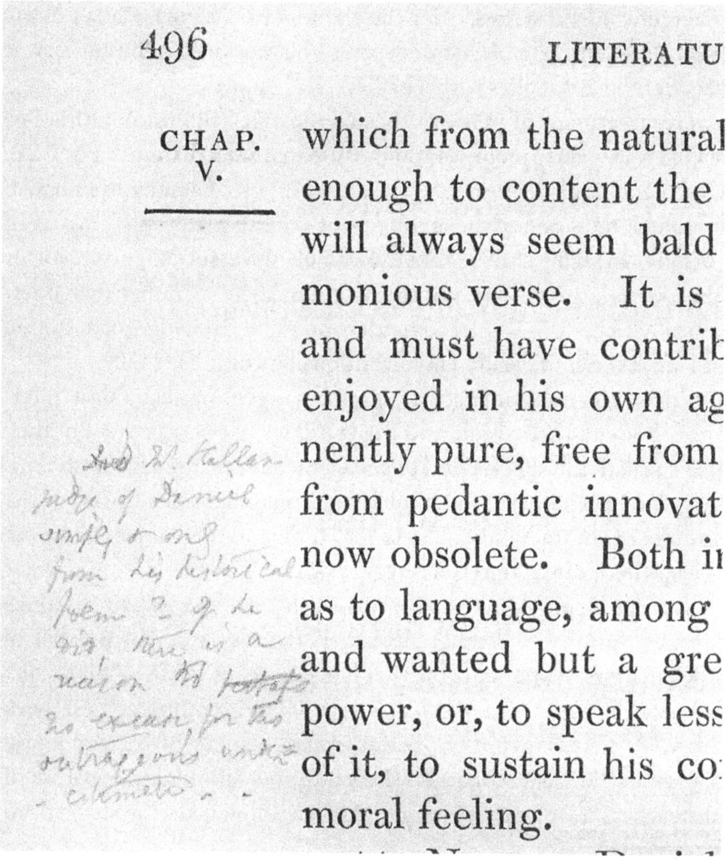

496 LITERATU

CHAP. V.

which from the natural
enough to content the
will always seem bald
monious verse. It is
and must have contrit
enjoyed in his own ag
nently pure, free from
from pedantic innovat
now obsolete. Both ii
as to language, among
and wanted but a gre
power, or, to speak less
of it, to sustain his co
moral feeling.

FIGURE 2. Elizabeth Barrett Browning's marginal annotations in Henry Hallam's *Literature of Europe* (3.496). Photograph: Armstrong Browning Library, Baylor University, Waco, Texas.

this opinion receives a "! ! ! ! ??" in the margin (2.306). Where Hallam suggests that Samuel Daniel ranks second to Edmund Spenser "due rather to the purity of his language than to its vigour," EBB underlines the last word and counters, "Vigour is not his characteristic—but he was a true poet—not a mere purist. These remarks are all tepid—to say the best of them" (2.314). Later, when Hallam discusses Daniel's awkward Italianate versification, she exclaims, "Did Hallam judge of Daniel simply and only from his historical poem? If he did, there is a reason tho ~~perhaps~~ no excuse, for this outrageous underestimate" (3.496) (fig. 2). And so on: Hallam finds Christopher Marlowe "energetic"; EBB writes, "Not the right word" (2.379). Hallam finds John Donne forgettable, obscene, and "the most inharmonious of our versifiers"; EBB replies with a baffled "???" (3.493).

Her treatment of many of these figures in "The Book of the Poets" reveals a tacit incorporation of the marginal disputes. For EBB, Gascoigne holds a more than "respectable" place among the English versifiers; he is one of the architects of English blank verse, a poet of "beauty and light" (4.458). Marlowe's blank verse "cadence revolves like a wheel, progressively, if slowly and heavily"—rather than energetically (454–55). Daniel is "tender and noble," not vigorous. Donne has "an instinct to beauty," not licentiousness or noise (458).

EBB's rejections of Hallam express an urgent philosophical difference about aesthetic value and the workings of poetic form. But they also speak to the special kind of engagement in marginalia. Both critical genre and intimate bibliophilic ritual, marginalia like EBB's pay the homage of contradiction. EBB is very funny on this subject in *Aurora Leigh*, where she characterizes marginalia as "the scholar's regal way / Of giving judgment on the parts of speech / As if he sate on all twelve thrones up-piled, / Arraigning Israel" (5.1224–27). Aurora's list of stock marginal comments that her late father has made—"*conferenda hæc cum his—/ Corruptè citat—lege potiùs*" (compare these with those—/ Cites corruptly—better read)—evokes EBB's own joyful disgust in the Hallam margins. Like Aurora's father's appreciation of his teachers, EBB's appreciation of Hallam often takes the shape of an arraignment.

More favorable appreciation does also appear in the Hallam books. On the back leaf of volume 3, for instance, EBB has made a running list of Hallam's sources with page numbers where he has mentioned them, as if to retrace his scholarly steps. Hallam's guidance is also manifest in her less emphatic marginal markings, those quieter signs of learning from the books and of trying to absorb the information they offer: her vertical and horizontal lines. These persist throughout the volumes, even on pages where EBB writes back. Often the lines mark out literary-historical cruxes, such as moments of origin and transition: the plot points of literary history that captured her attention.

One such example is Hallam's account of "consonant and assonant rhymes" in fifteenth-century Spanish poetry, which EBB marks with a vertical line in the margin:

> In their lighter poetry the Spaniards frequently contented themselves with *assonances,* that is, with the correspondence of final syllables, wherein the vowel alone was the same, though with different consonants, as *duro* and *humo, boca* and *cosa.* These were often intermingled with perfect or consonant rhymes. In themselves, unsatisfactory as they may seem at first sight to our prejudices, there can be no doubt but that the assonances contained a musical principle, and would soon give pleasure to and be required by the ear. (1.165)

These remarks about the satisfactions of the ear—both the medieval Spanish ear and the Victorian ear—are reflected in a letter that EBB wrote to Richard Hengist Horne in 1844. Defending her own assonances, she uses the same language to insist on the same point: medieval Spanish poetry models a broader range of prosodic pleasures than modern prejudices allow. "You who are a reader of Spanish poetry," she writes, "must be aware how soon the ear may be satisfied, even by a recurring vowel. I mean to try it."[30] The permission to half-rhyme borrowed from Spanish poetry is also a borrowing from Hallam's books. Though EBB refuted Hallam's readings of the English poets, she held on to these observations about the historical conditioning of the prosodic ear.

RHYME AND FALSE RHYME

As I have shown, for writers such as Hallam, Sismondi, the Schlegels, Hegel, and Henry Hallam's son Arthur, rhyme occupies a crucial place in European literary history, marking the beginning of the modern poetic tradition. In some cases, the origin of rhyme is characterized as a necessary but traumatic break from classical ways of being and knowing. In other cases, it represents the initiation of glorious new modes of intersubjectivity: new ways of feeling and communicating feeling. In the historical account preferred by Sismondi and Arthur Hallam—and derived, in part, from Warton—rhyme was born in medieval Arabia and the Levant, and as it passed through Spain, Provence, and Italy, it was enriched by each of those poetic cultures. This progression, described and then dismissed by Henry Hallam, is clearly in the background of EBB's conception of English poetry, whose first "intonation" she describes as a Wartonian compound of Eastern and Western sounds. But the origin of rhyme, which is not by any account an English origin, lies outside the historical and geographic limits of her subject.

Despite her narrower focus, EBB retains rhyme as a powerful literary-historical catalyst. Instead of denoting a break between the classical and modern periods (or pre-Christian and Christian man, as Hegel has it), it stands at another crossroads altogether. Rhyme is complicit in a disturbing change she observes in the post-Elizabethan poets: "The voices are eloquent enough, thoughtful enough, fanciful enough; but something is defective.... What is so? And who dares to guess that it may be INSPIRATION?" Whereas Elizabethan poetry possesses a tuneful "sweetness," EBB detects a "brackish" taste in the poetry of the next generation. In fact, "a deeper gulf than an Anno Domini yawns betwixt an Elizabethan man and a man of [the] era upon which we are entering"—and that gulf was produced by "the idol-worship of RHYME" (4.466).

A reader familiar with EBB's poetry might be momentarily confused by this argumentative turn, which echoes some of the eighteenth century's most violent antirhyme rhetoric.[31] Confusion would be a fair response. The vast majority of her own poems are rhymed, and those that she had published before 1842 were predominantly stanzaic. The ones that were not strictly stanzaic—like her translation of Aeschylus's *Prometheus Bound* (1833, 1850) and her Aeschylean "Seraphim" (1838)—featured rhymed strophes or rhyming dialogue; or, in the case of her juvenile "Battle of Marathon" (1820) and "Essay on Mind" (1826), Popean rhymed couplets.[32] The poems in the volume that followed "The Book of the Poets" were more inventive in their rhyming. *Poems of 1844* included almost thirty sonnets, a narrative poem in terza rima–inspired triplets, and the intricate medievalist ballad "Rhyme of the Duchess May." All of which is to say that EBB cannot possibly be an enemy of rhyme.

Instead, she is proposing a distinction between two categories of rhyme, one good and one bad. By conflating the decline of poetry with a frenzy for rhyming, she is suggesting that the transition from classical, quantitative meter to modern, accentual-syllabic rhyme was a less monumental literary-historical event than the break between the use of rhyme inspired by the Italians and the systematic abuse of rhyme arising from the "pestilential influence of French literature." This new schism allowed wits to ascend to the place of poets and compromised the art of prosody:

> Among the elder poets, the rhyme was only a felicitous adjunct, a musical accompaniment, the tinkling of a cymbal through the choral harmonies. You heard it across the changes of the pause, as an undertone of the chant, marking the time with an audible indistinctness, and catching occasionally and reflecting the full light of the emphasis of the sense in mutual elucidation. But the new practice endeavoured to identify in all possible cases the rhyme and what may be called the sentimental emphasis; securing the latter to the tenth rhyming *syllable*, and so dishonouring the emphasis of the sentiment into the base use of the marking of the time. And, not only by this unnatural provision did the emphasis minister to the rhyme, but the pause did so also. "Away with all pauses,"—said the reformers,—"except the legitimate pause at the tenth rhyming syllable. O rhyme, live for ever! Rhyme alone take the incense from our altars,—tinkling cymbal alone be our music!" (4.467)

"The idol-worship of RHYME," for EBB, is its perversion away from its proper usage as a richly melodic rather than a bluntly percussive sound effect. The "elder poets," those closest to rhyme's Mediterranean origins, used it in subtler and more vital ways than the Francophile idolators did. Rhyme didn't just serve as the punch line to an end-stopped couplet. Caesura, likewise, was unpredictable. Rhyme and patterns of pause could play off one another so their separate arabesques might sometimes miss and sometimes, all the more gratifyingly, meet.

As earlier chapters have shown, this understanding of rhyme's double nature had precedents. A decade before EBB's writing, a similar distinction between true rhyme and false rhyme—"diffused resemblances" versus the dull "recurrence of termination"—had been proposed by Arthur Hallam.[33] Thomas Carlyle, in his praise of Dante's terza rima, had likewise distinguished between "true song" and "false song," condemning "Rhyme that had no inward necessity to be rhymed."[34] All of these taxonomies of rhyme owed something to the theories of organic form in August Schlegel's and Samuel Taylor Coleridge's lectures on Shakespeare.[35] The organic idea was a rebuke to those who had disparaged Shakespeare's plays for their "barbarous shapelessness & irregularity." Both Schlegel and Coleridge argued that these evaluations of

Shakespeare resulted from the misguided application of classical and neoclassical theatrical standards to his plays: "The true ground of the mistake . . . lies in the confounding mechanical regularity with organic form," which, Coleridge writes, is "innate" and "shapes as it develops itself from within."[36] In this view, Shakespeare's strength lies in his resistance to external rules—in his faithfulness to the internal logic of the artwork and to the natural correlation between content and form. What previous critics have taken for a failure of order in Shakespeare is in fact something quite wonderful: the efflorescence of, in Schlegel's terms, "new kinds of poetry."[37]

The new kind of poetry that Shakespeare represented was organic down to the smallest details of its prosody (as, indeed, the concept of organicism entails). In the same lecture series in which he expounds the organic idea, Schlegel tells the story that EBB later rehearsed about the rough beauty and the multiformity of Elizabethan rhyme and then about the lamentable standardization and mechanization of the couplet. It is, in fact, a story about the diverging histories of blank verse and rhyme:

> In England, the manner of handling rhyming verse, and the opinion as to its harmony and elegance, have, in the course of two centuries, undergone a much greater change than is the case with the rhymeless Iambic or blank verse. In the former, Dryden and Pope have become models; these writers have communicated the utmost smoothing to rhyme, but they have also tied it down to a harmonious uniformity. . . . We must not estimate the rhyme of Shakspeare [*sic*] by the mode of subsequent times, but by a comparison with his contemporaries. . . . Many of his rhymes . . . are faultless: ingenious with attractive ease, and rich without false brilliancy. The songs interspersed . . . are generally sweetly playful and altogether musical; in imagination, while we merely read them, we hear their melody.[38]

Schlegel's argument is not just about poetry; it is also about criticism—the inability of contemporary commentators to properly hear Shakespearean prosody. This concern persisted from Schlegel's lectures in 1808, through Coleridge, Carlyle, and Arthur Hallam. As late as 1842, EBB was still fighting for this history of English prosody, and for the sweet aesthetic pleasures of organic rhyme.

Here, again, EBB was fighting against the historiographic vision of

Henry Hallam. Although Hallam pays many compliments to Shakespeare and speaks highly of Coleridge's and Schlegel's Shakespeare criticism (3.580), he exhibits the neoclassical biases that these Romantics railed against. In Shakespeare's early work he finds a "redundance of blossoms" and "unbounded fertility" (2.313). The little he has to say about the form of Shakespeare's plays amounts to a defense of their "regularity" against allegations of their "extraordinary barbarism and rudeness" (3.575–76). Both of these evaluations of Shakespeare uncritically reinforce the value system that Schlegel and Coleridge found so flawed.[39] And as we have seen, Hallam's "tepid" assessments of other Renaissance poets rankled EBB the reader, who strongly preferred the jubilant birdsong of the Elizabethans to the "correctness" and regularity of Dryden and Pope (4.457, 466, 473).

Indeed, Hallam's preference for Dryden could only have strengthened EBB's conviction of the historian's bad sympathies. In "The Book of the Poets," EBB holds Dryden responsible for "establish[ing] finally the despotism of the final emphasis" and all but silencing poetic music (Arthur Hallam had likewise accused Dryden of importing the "death-dance of Parisian foppery").[40] But for Henry Hallam the case is quite otherwise. He suggests, in a confessional aside, that a taste for Dryden is a mark of critical maturity: "The admiration of Dryden gains upon us, if I may speak from my own experience, with advancing years, as we become more sensible of the difficulty of his style, and of the comparative facility of that which is merely imaginative" (4.431–32). In coordinating Dryden's technical precision to his own well-developed critical faculty, Hallam appears to trivialize both organic form and the critics, like EBB, who love it.

Twentieth-century critics like Cleanth Brooks recast organic form as a theory of aesthetic autonomy and a bulwark against literary history. But as we can see, organic form was originally a literary-historical heuristic as much as it was a critical and theoretical concept. It was a way to understand Elizabethan style historically, as well as a model for thinking about the abstraction of literary form. As a historiographic theory, it presented EBB with a legitimate counternarrative to Hallam's history, which privileged neoclassical smoothness over the excesses he associated with Shakespeare. At the same time, the large contours of this debate offered EBB new ways to theorize poetic form—to think rhymingly about blank verse.

UNBLANK VERSE

EBB's most famous statement on poetic form is in Book 5 of *Aurora Leigh,* and it is in blank verse. Aurora is reflecting on the quasi-Virgilian development of her career, which has evolved through ballad, pastoral, and epic. Her pastoral "failed," she says, because it was too correct: "it was a book / Of surface-pictures—pretty, cold, and false / With literal transcript,—the worse done, I think, / For being not ill-done" (5.130–33). The antidote to such frigid correctness is a studied turning away from correctness, a surrender to poetry's self-shaping life force. Here Aurora adopts the verdant language of organicism, and her case study, like Schlegel's and Coleridge's, is Shakespearean drama:

> What form is best for poems? Let me think
> Of forms less, and the external. Trust the spirit,
> As sovran nature does, to make the form;
> For otherwise we only imprison spirit
> And not embody. Inward evermore
> To outward,—so in life, and so in art
> Which still is life.
>
> Five acts to make a play.
> And why not fifteen? why not ten? or seven?
> What matter for the number of the leaves,
> Supposing the tree lives and grows? exact
> The literal unities of time and place,
> When 'tis the essence of passion to ignore
> Both time and place? Absurd. Keep up the fire,
> And leave the generous flames to shape themselves. (5.223–36)

Aurora's answer to the question "What form is best for poems?" is unequivocal: "Inward evermore / To outward." The references to life, growth, and dramatic form confirm the Romantic pedigree of these lines, but they cannot distract us from their self-referential quality. "What form is best for poems?" is, after all, a question that a poem is asking—and, by example, answering. The lines reject "the despotism of the final emphasis," coiling smoothly around their enjambments and pausing at pointedly irregular intervals. Though they are anti-Augustan in their prosody they seem to harness all of Pope's formal wit. They are conscious of themselves as lines, flaunting line-ends even as they flout them.[41] Indeed, the stanza depends on a strong sense of its own insides and outsides to make its point about the insides and outsides of poems. In the second line, for example, the word "external" appears at the metrical halfway mark, the inmost part of the line, while "spirit" takes the outer edge. Three lines down the spatial joke gathers momentum. "Inward evermore / To outward," EBB writes, with "Inward evermore" pushing out to the margin and "To outward" moving in to the line's center. These chiastic motions might be too clever if they did not so seriously advance the stanza's metapoetic thesis.

The form that is best for poems appears here to be blank verse, as against fixed form—especially given Aurora's generic progress from ballad to epic. The rhymelessness and enjambments of blank verse suggest an inward-to-outward and sense-to-style directionality, whereas fixed forms might be seen to "imprison . . . not embody." But we know from Schlegel and his heirs that there is no essential relationship between rhyme and confinement, and EBB's lines make no claims for such a relationship. They themselves seem to flicker between fixed and unfixed form. In fact, there is something uncanny about this verse paragraph: its compromised, but still palpable, sonnetness. Taking the shape of fourteen iambic pentameters, it has the proportions of a sonnet. Like the stanza that opens *Aurora Leigh*, this one also has the shadow of a rhyme scheme, starting strong (ABCBC) before fading away.[42] If this is the poem's most explicit celebration of its blank verse body, why does the blank verse partake so much of the sonnet?

The strangeness of these lines is due not to a strange combination of a genre and a form (i.e., epic poem and rhymed stanza: a familiar pairing in both English and Continental European literature), or even, as many have argued of the larger work, to a strange combination of two genres (i.e., epic poem and novel).[43] It is due, rather, to the interpenetration of two apparently incompatible verse forms: blank verse and the rhyming sonnet. Whereas blank verse is the form most strenuously dissociated from rhyme, the sonnet stanza remains a powerful index for rhyme. A sonnet's rhyme pattern orchestrates its mood and argument (through octave, volta, and sestet, or quatrains and couplet), its language of allusion (signaling the Petrarchan, Shakespearean, or Spenserian tradition), and its production of the fruitfully finite poetic space of a stanza. The sonnet is exemplary of the closed poetic form, while blank verse is just about as close as the midcentury gets to a form that is open.

But EBB offers a different reading altogether. By writing blank verse and the sonnet into one another, she makes a prosodic argument for their common ground; and by using this blank verse–sonnet hybrid as a vehicle for her baldest defense of organic form, she makes the argument explicit. *Aurora Leigh*'s interstitial form insists that the rhyme of an Augustan couplet and the rhyme system of a sonnet are less alike than the rhyme system of a sonnet and the sound effects of blank verse. Whereas a heroic couplet's rhymes match, a sonnet's rhymes constellate—not only through the arrangement of end rhymes but also in the way that end rhyme lights up smaller and more scattered details of assonance and consonance.[44] And although a sonnet loves its rhymes, the rhymes need not correspond to the syntactic period; the caesura can hit the terminal position, but it can just as easily break up a line.[45] In other words, a sonnet behaves a lot like blank verse. The important poetic coordinates are not, for EBB, rhymed and unrhymed verse: they are organic rhyme and organic blank verse versus mechanical rhyme. Recognizing the organic (even arboreal) quality of EBB's rhymes in 1843, Robert Browning observed, "The grand rhymes *pair* in virtue of their essential characteristics only, and the *accidents* (of a mute or a liquid) go for nothing: just as tree matches with tree in a great avenue, elm-bole with elm-bole, let the boughs lie how they may."[46]

Thus, in the same way that her rhyming tends toward sonic openness, EBB's blank verse tends toward rhymed and stanzaic form. These tendencies emerge in her literary-historical research, are tested in the half-rhymes of the 1840s, and find expression also in the organic melding of sonnet and blank verse form in *Aurora Leigh*. As the critical anxiety around EBB's rhyming indicates, imperfect rhyme presses at rhyme's limits, the places where rhyme threatens to dissolve into something else: blankness. Therefore, it troubles the difference between rhymed and unrhymed verse, showing that difference to be only a matter of degree.

LITERARY HISTORY AS POETIC FORM

I'll end this chapter by revisiting beginnings, by considering another way that poetic origin stories might have helped EBB reach these theoretical and prosodic ends. I especially want to look at three moments in her own history of poetry that allowed her to rearticulate the story of rhyme with the story of blank verse—that let her make a persuasive historical case for the kinship of these forms.

The history of blank verse began, for EBB, before blank verse became English. Her marks in Hallam's books highlight the invention of *versi sciolti* (loosened verse) in sixteenth-century Italy and Spain, its importation into England by Henry Howard, Earl of Surrey, and its English cultivation in the Elizabethan period and beyond.[47] Rhyme has a different history: it originates in the early medieval period and spreads through Europe before arriving in the sonnets of Dante and Petrarch, "the morning stars of our modern literature."[48] But when blank verse and the sonnet enter English poetry, their paths begin to cross, and they keep crossing.

EBB makes much of the poets under whose aegis the two forms meet. First there is Surrey, who brought to England "the [Italian] sonnet structure, the summer-bower for one fair thought." Following Hallam, EBB also credits Surrey with "the first English blank verse, in his translation of two books of the Aeneid" (4.453–54). Although Surrey's prototype is "only heroic verse without rhyme," rather than "the arched cadence ... and underflood of broad continuous sound" that Shakespeare and Milton achieved (4.454), his double contribution remains remarkable: he stands at the English origin of both the quintessentially rhymed and the quintessentially unrhymed verse forms. His career is the conduit for their twin birth into English literature.

After Surrey comes the imperfect perfection of Shakespeare's organic rhyme. In "The Book of the Poets," he is one of the elder poets who preceded the corruption of versification, and EBB praises his "sonnets and songs" as "short sighs from [his] large poetic heart" (459). But he is also in that essay "the most wonderful artist in blank verse of all in England," an honor he earned by the same criteria that won him the epoch of beautiful rhymes: "Often when [his blank verse] is at the sweetest, his words are poor monosyllables, his pauses frequent to brokenness ... but the whole results in an ineffable charming of the ear which we acquiesce in without seeking its cause, a happy mystery of music" (463–64). Like Shakespearean rhyme, Shakespearean blank verse is musical, irregular, and sweet. The small repertoire of qualities that EBB ascribes to both his rhyme and his blank verse portrays Shakespeare's blank verse as continuous with—indeed, as one part of—his rhyme practice.

Milton also represents the affinity between rhyme and blank verse. In EBB's words,

> He stood in the midst of those whom we are forced to consider the corrupt versificators of his day, an iconoclast of their idol rhyme, and protesting practically against the sequestration of pauses. His lyrical poems, move they ever so softly, step loftily, and with something of an epic air. His sonnets are the first sonnets of a free rhythm.... His epic is the second to Homer's, and the first in sublime effects. (471)

This description of Milton's poetry suggests a subtle reading of his prosodic forms. His rebellion against the rhyme conventions of his period sends him pioneering in two directions: toward blank and unblank verse. Freed from the confines of false versification, Milton crafted both a blank verse that is transcendentally musical and a sonnet form that is grandly epic. The interchange that EBB notes between the sonic properties of the Miltonic sonnet and those of the Miltonic epic (against the defects of mechanical rhyme) presents a powerful literary-historical rationale for her own iconoclastic prosody.

These three literary-historical figures help concretize the relationship between historiographic narrative and poetic form. In Surrey, Shakespeare, and Milton, as EBB characterizes them, the genealogies of rhyme and blank verse converge—just as those forms converge on her page. Could a poet's loosened and off-kilter rhymes owe something to her transnational conception of blank verse? Might her blank verse epic organize sound in a deliberately stanzaic way? Thinking about prosody historiographically—that is, alongside literary history writing like Hallam's and EBB's, and with an eye to the long and storied lives of poetic forms—makes these strange questions feel a little less strange.

5

William Morris's Fleshly Rhymes

Throughout this book, I have been emphasizing rhyme's role in the romantic origin story and the way the early rhyming of medieval love poetry—"romantic rhyme," as Hegel called it—came to be identified with European literary modernity. As I have been arguing, Victorian poetic theory absorbed these historiographic narratives, so that ideas about the nature and effects of rhyme became inseparable from ideas about its origins. In chapter 2, I showed how this genetic model operated in the context of literary history writing itself: Sismondi's presentation of Jaufré Rudel's stanza made the form of rhyme—its evocation of distance, its mnemonic function—appear to be a poetic materialization of desire. In chapter 3, I suggested that Tennyson developed the *In Memoriam* stanza on a related genetic principle. This chapter returns to the association of rhyme and love in Victorian poetry to examine its significance for Pre-Raphaelite poetics.

The Pre-Raphaelites were fascinated by romantic literary history. Dante Gabriel Rossetti translated Dante and other early Italian poets, he modeled his *House of Life* sequence (1870–81) on Dante's *Vita nuova,* and his paintings obsessively revisit Dantean characters and images. Christina Rossetti's sonnet sequence *Monna Innominata* (1881), dense with allusions to Dante and Petrarch, is also framed by a historiographic story of amatory poetry, extending from the Provençal troubadours through the Italian poets to Elizabeth Barrett Browning.[1] And both Rossettis used rhyme for affective purposes. Think of the devastated monorhymes of Dante Gabriel's "The Woodspurge" (1856); or the way Christina's rhyme patterns become figures of distance, enacting not only the longing of *amour de loin* but also its refusals of intimacy.[2]

Of course, Pre-Raphaelite poetry doesn't always spurn intimacy. In Christina Rossetti's *Goblin Market* (1862), instead of distant yearning there is "balked desire" and deranged hungering, sucking, gorging, squeezing, mauling.[3] The poem overwhelms with a profusion of anaphora, similes, and erratic rhythms and rhymes, amplifying the sisters' experiences of thirst, privation, violence, and sensory overload with its spectacularly superfluous prosody.[4] Likewise, Dante Gabriel's "The Blessed Damozel" (1850) is about lovers separated by death, but the poem repeatedly closes that distance, bringing the reader into contact with the dead woman's living, and sexual, body: the "ungirt" robe, the warm bosom, the hair that "[fell] all about my face."[5] Distant love here flickers into a very proximate love. Or the reverse: in his infamous "Nuptial Sleep" sonnet (1870), the postcoital scene reveals two lovers whose lower bodies are still "knit" together. In their extreme physical intimacy, they nonetheless find distance enough to love and kiss across:

> Their bosoms sundered, with the opening start
> Of married flowers to either side outspread
> From the knit stem; yet still their mouths, burnt red,
> Fawned on each other where they lay apart.[6]

Rossetti's ABBA sonnet quatrain evokes the near-and-far of Tennyson's *In Memoriam* stanza, but turns it into a dynamic picture of naked bodies: the A's outspread like sundered bosoms, the B's like entangled legs; and then the A's like fawning mouths reuniting. As observed by the Pre-Raphaelites' sternest Victorian critic, Robert Buchanan, form is drawn into the poetry's unashamed "fleshliness." Rossetti's error, according to Buchanan, was to think that "poetic expression is greater than poetic thought, . . . the body is greater than the soul, and sound superior to sense."[7]

William Morris, like the Rossettis, sought to develop a poetics of fleshly form. But Morris's poetic imagination was more profoundly genetic: he looked beyond individual sources (and even traditions) toward a synthetic picture of literary history; and his use of prosody was enriched by historiographic theory. In Morris's narrative love poetry, the form of rhyme is closely bound to the content of romantic love. For Morris, the relationship between the rhyme-form and the love-content is a matter not only of literary-historical precedent (love poems often rhyme) or of analogy (the form of rhyme somehow resembles the form of love), though it is these things, too. More importantly, rhyme and love are bound together metonymically by a historiographic idea: the momentous arrival of romantic literature. To look closely at this idea and how it shapes Morris's erotic verse is to see a particularly Pre-Raphaelite intensification of historiographic form.[8]

The historiographic association between rhyme and love in Morris's poetry raises some compelling interpretive questions. If rhyme and love share an origin story, can rhymes be used to say something about the historicity of love? Does the appearance of rhyme in a poem's diegetic world tell us something about the quality of its characters' feelings? Could those feelings read, in any meaningful way, as historical? In other words, what are the limits of rhyme's signifying power? How much history (how much historical feeling) can rhyme hold?

KISS RHYMES TO BLISS

Let me begin with a quintessential example of Morris's rhyming. In "The Defence of Guenevere" (1858), the first poem in Morris's first volume of Pre-Raphaelite poetry, two icons of courtly love transgress. As Guenevere recalls the scene in a retrospective monologue, it happened in a garden on a spring day when the birds were singing, and the garden wall "shut the flowers and trees up with the sky, / And trebled all the beauty." Guenevere tells her story in the rhymed form of terza rima, and the rhyme words *kiss* and *bliss* mark the moment when chivalry's remote desiring turns, catastrophically, toward consummation:

> . . . In that garden fair
>
> Came Launcelot walking; this is true, the kiss
> Wherewith we kissed in meeting that spring day,
> I scarce dare talk of the remember'd bliss,
>
> When both our mouths went wandering in one way,
> And aching sorely, met among the leaves;
> Our hands being left behind strained far away.[9]

In these lines, the versification seems to follow, and even intensify, the narrative of sexual encounter. To understand this effect, so characteristic of Morris's poetry, let me review—in order to put aside—some familiar models for thinking through rhyme's meaningfulness: the semantic, the allegorical, and the mimetic.

We might observe that the rhyme of *kiss* and *bliss* works like other rhyme clichés (*bright* and *light, trees* and *breeze*) to create an accord that is both sonic and semantic; as Byron wrote in canto 6 of *Don Juan,* "'Kiss' rhymes to 'bliss,' in fact as well as verse."[10] Hugh Kenner called this kind of pairing a "normal rhyme" because its correspondence seems natural and almost inevitable.[11] It is a positive version of the alogical relationship that W. K. Wimsatt attributed to Pope's couplets in his "One Relation of Rhyme to Reason."[12] Wimsatt was interested in the semantic juxtaposition of rhymes like "queen" and "screen," where disjunctive meanings create deflationary or comical effects. A similarly formalist account of Morris's *kiss* and *bliss* rhyme would locate meaning in and across the rhyme words themselves.

We could also approach rhyme's meaning through allegory. Morris's use of Dante's terza rima for this poem invites us to read beyond the rhyme words to see the whole rhyme scheme as significant. Dante himself had described his *Divine Comedy* as an allegory, and nineteenth-century Dante critics, such as August Schlegel, had celebrated the three-part terza rima pattern as a central aspect of the poem's Trinitarian meaning: its elaborate allegorical construction, at every scale of form, according to multiples of three.[13] By the time Morris wrote the "Defence of Guenevere," terza rima's meaning-bearing capacity had been exploited for a variety of other ends, including the allegorical representation of another tripartite form: the adulterous love triangle. Morris follows an example set by Byron and Robert Browning before him in using terza rima specifically for a story about adultery, so that the rhyme scheme becomes in this context a prosodic performance of mediated desire.[14]

The allegorical reading does have a biographical rationale. William Morris spent his remarkable career (as a poet, a painter, a textile designer, a craftsman, a bookmaker, and eventually a socialist theorist) finding meaning in aesthetic forms. He studied Ruskin's *The Stones of Venice* and considered the chapter on "The Nature of Gothic" to be "one of the very few necessary and inevitable utterances of the century."[15] Ruskin, under the influence of Sismondi, had discovered in the contours of gothic architecture the expression of spiritual freedom and joy in labor—a meaning that was for him both historical (in that it pointed to the medieval culture that enabled it) and formal (in that it manifested itself in a glorious wildness and asymmetry of design).[16] In Morris's visual arts and crafts, his patterns and colors, critics have found a range of allegorical meanings, from the pleasure and pain of the human body to class struggle and the communitarian ideal. There is reason to believe, as Walter Crane put it in 1911, that Morris's poetry is also a kind of design work: "*decorative patterns* in forms of speech and rhyme."[17] Thus, reading Morris's rhyme patterns as similarly allegorical forms—even without the Dantean precedent—would make sense in the context of Morris's aesthetic program.

But there is something about the rhyming of *kiss* and *bliss* in "The Defence of Guenevere" that makes both the semantic and the allegorical explanations feel incomplete. In the allegorical explanation, the relationship between form and meaning is too arbitrary. Any tripartite form might do to represent the structure of adultery—a triptych painting, for example, or a braided wallpaper design. The meaning doesn't depend on rhyme *as* rhyme. The trouble with the semantic explanation is that it is too local: each rhyme pair produces its own meaning, rather than pointing to a more stable meaning in the rhyme form. It doesn't account for the self-reflexiveness of the *kiss*/*bliss* rhyme, its heightened mimesis: *kiss* meets *bliss* in tandem with the lovers' adulterous gesture. A latent analogy between kissing and rhyming—between the magnetism of desire and the magnetism of rhyme—becomes explicit.[18] The strangely eloquent rhyme of *kiss* and *bliss* tells the story of these two specific lovers, but it also draws attention to the fleshly qualities of rhyme itself: its libidinal energies, the way rhyme words "ache" and "strain" toward one another like Guenevere's and Launcelot's wayward lips; how the closure of rhyme is also a kind of bliss.

This analogy between kissing and rhyming suggests a mimetic use of form. But is such formal mimesis a matter of the poet's sleight of hand—an elegant transfer of meaning from the poem's diegetic world to its form? Or is it the reader's wishful interpretation? The canonical answers to such questions remain Alexander Pope's and Samuel Johnson's: when we notice mimetic form, either the poet has made sound "*seem* an echo to the sense" or the reader's "mind [is] govern[ing] the ear."[19] The first posits an ingenious poet who has made a poem's form seem to mirror its content; the second envisions an overenthusiastic reader who has read too much into the form.

Genetic formalism offers a different possibility altogether: that a form like rhyme has its own meaning or content, independent of the reader and the writer and even the poem. I have already proposed that in the nineteenth century, rhyme contained the idea of romantic love. But it might be more precise to say that *the idea of rhyme* in the nineteenth century was so connected with *the idea of love* that love could be considered part of the content of rhyme. Rhyme presented itself in that period as a way to speak about love in advance of any particular thematic material or stanzaic form (in advance, for example, of being used for something like an amatory sonnet). The close connection in the nineteenth-century literary-historical imagination between the origin of rhyme and the origin of romantic love meant that rhyme was more than just an allegory or analogy for love; it was, among other things, love's aesthetic form.

This chapter is an effort to read William Morris's poetry in a way that is attuned to this historiographic conception of rhyme. In what follows, I will further specify the relationship between romantic rhyme and romantic love in nineteenth-century thought, and then I'll examine some of the ways that relationship shaped the later poetry of William Morris. My focus will be Morris's magnum opus *The Earthly Paradise* (1868–70)—an epic romance that was widely read and well loved in the nineteenth century but is rarely read now, even as Morris's prose romances and utopian fictions are experiencing a renaissance. One reason why *The Earthly Paradise* has fallen by the wayside is its genuinely daunting length; it runs to 42,000 lines and four volumes, making it one of the longest poems in English (compare the 10,000 lines of Milton's *Paradise Lost*). I propose that there's another reason *The Earthly Paradise* has lost its readership: we don't know how to read the poem Morris was writing. We don't know how to read it, because it makes use of a set of assumptions (about form, about love, about history) that were very familiar to Morris's contemporaries but are less familiar to us. Recovering these assumptions brings us closer to both the form and the feeling of Morris's poem.

ROMANTIC HISTORIES

The Earthly Paradise is structured as a frame narrative on the model of Chaucer's *Canterbury Tales* (1400), Boccaccio's *Decameron* (1353), and Edward Lane's 1840 translation of *The Thousand and One Nights* (also known as the *Arabian Nights*).[20] The story Morris tells is about a group of medieval Norse wanderers leaving behind their plague-ravaged homeland in search of an Earthly Paradise, where they hope to find eternal life. After many years of travel, they arrive on an island populated by Greek elders who have preserved the culture of antiquity into the Middle Ages. Reconciled to the failure of their enterprise, the wanderers decide to live out their remaining days on this classical Greek island. It is agreed that the Norse Wanderers and the Greek Elders will tell each other stories from their respective cultures, and the poem carries on this way: for each month, two stories are told, one from medieval literature and one from classical literature—so that the twenty-four tales form a kind of anthology of myths and legends, often tragic love stories, from antiquity and the Middle Ages (several of the characters are familiar ones: Perseus and Andromeda, Pygmalion and Galatea, Paris and Oenone, Cupid and Psyche). The whole medievalist apparatus is doubly framed by the voice of an external narrator, a philosophical and lovelorn "idle singer," whom we take to be Morris the Victorian poet. In lyric interludes between the months, we rejoin Morris to reflect on the beauty of erotic love and the finitude of life on earth.

The Earthly Paradise is obviously a poem about literary history. Like Chaucer's and Boccaccio's works, it collects diverse stories from a range of literary traditions into a relatively organic whole. But Morris's juxtaposition of classical and medieval tales and the strange manner in which those tales interact make the poem historical in another way. The poem makes aesthetic use of theories of literary history that were current in Morris's time, especially the historiographic theory of the invention of romantic literature that I have been describing throughout this book. From our vantage point, the various meanings of *romantic* (relating to the romance genre, to the Romance languages, and to romantic love) hold an interest that is mainly etymological: they offer historical insight into the name by which we came to know nineteenth-century Romanticism.[21] In the nineteenth century, as I have shown, the meanings attaching to the word "romantic" had more coherence. "Romantic" evoked an origin story about the forms and feelings of modern European literature and a powerful idea about the periodization of culture. "Romantic" meant the end of the classical world and the beginning of a new medieval one. The new medieval world rang with Provençal rhyme.[22]

This fuller sense of the word "romantic" informed the most important nineteenth-century response to *The Earthly Paradise*. In Walter Pater's 1868 review of the poem (a landmark essay that became the foundation of his aestheticist philosophy in *The Renaissance*), Pater associates Morris's poetry with "the great romantic loves of rebellious flesh," the medieval moment when a "mystic passion" for "the fleshly lover" began to rival Christian mysticism.[23] Later, in an 1889 essay on classical and romantic tendencies in literature, Pater returns to the historical meaning of the word "romantic": "In the literature of Provence," he writes,

> the very name of *romanticism* is stamped with its true signification: here we have indeed a romantic world, grotesque even, in the strength of its passions, almost insane in its curious expression of them, drawing all things into its sphere, making the birds—nay, lifeless things—its voices and messengers; yet so penetrated with the desire for beauty and sweetness that it begets a wholly new species of poetry, in which the *Renaissance* may be said to begin.[24]

Pater's account of this impassioned "romantic world" with its new poetic language—rhymed poetry—draws on the periodizing theories I explored in previous chapters, particularly Warton's historiography of romance and de Staël's opposition of classic and romantic. In his 1774 *History of English Poetry*, Warton's use of "romantic" as a historical category opposing the classical was an early instance of that meaning in English.[25] Warton understood literary history as two broad periods punctuated by the medieval invention of "romantic fiction," a species of literature "entirely unknown to the writers of Greece and Rome."[26] Romantic fiction was a fusion of Gothic and Arabic influences, and two of its hallmarks were chivalry and romantic love. Since the ancients had no equivalent for the quality of passion Warton found in Provençal lyric and Arthurian romance, he concluded that romantic love must have entered Europe from the outside, after the fall of Rome. Warton's historiographic theory thus pulled together and coperiodized the histories of love and literary form.[27]

After Warton, versions of this story resurfaced in the lectures and writing of the Coppet group, where the "grand division" (August Schlegel) of classic and romantic became a fuller aesthetic theory, and where the question of the origin of romantic love became more closely linked to the romantic poetics of rhyme. Recall de Staël's and Sismondi's descriptions of rhyme's erotic character—its desiring structure, its romantic appeal to memory and hope—and Sismondi's careful work to relate that phenomenology of rhyme to the form's European origin in Provençal love poetry.[28]

In Hegel's *Aesthetics*, an important source for Pater, both the phrases "romantic love" and "romantic rhyme" gain conceptual rigor. Like Warton and the Coppet group, Hegel saw "romantic love" as a medieval development—one of many indices of what he considered the romantic phase of art. In his "The Concept of Love," a section of the *Aesthetics* that deals with chivalry, Hegel connects romantic love to a new "inner infinity of the person," an experience of the self's subjectivity and of the beloved's exquisite particularity that he finds only in romantic art. "As this subjective spiritual depth of feeling," he writes, "love does not occur in classical art, and when love does make its appearance there it is generally only a subordinate feature in the representation or only connected with sensuous enjoyment." He proceeds to define romantic love through classical art's negative examples—the unromantic loves of Penelope, Andromache, and Paris and Helen; the unromantic love lyrics of Sappho and Anacreon. In Sappho, love is "indeed heightened to lyrical enthusiasm," but it is too centered on the enflamed and suffering body rather than the "deep feeling of the subjective heart and mind." In Anacreon, there is not enough suffering, and the lover is too indiscriminate in his desires. So Hegel defines romantic love as a passionate, inward, all-encompassing experience that is also fundamentally historical.[29]

As I explained in chapter 2, Hegel's idea of "romantic rhyme" is historical, too. He uses the modifier "romantic" to differentiate the new rhyme systems of medieval poetry from those isolated instances of rhyme-like sounds that occasionally ornamented classical Latin poems. Rhyme is bound up with a range of historical conditions (the "corruption" of classical quantitative prosody, the emergence of Christianity, the rise of chivalry, the appearance of new European vernaculars and lyric forms) that make the "personal inner life of feeling" intrinsic to its operation. Though Hegel sees Germanic alliteration as a nascent form of rhyme, the more fully realized rhymes of the romantic stanza embody the erotic pain and pleasure they were developed to express. Those rhymes dance a courtship dance with one another, and they also toy with our own quasi-erotic readerly appetites: "[I]t is as if the rhymes now find one another immediately, now fly from one another and yet look for one another [so] the ear's attentive expectation is now satisfied without more ado, now teased, deceived, or kept in suspense."[30] His term "romantic rhyme" (*romantischen Reimes*) thus manages to hold together both historical and erotic valences without becoming a pun. In "romantic love" and "romantic rhyme," "romantic" acts as an affective, but also a historiographic, marker.

This idea of rhyme as doubly romantic—as both *loving* rhyme and *medieval* or *modern* rhyme—prompted some brilliantly winking poetic performances in the nineteenth century. Keats's "Isabella; or, The Pot of Basil" (1818), for instance, represents another familiar story of courtly love by depicting kissing-as-rhyming. After pining and sickening for one another over the course of eight gorgeous ottava rima stanzas, Lorenzo and Isabella finally consummate their desire: Lorenzo's "timid lips grew bold, / And poesied with hers in dewy rhyme: / Great bliss was with them, and great happiness / Grew, like a lusty flower in June's caress."[31] Keats suggests quite clearly here that a kiss is an embodiment of romantic rhyme, that rhyme is a kissing kind of speech, and that rhyming and kissing bear a special relationship to the redolent atmosphere of medieval love.

Another famous example (made much of by Pater and Vernon Lee) is the Helena scene in Goethe's *Faust II* (1832), where the modern Faust is teaching the classical Helena how to speak in the historically foreign idiom of rhyme.[32] As Helena learns to complete Faust's rhymes, their swooning dialogue becomes a love marriage (and an allegory for "the reconciliation of the Classic and Romantic elements in Art and Literature," in the gloss of Goethe's nineteenth-century translator, Bayard Taylor, whose English version I quote here).[33] Helena's absolute inexperience with rhyme allows Goethe to defamiliarize it at the same time as he eroticizes it. Helena's untrained ear hears rhyme as affection, submission, pleasure, and touch: "strangely-sounding speech, friendly and strange: / [wherein] Each sound appeared as yielding to the next, / And, when a word gave pleasure to the ear, / Another came, caressing then the first."[34] Faust's answer adds to this repertoire of qualities "delight," rapture, and satisfaction:

> If thee our people's mode of speech delight,
> O thou shalt be enraptured with our song,
> Which wholly satisfies both ear and mind!
> But it were best we exercise it now:
> Alternate speech entices, calls it forth.[35]

And when Helena asks, "Canst thou to me that lovely speech impart?" their exchange falls into reciprocally answering (and nuptially binding) rhymes:

> FAUST
> 'Tis easy: it must issue from the heart;
> And if the breast with yearning overflow,
> One looks around, and asks—
>
> HELENA
> Who shares the glow.
>
> FAUST
> Nor Past nor Future shades an hour like this;
> But wholly in the Present—
>
> HELENA
> Is our bliss.
>
> FAUST
> Gain, pledge, and fortune in the Present stand:
> What confirmation does it ask?
>
> HELENA
> My hand.[36]

Keats's kissing scene and Goethe's marriage scene, in their staging of the historical and affective meanings of rhyme, depend upon the kind of genetic thinking that Romantic theorists elaborated historiographically. This isn't to say that rhyme always had to mean the same thing as romantic love in the nineteenth century; there are plenty of rhymed poems that don't treat erotic themes and don't activate the associations I've described. But it is also true that rhyme, love, and romantic periodization shared the same conceptual space in nineteenth-century thought, and the associations among them were there to be activated by poets, as Keats, Goethe, and Morris activate them. Such ideas are not as closely associated now, because we are no longer pursuing the origins of love and literary form. Nonetheless, nineteenth-century theories of rhyme can do more than help us read nineteenth-century poetry better. They can productively estrange for us the relations of form to history and content to form.

ANCIENT RHYME IN *THE EARTHLY PARADISE*

In light of the romantic model of periodization, the organization of *The Earthly Paradise*—its apparently tidy division between classical and medieval tales—becomes legible as a contrast between classical and *romantic* literature, with all the historical and affective tonalities that word conveys (Pater saw this contrast clearly). The classical tales are drawn from Greek and Latin myth; while the medieval tales, from Norse, Arabic, Italian, German, and other sources, represent the range of poetic cultures that make up Warton's romantic creation myth. This structure draws out parallels—you might even say rhymes—between the classical and romantic tales: in both we find tyrannical kings, wronged children returning as adults to claim their birthright, dragons, enchantresses, and the agony and ecstasy of love. There is contrast, but also, in Herbert Tucker's words, a "chiastic symmetry."[37]

There are striking stylistic similarities across the two sets of tales as well. In both we find recurrences of rhyme words, including that sexy pair from "The Defence of Guenevere," *kiss* and *bliss*. As it does in the "Defence," the *kiss/bliss* rhyme appears in many of the medieval tales to enflame a romantic moment. In one tale, "The Land East of the Sun and West of the Moon," for instance, Morris uses the rhyme half a dozen times—and most climactically when the lovers at the center of the tale, a farm boy and the swan maiden he loves, cross over into her enchanted swan world. His "lips did meet / In one unhoped, undreamed-of kiss, / The very heart of all his bliss."[38] But the same rhyme also appears in the majority of classical tales. In the first poem, "Atalanta's Race," the stubborn princess loses a footrace to her handsome suitor. As she falters near the finish line, she finds herself falling into his embrace: "A strong man's arms about her body twined. / Nor may she shudder now to feel his kiss, / So wrapped she is in new unbroken bliss" (186). The same rhyme shows up in "The Story of Cupid and Psyche," "Pygmalion and the Image," "The Death of Paris," and many more of the classical love stories. This pattern could be understood as macroprosodic: although we can't quite hear the rhyme of *kiss* and *bliss* as it chimes with every other *kiss/bliss* pair in every other tale where it appears, there is nonetheless the structure of a long-distance rhyme connecting the stories: an overarching call-and-response that serves to affiliate one pair of lovers, and one love scene, and one kind of love, with the next. In fact, the pattern of *kiss/bliss* rhymes guarantees that love *sounds* the same in both the classical and romantic tales.

Morris has thus established the broad historical distinctions of classical and romantic only to blur them. Despite his schematic organization, it becomes apparent that he is not offering rigorously classical or medieval tales. As many readers have observed, the classical tales do not look and sound classical, because they are being retold in the medieval context of *The Earthly Paradise*'s plot: they are, in Florence Boos's coinage, "medieval-classical."[39] The classical tales' excess of medievalist detail extends to the texture of verse: always rhyming couplets and rhymed stanzas, often Chaucer's rhyme royal. Of course, Morris couldn't have written in a strictly classical form—quantitative Greek prosody has no English equivalent—but he uses none of the familiar strategies by which nineteenth-century poets typically approximated lost Greek rhythms: dactylic hexameters, Sapphic stanzas, Pindaric strophes, unrhymed blank verse, and so on. Morris the craftsman is *not* reaching for the feeling of classical Greek prosody, even though classical Greek is the imagined language of most of the poem.

For Walter Pater, this is exactly as it should be. In his review, Pater argues that Morris's historical style is predicated on his "charming anachronisms." In representing the classical world, Morris treats it as a world at a distance, one that can only be apprehended and represented through the filters of the distinct historical periods that have intervened. The effect Morris strives for is a "composite experience" rather than an "actual revival" (much like Hallam's description of Tennyson's historiographic forms).[40] When Morris renders his classical epic *The Life and Death of Jason* or the classical tales from *The Earthly Paradise* in medievalist style, he is approaching ancient Greece in the truest way that a modern artist can: through layers of history. For Pater, medievalist detail in a classical tale is a lovely aesthetic solution to the problem of historical difference.[41]

This explanation, attractive as it is, doesn't quite account for the force of rhyme's anachronism in *The Earthly Paradise*. Throughout the poem, Morris reminds us insistently that what we're reading is not just poetry, but poetry in rhyme. In the opening lines of the poem, Morris's idle singer tells us that he will be singing his stories in "murmuring rhyme." The interludes that return us to the storytelling frame between tales often describe the tales themselves as rhymes. After the classical tale for June, "The Love of Alcestis," the Wanderers are moved by "the measured falling of that rhyme" (11); after the classical "Son of Croesus" tale, we find the story's auditors "Soothed by the sweet luxurious summer time, / And by the cadence of that ancient rhyme" (5–6). "Pygmalion and the Image," another classical tale, is similarly described in the lyric that follows it as an "ancient rhyme" (1). All of these examples toy with a combination of metapoetic realism and historical incongruity. On one hand, the narratives *are* made up of rhymes, so the familiar synecdoche of "rhyme" for "poem" makes some sense. On the other hand, "ancient" seems in these moments to carry a real historical specificity: not just generically old, but of antiquity. We are forced to acknowledge the friction with which "ancient" modifies "rhyme"—the weirdness of a classical tale, told in a classical language, cast in modern rhyme.[42]

Rhyme's appearance as an odd and untimely medium is exacerbated by the historical realism of the Greek environment in which the stories are exchanged. Many details of the Elders' city suggest that the Wanderers have experienced a kind of time travel in arriving there—or at least that the Elders have undergone an uncanny slowing-down of historical time. They are "clad in ancient guise" (19), and they still perform the daily rituals of the classical world in agora, council-house, and temple, "[w]herein the gods worshipped in ancient lands / Still have their altars" (70–71). They are surrounded by Grecian architecture and art, pillared buildings made of marble and emblazoned with gold images of the old gods (37–38). They also speak Greek, but they seem aware of the antiquity of their language, observing that a few of the Wanderers can also speak "the ancient tongue / That through the lapse of ages still has clung / To us the seed of the Ionian race" (77–80). Notwithstanding this acknowledgment of their belatedness, the Elders' language remains classical Greek, and that appears to be the only language with which the two groups can communicate.

We are left with what feels like a logic problem. If the tales we are reading are being related in ancient Greek, and we are reading them in modern rhyme, perhaps they have undergone a translation process. If so, we should take their rhyming lightly. Yet we know that they have not been translated into rhyme, since the Wanderers are moved precisely by the rhymes they hear. The result is that we have to imagine we are overhearing these poetic tales in classical Greek, and that the

Greek falls impossibly into rhymes and stanzas like romantic poems. Morris further intensifies the anachronistic effect by putting rhymed poems and songs into the hands and mouths of his classical characters. In some more ambiguous cases these are embedded songs; in other cases, Morris tells us outright that rhyme is there—as when Orpheus appears in "The Hill of Venus" "crooning o'er snatches of forgotten rhyme" (506).

From this catalog, it may sound as though rhyme has been dehistoricized by Morris and detached from its medieval associations, but this is not the case. Rhyme remains potently historical, even in the poem's Greek world. Morris uses rhyme as a transhistorical language of desire, but he does it, paradoxically, by evoking rhyme's historicity. He uses ideas about rhyme's history and its historical forms to shape personal histories of love. This work is most visible in the classical tales, where rhyme is denaturalized—where the historical and erotic content of rhyme stands in relief against the classical background.

ORIGINS OF LOVE

"The Story of Acontius and Cydippe" is a classical tale that is saturated with medievalist description and feeling, with a kind of romantic intensity that strains against the minimalist plot. Here is the plot: it is springtime in "a garden fair," and a boy (Acontius) sings a song, sees a girl (Cydippe), kisses her, grows sick with love, can't eat, can't sleep, finds out she is about to take vows of chastity, and thinks he will die from the pain of it. Venus intervenes by giving Acontius an apple on which he writes "Acontius will I wed today." As Cydippe is about to take her vows, he throws the apple into the folds of her dress. She picks it up and reads its message out loud, and her utterance has the force of a contract. The town elders want to punish the two for their transgression, but then they realize that romantic love is its own punishment: it distracts from all the other beauties of the world, and it makes solitude unbearable.

Most of the five hundred couplets of this tale are given over to Acontius's pitiable condition, and the rhymes are conventional and often lovely: *kiss* and *bliss* (of course), *desire* and *fire*, *breath* and *death*. But I'm less interested in the local effects of the rhymes than in what rhyme does in the plot. I said that Acontius sings a song, then falls in love. His song, which breaks from the couplet form of the tale into a quasi-Provençal canzone—about flowers, kissing, and the pain of love—seems to *generate* the passionate feeling that overtakes him. That is, he idly begins to sing a song of love, and the song brings love into his world. These are the lines that follow Acontius's song:

> What was it that through half-shut eyes
> Pierced to his heart, and made him rise
> As one the July storm awakes
> When through the dawn the thunder breaks?
> What was it that the languor clove,
> Wherewith unhurt he sang of love?
> How was it that his eyes had caught
> Her eyes alone of all; that nought
> The others were but images,
> While she, while she amidst of these
> Not first or last, when she was gone,
> Why must he feel so left alone? (71–82)

Acontius's sudden, catastrophic, and seemingly random love for Cydippe either comes out of nowhere or it comes out of his song. It is an event, like a clap of thunder, that "clove" Acontius's world. Here we have not just the echo of medieval lovesickness (Dante seeing Beatrice, Petrarch seeing Laura, Troilus seeing Criseyde), but also an echo of the story of romantic love. A song of love is sung in Provence, and love appears, and it breaks history (and the history of European literature) in two. Morris evokes the eventfulness of love, but in this case the history love periodizes is a personal one, not a European or world-historical one. Acontius's life is divided into a before and after: after he has seen Cydippe "his old life seemed passed away" (93).[43]

This is a story about the *vita nuova* of love: the new forms of language that love produces and the forms of love that poetry makes possible. For Victorians these novelties belonged to a romantic world. By turning a literary-historical story (the rupture between classical and romantic literature) into the story of one person's life, by scaling it down to individual experience, Morris aestheticizes the historiographic idea. Here, and throughout *The Earthly Paradise*, the origin of the "romantic" can be traced to the moment when eye catches eye, and cheek burns, and the colors of the flowers grow painfully intense, and speech turns into rhyme.

"The Story of Acontius and Cydippe" illustrates with extreme clarity how romantic form and romantic feeling might shape a classical narrative. Elsewhere in the classical tales, rhyme's romantic effects are subtler. "Pygmalion and the Image," one of the classical tales described in the frame as an "ancient rhyme," has no Provençal love song to catalyze the passion of the protagonist. Nonetheless the tale relies on similar notions of love, language, and literary history, and it brings them together in the sound and shape of rhyme.

"Pygmalion and the Image" is Morris's version of the story from Ovid's *Metamorphoses* about a sculptor who falls miserably in love with a sculpture he has made. Finally, through Venus's intervention, the statue comes to life, and she becomes his living wife. Morris's departures from Ovid and his medieval source mostly involve descriptive amplification and a softening of the hard-edged misogyny of earlier versions, especially Ovid's. Morris's tale still begins with Pygmalion's contempt for real, living women, and it still ends with him married to the art object he has designed, but it lays unique emphasis on the statue's articulation of desire. In Ovid's version, Pygmalion places the statue on his bed and palpates her into liveliness; in Morris's version, Pygmalion arrives home to an already living woman who says, "Pygmalion come to me, / O dear companion of my new-found life, / For I am called thy lover and thy wife" (495–97). In a long monologue, she then offers her "new-made" soul to him, and instructs him on how to caress her: "[L]ay thy hand this heaving breast upon!"; "Sweep mine hair round thy neck"; "Draw me to thee, sweet / And feel the warm heart of thy living love / Beat against thine" (500–509). In Morris's story the statue comes to life murmuring words and doesn't stop talking until the poem ends.

Despite the story's focus, then, on a sculptor and his statue, Morris seems less concerned with visual representation than with problems of poetic language. For most of the narrative, Pygmalion himself is excessively *in*articulate. He is a lovesick Troilus (the Chaucerian echo reinforced by the poem's rhyme royal stanzas), and one symptom of his lovesickness is an inability to name the problem he is suffering from. A kind of aphasia seizes him as he finishes carving his statue's body. He experiences a "burning longing … / A strange and strong desire he could not name" (75–77). Morris repeats variations on this phrase several more times, as "higher 'gan to flame / That strange and strong desire without a name" (130–31). Pygmalion knows that he is

FIGURE 3. Edward Burne-Jones, *The Godhead Fires* (1878); Venus gives life to Galatea. From Pygmalion and the Image, 2nd series (ca. 1875–78). Photograph: Birmingham Museum and Art Gallery.

feeling something painful—a "nameless hope" (379)—but he doesn't have the words to say what it is, because the feeling itself doesn't have a name. When he prays to Venus, he "can frame no set of words" to ask for what he wants.

Is it possible that Pygmalion can't say what he wants or how he feels because he is feeling medieval feelings in a premedieval world? Morris suggests that his love is *unspeakable* not because it's perverse—a human man's love for an inanimate statue—but because it's proleptic: a classical person experiencing romantic love. It isn't only the pining that Pygmalion can't name; it's also the mad joy he feels when he first embraces his statue come to life. In that moment, Pygmalion's ecstasies are "passing all words, yea, well-nigh passing thought."

Galatea is more articulate than Pygmalion, but there's something strange about her speech, too. When Venus grants her life (along with a "dowry of desire and thought") Galatea begins "To murmur in some tongue unknown to man" (588) (fig. 3). A reader might be inclined in this moment to understand her murmuring as an inchoate form of human speech or a sort of godspeech she speaks before she learns to talk like a woman and to narrate the story of her new life to Pygmalion. But like Pygmalion's love problem, Galatea's murmuring problem is also a problem of history: the premature arrival of something like rhyme. The word "murmur" appears all over *The Earthly Paradise.* Trees murmur, bees murmur, the sea murmurs, and lovers murmur—as Psyche "murmur[s] low" when she is visited by Cupid in the night. Murmuring is also the way that Morris, in the frame of *The Earthly Paradise,* had described the prosodic atmosphere of the entire poem: it is written in "murmuring rhyme." So when Galatea is making sounds in "some tongue unknown to man," and those sounds murmur, they remind us that we are reading rhymed poetry. Galatea murmurs, just like love murmurs and rhyme murmurs. And even before Galatea's murmuring becomes intelligible, it has a content: the "desire and thought" that make her alive.

Such suggestiveness resolves into concrete form in the poem's last stanza, where sound and body, love and language merge:

> What words he said? How can I tell again
> What words they said beneath the glimmering light?
> Some tongue they used unknown to loveless men
> As each to each they told their great delight,
> Until for stillness of the growing night
> Their soft sweet murmuring words seemed growing loud,
> And dim the moon grew, hid by fleecy cloud. (638–44)

The stanza begins with the narrator's decorous refusal or inability to describe the love scene, and it ends with a dramatic blackout. Morris is only a little bit coy about whether Pygmalion and his lover are speaking or kissing. Galatea's earlier "tongue unknown to man" becomes here "some tongue ... unknown to *loveless* men" (my emphasis), now certainly a secret erotic language for those in love.

The lovers' climactic union is met with a crescendo of sonic orchestration. In addition to the rhyme royal end rhymes that seem to murmur their own story about the lovers' experience—"light," "delight," "night," "loud," "cloud"—internal rhymes, almost rhymes, and identical rhymes fill the stanza's space with paired patterns of sound. "What words he said" repeats, with an incremental difference, in "What words they said" in the line below. There's the half-rhyme of "some tongue," the internal rich rhyme of "each to each," the internal true rhyme of "until" and "still," the very internal rhyme of "murmur." The whole stanza seems to draw together in a murmuring of coupling sounds. Phrases, words, and even pairs of syllables within words find their mates. Finally, the closing rhyme pair "loud" and "cloud" evokes the erotic logic of the *kiss* and *bliss* rhyme: from frenzied desire to rest. *First* kiss, *then* bliss; *first* "growing loud," *then* "fleecy cloud."

In the context of this stanza, the sound patterns of the penultimate line read as unusually mimetic: "Their soft sweet murmuring words seemed growing loud." We can hear the line move from the sibilant whisper of "soft sweet" to the onomatopoeic murmur of "murmuring words" to the relatively open vowels of "growing loud"—made louder by the terminal emphasis on the rhyme word "loud." We also might experience these words in the mind's mouth, an intensified version of the poetic imagery that I. A. Richards called "articulatory": "the feel in the lips, mouth, and throat, of what the words would be like to speak."[44] The idea of articulatory imagery isn't all that risqué in *Principles of Literary Criticism*. In this case, though, it's the feel of words in the mouth that are *about* the feel of words in the mouth: the whispers and murmurs of "some *tongue* ... unknown to loveless men." At the same time as the stanza purports to exclude the reader from its private space, its language registers in the reader's body.

This kind of thing horrified Robert Buchanan, that Victorian critic who, as we saw, charged the Pre-Raphaelites with an obscene "fleshliness." He thought their poems were too full of kissing lips and "munch[ing]" mouths, too "sickening[ly]" eager to "reproduce the sexual mood," too fixated on form, sound, and flesh.[45] Buchanan was ungenerous, but he wasn't totally wrong. Morris *is* reproducing the sexual mood here, and he's doing it through the poem's form. In fact, the final couplet's abrupt shift from auditory and articulatory imagery to a visual image (the moon disappearing behind a cloud) makes us recognize how mimetic that ear and mouth imagery was. In this, the most *romantic* couplet of the poem—as the lovers murmur to one another their "great delight"—the erotic and prosodic details converge.

William Morris's "murmuring words" couplet in "Pygmalion and the Image" bears some resemblance to a verse in another Victorian poem that became the locus classicus of mimetic form for the New Critics. The verse is Tennyson's, from *The Princess*: "The moan of doves in immemorial elms / And murmuring of innumerable bees." John Crowe Ransom, René Wellek and Austin Warren, and W. K. Wimsatt all pointed to these lines as exemplary of a special kind of verbal mimesis that occurs when an onomatopoeic effect extends across an entire line. Instead of just the word "murmur" murmuring, the whole line seems to murmur like the humming of bees. I say "seems to" because it is an effect—and Ransom's joke was to show how the effect disappears when the relation between sound and sense is compromised. Rewriting the line as "murdering of innumerable beeves," Ransom tried to prove that the reader's mind does indeed govern the ear.[46]

The same could be said for these lines from "Pygmalion and the Image." Knowing that the stanza's semantic meaning is love and sex, we hear the versification as loving and sexy. It's an arbitrary relationship between form and content made to seem natural. Except that there is a difference here. To a Victorian mind and ear attuned to literary-historical myth, rhyme intrinsically is a form of desire; literary history made it so. From this perspective, Pygmalion and Galatea's love scene doesn't trick us into thinking that rhyme is romantic. Instead, it concentrates our attention on rhyme's already fleshly form.

6

Coventry Patmore's Passionate Pause

One of Coventry Patmore's most affecting elegies for his wife Emily hardly mentions her at all. Instead of treating the object of grief directly, Patmore's "The Toys" (1877) focuses on an episode in the grief-life of the widower and his little son. After punishing his son too harshly for "having my law the seventh time disobey'd," the remorseful father visits the child's bedroom. There, beside the sleeping boy, whose lashes are still wet with tears, he finds evidence of the child's efforts at self-consolation:

> . . . on a table drawn beside his head,
> He had put, within his reach,
> A box of counters and a red-vein'd stone,
> A piece of glass abraded by the beach
> And six or seven shells,
> A bottle with bluebells
> And two French copper coins, ranged there with careful art
> To comfort his sad heart.[1]

This spectacle moves the father to recognize a parallel between the child's self-soothing game and "the toys" with which adults "ma[k]e our joys," and to ask God, the father of us all, for forgiveness.[2]

Patmore's poem, sentimental as it is, offers a rigorous account of elegiac prosody, where aesthetic form is both proof of and proof against unbearable pain. In his double grief at the mother's absence and the father's anger—"His Mother, who was patient, being dead"—the child finds comfort in arranging his playthings into sequences of measured lines.[3] The poem is reticent about the nature of the toys that occupy grown-ups, but the child's trinkets suggest an analogy with the materials of the poetic line. The analogy is so strong, in fact, that it seems to transform the poem before our eyes: we find ourselves reading a lineated arrangement of counters, stones, glass, shells, coins, and flowers rather than words, feet, and rhymes. Grief is expressed—but also counted, ordered, and *felt*—in those objects and the "careful art" of their organization.

Although Patmore is now recognized as an important nineteenth-century elegist and prosodic theorist, for most of the twentieth century he was the patriarchal poet of *The Angel in the House* (1854–56): he was responsible for inventing the angel who leaned over Virginia Woolf's shoulder and whispered that women don't write. To become an author, Woolf explained in "Professions for Women" (1939), she had to kill Patmore's angel. Toward the end of the twentieth century, Woolf's Patmorean image became an icon of feminist recovery criticism. In *The Madwoman in the Attic* (1979), Sandra Gilbert and Susan Gubar invoked Woolf's battle with the angel to explain the psychological obstacles faced by all nineteenth-century women writers.[4] Our main anthologies still use Patmore in this way: lines from *The Angel in the House* are excerpted alongside conservative conduct manuals to teach students about the Victorian "Woman Question."[5]

While this version of Coventry Patmore has continued to have pedagogical utility, the criticism has been gaining in range and detail. Those who have written in recent years on *The Angel in the House* have approached the poem not just as a record of Victorian patriarchy but also as a generic experiment, and a surprisingly rich exploration of the form and temporality of conjugal love.[6] And there has been renewed interest in the elegies of *The Unknown Eros* (1877), too. But the majority of Patmore studies today focus on his poetic theory; the 1857 "Essay on English Metrical Law" has become a key text for scholars working on Victorian versification.[7] For Adela Pinch, among others, Patmore's essay is "the most important nineteenth-century account of meter after Wordsworth."[8] It is easy to see why the "Metrical Law" has acquired the status it has: it consolidates a huge amount of nineteenth-century thinking about prosody, at the same time as it advances a relatively idiosyncratic theory of its own—one that directly influenced poets as diverse as Gerard Manley Hopkins, Alice Meynell, Francis Thompson, and Thomas Hardy. Scholarship on the "Metrical Law" has shared the emphasis of prosody studies more broadly in favoring meter over other aspects of versification, despite Patmore's own philosophical investment in rhyme. This chapter shifts the focus to rhyme, in order to uncover the historiographic and affective features of Patmore's thought.

Among the writers this book treats, Patmore is exceptional for the total integration of the philosophical, historical, and practical aspects of his work. Elizabeth Barrett Browning wrote literary history that became in her hands a poetic theory, but she did not venture (despite a wealth of marginalia and correspondence on the subject) a systematic theory of prosody. Meanwhile, Arthur Hallam wrote literary historiography and literary criticism that are interconnected, but—although he wrote many poems of his own—it would be left to Tennyson, a poet famously allergic to theorizing, to write poetry on the historiographic model of form that Hallam laid out. Patmore's "Metrical Law" is a theory of prosody that engages with many of the poets and thinkers I've already discussed (most notably, Tennyson, Arthur Hallam, and Hegel). What is more, Patmore set out to develop a poetic form that directly answered his theory of prosody, and he spent the last several decades of his career writing exclusively in that form. Patmore called the poems that embodied his prosodic theory "odes." This chapter explores the significance of that word for Patmore: why the ode was itself a theory of literary history, why the ode was an ideal poetic counterpart to his prosodic system, and why the form of the ode lent itself so readily to elegiac feeling.

I begin by looking at Patmore's "Metrical Law," which I propose is really an attempt to grapple with what it feels like to be at the end of a poetic line—not just the end of a line on the page but also the end of a literary-historical line.[9] In Patmore's poetics, these two different kinds of line-ends converge: Patmore sees end-of-line rhyme and end-of-line pause as the definitive, and underappreciated, elements of modern English prosody. I then examine the role of rhyme and pause in Patmore's concept of the ode, which he understands (like Hallam's and Tennyson's lyric) as a protean genre defined by affective form. Here, I consider two competing models of the ode—Edmund Gosse's classicist one and J. G. Herder's historicist one—in order to clarify Patmore's historiographic position. Finally, I return to the poems of *The Unknown Eros*, showing how another elegiac ode, "The Azalea," enacts his theories of literary history and affective form. In poems like "The Azalea," where Patmore builds elaborate patterns of feeling out of irregular rhyme and extended pause, he makes a case for the expressive resources of modern English prosody against the old, imported schemes of classical and romantic literature. Read alongside his theoretical work, Patmore's odes announce a new era in the history of poetic forms—and point toward the future of modernist free verse.

THE "METRICAL LAW"

Patmore considered his "Essay on English Metrical Law" to be his definitive statement on poetic form, and he consequently republished it (in slightly modified versions) throughout his career. By his own account, the essay was inspired by a deficiency in the field of prosody criticism. No theory, from the Renaissance onward, had sufficiently explained "the mechanism" of modern English verse. While metrical theorists had agreed that so-called accentual-syllabic English poetry is measured differently from so-called quantitative Greek poetry, the true quality of that difference had remained elusive. The fundamental problem, as Patmore saw it, was the nature of the accent. Was it a length? A tone? A weight? A loudness? A combination of more than one of these attributes? "The only tenable view," Patmore concludes, is that accents correspond to regular periods of spoken time, what he calls "isochronous intervals" (meaning intervals of the same duration). We hear the progress from one isochronous interval to the next as "an 'ictus' or 'beat,' actual or mental, which, like a post in a chain railing, shall mark the end of one space, and the commencement of another." Many scholars have pointed out that Patmore's major intervention here is the assertion that the ictus "*has no material and external existence at all,* but has its place in the mind, which craves measure in everything."[10] Rather than inhering in the line itself, the beat is something we bring to the line—an "idea (or idealization)" of meter, as Yopie Prins explains it.[11]

Locating the beat in the mind rather than in the poetic syllable allows Patmore to imagine counterintuitive ways to scan a line. Most significantly, it lets end-of-line pauses—or catalexis—count in the same way that so-called accents do: as "*subjects*" rather than "*interruptions* … of metrical law" (22). Even poems with irregular line lengths can be understood as existing in a grid of isochronous sections; the time that isn't occupied by syllables is occupied by periods of rest. This makes sense when we think of a 4-3-4-3 ballad or hymnal meter (where the three-beat lines are the same as the four-beat lines; they just

TABLE 1. Voiced vs. Unvoiced Syllables

1	2	3	4	5	6	7	8	9	10	11	12	13	14	15	16
Through	del	i	ca	test	e	ther	fea	th'ring	soft	their	sol	i	ta	ry	beat
Is	this?														

happen to end in what Derek Attridge calls an "unrealised beat")—but its more extreme instances are harder to fathom.[12] In an "irregular" iambic ode, Patmore's limit case, there may be terminal pauses of durations up to fourteen syllables, and he insists that a sensitive reader will wait these pauses out. For example, in his own ode "To the Unknown Eros," we can find a line of sixteen voiced syllables ("Through delicatest ether feathering soft their solitary beat") and another line of only two ("Is this?").[13] Patmore would allot both these lines the same sixteen-syllable reading time, so that from the perspective of isochrony they would be understood as in table 1. Accounting for both the voiced and the unvoiced syllables, the second line would read, "Is **this**? [*dah-**dah** dah-**dah** dah-**dah** dah-**dah** dah-**dah** dah-**dah** dah-**dah***]"[14] One subsequent prosodic theorist called such a suggestion "theorizing run mad."[15]

But the pause, for Patmore, is not only a metrical abstraction; it is a key to how poems manage emotion. The longer the catalectic pause is in relation to the syllable count of the line, the more powerfully does the poem strike us as sad. Providing an example from his own early poetry, Patmore declares definitively that "the six-syllable 'iambic' is the most solemn of all our English measures. It is scarcely fit for anything but a dirge; the reason being, that the final pause in this measure is greater, when compared with the length of the line, than in any other verse." Here are the lines from "Night and Sleep" that he uses to make his case:

How strange it is to wake
    And watch, while others sleep,
Till sight and hearing ache
    For objects that may keep
The awful inner sense
    Unroused, lest it should mark
The life that haunts the emptiness
    And horror of the dark. (27)

When reading a six-syllable iambic—that is, with three accented syllables per line—we understand that we are really reading a four-beat line, and we are invariably moved by the pregnant pauses. And if the six-syllable iambic is a recipe, specifically, for solemnity, the irregular ode—with its jagged line lengths and its correspondingly varied pauses—is the most open to "the variations of the high and stately lyrical feeling which alone can justify the use of this measure" (28). As he will state the case in the 1890s, the irregular ode requires a "metre-making passion," and there should be an exact correlation between the intensity of feeling and the length of pause, from "the long-drawn sigh of two syllables to the passionate cataract of sixteen, in which pause altogether disappears."[16] This would perhaps be a line with *no* words—in other words, a stanza break. The affective content of the poem resides in the pauses that we feel and count and do not voice. Patmore's strong claims for the correlation between form and feeling—specifically pause and feeling—were met with some friendly ridicule by Tennyson, who sent him a sprightly little jingle in the same six-syllable iambic that should only have been fit for a dirge: "How glad I am to walk / With Susan on the shore! / How glad I am to talk! / I kiss her o'er and o'er." "Is this C.P.'s most solemn?" he asks.[17] Clearly, Tennyson felt that Patmore was asking the pause to bear too much affective weight.[18]

And Patmore seems to have his own doubts in the "Metrical Law"—for as soon as he has established that the beat is in the mind, and that emotion is in the pause, and that the pause can and must tick out uncomfortably long, his essay abruptly switches tracks. Suddenly he is writing about rhyme and alliteration, and in increasingly ecstatic terms.[19] Rhyme, like alliteration, is "no mere 'ornament' of versification: it is a real and powerful metrical adjunct when properly employed," he pronounces. "Rhyme is so far from being extra-metrical and merely 'ornamental,' as most persons imagine it to be, that it is the quality to which nearly all our metres owe their very existence" (31, 40–41). Rhyme makes a stanza where no stanza could otherwise be, and rhyme designates the limit of the line. It is, finally, "the highest metrical power we have" and "the great means, in modern languages, of marking essential metrical pauses" (41, 31). Rhyme, to sum up, is a condition of possibility for the structure of the stanza, the meter, the line, and the pause.

Patmore's understanding of the regulating power of rhyme is gleaned from a long line of rhyme theorists before him. From Samuel Daniel, he takes the notion that rhyme is a binding principle. In one of the passages from "The Defence of Rhyme" (1603) that Patmore excerpts, Daniel writes that the "like sounding accents" of rhyme "seeme as the jointure without which [verse] hangs loose and cannot subsist, but runs wildly on, like a tedious fancie without a close." So rhyme acts as a check on the incontinent metrical line, but it also—significantly—acts as "due stayes for the mind" (quoted in Patmore, "Metrical Law," 40). This idea of rhyme is nothing like Patmore's idealization of meter; rather than a projection coming out from the mind to organize the verse, it is a power that comes out of the verse to organize the mind. A historical analogue is supplied by Hegel, who argued that rhyme became a prosodic necessity when absolute classical quantity gave way to the more arbitrary accentual system. Rhyme came as "a new power, working *ab extra*," whose "very grossness, as compared with syllabic quantity, is a great advantage, inasmuch as the greater spirituality of modern thought and feeling demand a more forcible material contrast" (Patmore, "Metrical Law," 42). From their different perspectives, both Daniel and Hegel represent rhyme as a means of rescue from a metrical system that is otherwise too lawless or indefinite to hold.

It appears that the rhyme portion of Patmore's "Metrical Law" essay works in a structurally similar way. As his argument about meter unfurls, it reaches a point of no return, of too much abstraction: the fourteen-syllable pause that no reader would ever naturally want to (or know how to) read. Into this crisis of a prosodic theory that cannot be applied, rhyme descends as a kind of deus ex machina. Rhyme is the crucial exception to the rule that the metrical accent has no inherent weight. We know exactly how to inflect a syllable when that syllable rhymes. And if we can't recognize the end of a line by the end of a long pause, we can recognize it by a resounding rhyme. The rhyme portion of the "Metrical Law," like Hegel's historical rhyme, offers a "more forcible material contrast" to the theory of isochronous intervals. Like Daniel's rhyme, it offers "stayes for the mind."

Indeed, Patmore's discussion of rhyme helps us think of it as a more positive, more concrete counterpart to his pause. In addition to marking the end of a line in a more legible way than catalexis can, rhyme is also a vehicle for feeling. Patmore insists on this point both in the "Metrical Law" and in an earlier review of *In Memoriam*, where he repeats, as an article of faith, Arthur Hallam's statement that the structure of rhyme "appeal[s] to Memory and Hope." In fact, Patmore's idea of rhyme has so much in common with his idea of pause that one wonders if the pause argument is a bit of a sleight of hand. If we agree that we feel moved by his solemn six-syllable iambic, for instance, is it possible to say that the end-of-line pauses are affecting us more or less than the end-of-line rhymes, which call to their partners across the space of the page?

Patmore's later prose confirms a significant conceptual overlap between pause and rhyme. Having stated in the "Metrical Law" that rhyme is "the quality to which nearly all our metres owe their very existence" (41), he formulates it thus in an 1890 preface to his poems: "Nearly all English metres owe their existence as metres to 'catalexis,' or pause." The substitution of "pause" for "rhyme" seems to suggest that a refinement or change of opinion has occurred during the intervening years—that perhaps Patmore has revised his thinking about the importance of rhyme. But a subsequent sentence calls that supposition into question. In reference to the odes his preface is introducing, Patmore explains, "[T]he verse in which this volume is written is catalectic *par excellence*, employing the pause (as it does the rhyme) with freedom only limited by the exigencies of poetic passion." The grammar of this second sentence, where "rhyme" has a nearly appositive relationship to "pause," indicates that Patmore has not at all changed his mind between the "Metrical Law" and the preface; rhyme and pause move in synchrony to what he calls "the exigencies of poetic passion." At the end of the preface, Patmore refers his reader for further details about his catalectic meter "to the Essay printed as an appendix to the later editions of my collected poems"—that is, to the "Metrical Law."[20] In his conflation of pause and rhyme, then, Patmore believes that he is simply stating the same principle for a second time.

Thus, although in the "Metrical Law" he acknowledges circumstances in which catalexis appears in modern poetry without rhyme, Patmore's ideas of rhyme and pause are generally linked phenomena. We might understand rhyme as the pressure and pause as the release, or rhyme as the image and pause as the afterimage.[21] Or, to put it yet another way, we might think of pause as the medium through which rhyme's "Memory and Hope" are experienced.

I would suggest that Patmore's theory of pause keeps dissolving into a theory of rhyme because modern European poetry, as a historical formation, is basically unthinkable without rhyme. In Patmore's quest to discover the secret workings of English prosody, he is confronted with the historical entanglement of accentual-syllabic meter with rhyme. This history is not just a subtext of the "Metrical Law"; it is its explicit premise. At the outset of the essay, Patmore makes the point that classical meter is irreconcilable with modern European meter and ultimately unhearable by modern ears (such hearing is "a lost skill," as Isobel Armstrong puts it), and he bemoans the neglect of rhyme in contemporary theories of English poetry.[22] In particular, he praises the Renaissance critic George Puttenham for his "explicit acknowledgment of the fact, so often lost sight of by his successors, that English verse is not properly measurable by the rules of Latin and Greek verse," and for a "much clearer discernment of the main importance of rhyme and accentual stress, in English verse, than is to be found among later writers" (4). When he discusses "accent," Patmore carefully negotiates the different meanings of that word in relation to classical versus modern prosody, concluding, "We are of course chiefly interested in its meaning as it is concerned in English and most modern European verse" (13).

So while some readers have found in Patmore's principle of isochrony the persistence of a classical model of prosody, I would characterize his argument somewhat differently.[23] For Patmore, the English line read right can be understood as borrowing an element of time-measure from classical duration, yes, but isochrony is an incomplete description if it doesn't take into account the modern interplay of rhyme and rest at the end of a line. This distinction is the motivation of the essay, the historiographic problem that demands a theory. Patmore doesn't want to find common ground between Greek and English meter. He wants to approach English meter on its own terms.

To think of Patmore's metrical theory as a theory of literary history is to recognize that his historical scale is large indeed. The relationship he draws between Greek and English meter is less comparative—one prosodic system juxtaposed with another—than narrative: the journey from classical Greece to Victorian England as a long process of change, loss, and emergence. If this narrative resonates with my earlier accounts of the prosodic historiography of Arthur Hallam and Hegel, it is because these thinkers are Patmore's avowed sources. Patmore scrupulously observes the historical break that Hallam and Hegel describe, and he understands that break to condition the way we read and scan, or ought to read and scan, modern poems.

But the most interesting thing about Patmore's metrical theory is that it doesn't rest at theory, or even a reading practice; he means it to be applied to the writing of poetry, too. The odes of *The Unknown Eros,* which Patmore began writing in the early 1860s, were intended to demonstrate his idea of isochrony; Patmore advertised this fact on many occasions, including in the preface of 1890 mentioned above—and critics have generally taken him at his word. I want to argue, though, that beyond simply showing what isochrony looks like, the odes present themselves as a literary-historical event: a significant moment in the same prosodic drama that Patmore (after Hegel and Arthur Hallam) worked to theorize. In this regard, Patmore's poetic relationship to literary history is distinct from that of a poet like Elizabeth Barrett Browning. Whereas EBB uses poetic forms (blank verse, assonance, half-rhyme) to present an argument about the literary-historical past, Patmore's prosody makes a claim for the present as *also* literary history—indeed, as a new stage in a larger literary-historical process. He does this through the genre of the ode.

ODE HISTORIES

Patmore's ode is a historiographic genre, a key to his interpretation of literary history. Against theories of the ode, now dominant, that chart the reverberations of classicism through the centuries, Patmore did not regard the ode as a stable transhistorical object. Rather, the ode expressed for him, through its continuously varying prosodic forms, historical and linguistic specificity. Seen through this idea of the ode, borrowed from Continental aesthetics, literary history becomes legible as a series of untranslatable cultural differences across space and time. Patmore's project is to develop a form of ode—never yet achieved—that expresses not the spirit of ancient Greece or Renaissance Europe but the distinctive character of modern English prosody, with its distinctive language of feeling.

Patmore's odes don't look or behave like classical or neoclassical odes. They are often narrative and elegiac rather than vocative and encomiastic; and they don't exhibit the structural features that we tend to associate with the Pindaric or Horatian model, and with aspirations toward those models.[24] Instead of a regular sequence of strophes or stanzas (often the first visual cue that you're reading an ode), they are printed in long, unbroken blocks of verse; their line lengths are extremely irregular, and they are densely but irregularly rhymed. As many twentieth-century readers remarked, they look like free verse.

In his important 1905 study of Patmore, the poet and critic Edmund Gosse suggested that "ode" was the wrong word altogether—and the disagreement between Gosse and Patmore tells us much about ode theory at the end of the century. Although Gosse noticed some resemblances between Patmore's ode form and Abraham Cowley's irregular Pindarics (which were the first major attempt to translate Pindar's form into English, and which Patmore found ridiculous), Gosse proposed that "the true analogy of his *Odes* is with the Italian lyric[s] . . . of Petrarch and Dante."[25] In other words, Patmore's so-called ode was better understood as a kind of sonnet or canzone, built "rather upon a musical than a metrical system," and with a medieval rather than classical origin.[26] (This claim has resurfaced frequently in Patmore criticism.[27])

But, in choosing to call his poems "ode," Patmore did not mean what Edmund Gosse meant, or what we tend to mean, by that term. By now, we have settled on a basic literary-historical trajectory. Stephen Fogle and Paul Fry, writing in the *Princeton Encyclopedia of Poetry and Poetics*, connect the genre to classical sources: Pindar, Horace, and to a lesser degree, Anacreon; and they state clearly that "[t]hroughout Europe, the history of the ode commences with the rediscovery of the classic forms"—by sixteenth-century Italians and by the Pléiade in France. The tone is serious, the orientation is vocative, the form is usually polymetric. In nineteenth-century England, the models remain largely Pindar and Horace, even if, as with Keats and Shelley, sonnet form is sometimes brought in as an additional element.[28] This history of the ode corresponds with the entry in the *Encyclopedia Britannica* from 1911. That essay, also written by Edmund Gosse, remains an authoritative definition of the genre. It is now the basis for the "ode" entry on Wikipedia (in common with many nineteenth- and early twentieth-century *Encyclopedia Britannica* articles now in the public domain).[29] Yet Gosse's perspective on the ode was far from disinterested.

Before Gosse's reading of ode history was enshrined as definitive in the encyclopedia, and before he wrote his important early study of Patmore cited above, his ode essay appeared in an earlier form as the introduction to an 1881 anthology called *English Odes*. Gosse was just becoming acquainted with Patmore as he was editing the anthology, and since he wanted to include one of Patmore's poems (even though he already had doubts about its classical affiliations), the two had occasion to quibble about the meaning of "ode." In a letter to Gosse, Patmore seems irritated by Gosse's narrow definition of the genre. He writes,

> DEAR SIR,
>
> The Ode called the "Unknown Eros" is at your service for your selection. Your volume is likely to be a valuable one, provided that you extend it so as to include such Odes as Spenser's "Epithalamium" (the one on his own marriage); but if you limit it to Odes proper, according to the "Pindarique" notion, I do not see where you are to get enough for even a small volume.
>
> Trusting you will not think this remark obtrusive,
>
> I remain,
Dear Sir,
Yours truly,
C. PATMORE.[30]

Gosse probably felt obliged to accept Patmore's suggestion when he devoted the first several pages of his volume to Spenser's poem, because in the introduction he hedges: "It is difficult to say whether we owe this exquisite rhapsody to the Greek or to the Italian side of the genius of Edmund Spenser; the poem is unique, and had no tolerable imitators." Gosse makes it clear that Spenser is not part of his ode tradition: nobody follows Spenser, and Spenser's own antecedents are open to doubt. Moreover, Gosse maintains that "the importer of the ode as we usually understand it was Ben Jonson"—a poet writing in the century after Spenser.[31]

The question of Greek versus Italian heritage was fundamental to Gosse's historiography of the genre, because too strong a hint of the Italian meant disqualification. As Patmore implied, Gosse's ode history is really a history of Pindarism through the ages. It is a story of more or less faithful adherence to the model established by Pindar—of classical poetry and a long legacy of neoclassicism. Although Gosse acknowledges that Pindar was not the original inventor of the Greek ode, he sees him as the first to "exercise it in all its grace and all its majesty." When Renaissance Europe rediscovered the ode, "Pindar was recovered, indeed, but recovered in … confusion," and those who attempted to imitate his style in Latin or Greek invariably failed due to their misunderstanding of Greek prosody. In Gosse's account, French was the first modern language in which odes were written, with Pierre de Ronsard in 1550 citing Pindar as a model. Because Italian literature already had its own "stately lyrical forms of verse" developed from earlier medieval forms, it did not participate in this early recovery of Pindar.[32] Italy, then, had something *analogous to* but different from an ode; it didn't yet have what Gosse would consider, in Patmore's phrase, "Odes proper." The classical ode therefore bypasses Italy in its first European development. For this reason, Spenser's poem is an ode if it draws on Greek sources, but it is less than an ode if it draws on Italian ones. This heavy editorial emphasis on the legacy of Pindar is confirmed by the book's frontispiece, which shows two Grecian women framing a lyre emblazoned with the word *Pindar*.

Gosse's Pindaric model constrains not just his history of the genre but also its formal parameters. Officially, he describes the ode as "any strain of enthusiastic and exalted lyrical verse, directed to a fixed purpose, and dealing progressively with one dignified theme," but he discounts many dignified poems (even ones called "odes" by their authors) that do not attempt to replicate the shape of Pindar's Greek verse.[33] Indeed, the English ode is presented as a drama of typographical error and triumph: Abraham Cowley's copy of Pindar was printed without choral divisions, so that poet misunderstood the ode's structure and initiated a rash of outrageously irregular Pindarics. William Congreve had a better edition of Pindar and set the tradition right, pointing English poets toward "for the first time, the metrical secret that had evaded Cowley."[34] When the Romantics inherited the genre, they irresponsibly let that secret slip away:

> All attempt to restrain [the genre] within the exact bounds of Greek tradition was abandoned, and the odes of Wordsworth and Coleridge are as absolutely irregular as Cowley's own. When Shelley came to write his "Ode to Naples," the very meaning of the terminology had been so far forgotten, that he commenced with two epodes, passed on to two strophes, and then indulged in four successive antistrophes![35]

From the vantage of Pindaric purity, the generic and formal experiments of Romanticism become a scandal. Needless to say, Patmore's

"To the Unknown Eros" is barely an ode at all—it is "constructed rather upon a musical than a metrical system"—but a paucity of Victorian examples seems to force Gosse's hand.[36]

Gosse's unyielding position on the ode accorded with his more general thoughts about the uses of literary history. In an earlier essay, "A Plea for Certain Exotic Forms of Verse" (1877), Gosse had argued for a turn away from the "blustering blank verse" of the "Spasmodic School" and back toward historical fixed forms.[37] Here, too, Gosse is surprisingly vehement, expressing disgust for any variation from the original pattern. His impatience for adaptation finds a scapegoat in Sidney Dobell, whom he describes as "the very helot of stylistic depravity," partly because, in addition to spasmodic verse, he "wrote sonnets of fifteen, sixteen, eighteen lines, and rhymed them as seemed good in his own eyes." Remarkably, Gosse considers even the Shakespearean sonnet to be an unfortunate deviation from the "old pure" Italian form. He advocates fidelity to "the exact shape" of an original model, granting no concessions for linguistic or historical differences. "We have a right to demand," he insists, "that if [poets decide to compose sonnets] they should follow in the time-honoured footsteps of Petrarch and Milton."[38] Gosse, in an anti-Romantic mode, feels that strict formal requirements deter bad poets and stimulate good ones, and he encourages the discovery of (and obedience to) more fixed forms from the past.

Like the Shakespearean sonnet, which reinterpreted the Italian form for a rhyme-poorer language, the English Pindaric has always confronted its linguistic and historical distance from its source. Even Cowley, as he translated Pindar into irregular rhymes, explained that because of "the great difference of time betwixt his age and ours" and because "our Ears are strangers to the Musick of his *Numbers*," exact translation is impossible. The best we can do is "supply the lost Excellencies of another *Language* with new ones in [our] own."[39] In fact, Gosse thought Cowley could have done better, by retaining Pindar's triads (if he could see them), instead of finding a new music for the old poems.

Gosse saw genres and forms as transhistorical: they move through history impervious to history itself—or they should try to. It is not so much that he denied changes in history and prosody; it is rather that he advocated a valiant perseverance in the face of inevitable decline.

A mournful poem of Gosse's own, called "Greece and England" (1879), makes this point well. The poem starts with a series of questions—in modern rhyme—about the lost beauties of ancient Greece:

> Would this sunshine be completer,
> Or these violets smell sweeter,
> Or the birds sing more in metre,
> If it all were years ago,
> When the melted mountain-snow
> Heard in Enna all the woe
> Of the poor forlorn Demeter?[40]

A few stanzas later, the answer is a resounding *Yes!* Yes, the sunshine would be completer and the birds sing more in metre, but we must make do with partial sunshine and less poetic birds:

> Ah! it may be! Greece had leisure
> For a world of faded pleasure;
> We must tread a tamer measure,
> To a milder homelier lyre;
> We must tend a paler fire,
> Lay less perfume on the pyre,
> Be content with poorer treasure![41]

When this poem was noticed in the *Spectator* in February 1880, the reviewer could only conclude that Gosse "has more poetical affinity with Greece and Rome, than with England.... He sees the past more vividly than he sees the present."[42] This sensibility is apparent everywhere in Gosse's criticism of the ode. The classical ode remains for him an ideal to aspire toward. Even if its splendor can never exactly be recaptured, Pindar's prosody can at least be imitated in the "tamer measure" of our "homelier lyre."

I have treated Gosse's views on historical forms at some length, because his idea of the ode has remained dominant and has directed the reception of Patmore's poems. His views on the sonnet have not had the same lasting power, but they help us see the radical purism that shaped his attitude toward genres and their forms. It is worth remembering that Gosse's transhistorical ode was a reading of literary history before it acquired the status of a definition. I'll turn now to Patmore's radically different idea of the ode, and the radically different vision of literary history that it entailed.

PATMORE'S ENGLISH ODE

One might think that by calling his later poems "odes," Patmore was signaling a desire to insert himself into the august poetic lineage that Gosse describes. And yet, Patmore felt he was doing something completely novel. In letters from the period in which he was composing them, he writes of the odes, "I have hit upon *the* finest metre that was ever invented," a meter that "opens up quite a new prospect to me of the possibilities of poetry."[43] From a perspective like Gosse's, this seems to be a contradiction. On one hand, Patmore claims for himself an antique genre, one with its own formal prerogatives; on the other hand, he claims an unprecedented metrical invention. Throughout the later part of his career, Patmore moved between generic and formal names for his new meter. It was an "irregular ode" (1850), an "iambic ode, erroneously called irregular" (1878); it was "catalectic verse" (1890), and "the iambic tetrameter with unlimited catalexis, which is commonly called the 'irregular' ode, though it is really as 'regular' as any other English metre, and even much more so, if its subtle laws are truly considered and obeyed" (1894). In his effort to name this new thing, Patmore was clearly both attracted to and wary of the term "ode."

Part of Patmore's problem had to do with his own historical imagining of the genre. Like Gosse's Pindaric ode, Patmore's irregular ode was an ideal; unlike Gosse's Pindaric ode, it was an ideal that had never previously been attained. If Gosse's ode yearned backward toward the lost Greek past, Patmore's ode yearned forward into the English future (which isn't to say that Patmore's relationship to English poetry and the English past was never nostalgic).[44] There is an early pang of this prospective yearning in Patmore's 1850 review of *In Memoriam*. As with the "Metrical Law," Patmore frames this essay historiographically, beginning with the observation that "There are certain great epochs in the history of poetry. . . ." He then undertakes a lengthy, chronological survey of the "established metres" in English in order to justify his claim that Tennyson's is "the first poem of historical importance which has appeared since 'The Excursion.'" The historical claim for Tennyson's poem rests on the question of form: Tennyson's "complete metrical science and feeling," which exceeds that of most other English poets.[45] Through minute descriptions of the ballad stanza, rhyme royal, the sonnet, the Spenserian stanza, the Augustan couplet, the "Pindarique

Ode," Patmore illustrates the affective capacities of rhyme, line length, and pause, as they have been used or squandered over the history of English poetry.[46] Patmore has nothing nice to say about the English "Pindarique Ode"—he thinks it is a clumsy forgery of feeling—but he has high hopes for a better "irregular Ode," one that will operate on the isochronous principle found in music. Wordsworth offers a glimpse of what is possible, even if his "Intimations" ode is less prosodically scientific than Patmore would wish—and less so than *In Memoriam*. "Good examples of the irregular ode are so scarce," Patmore laments, "the ode of Wordsworth's to which we have just alluded being the only generally satisfactory one in the language."[47] Patmore knew exactly what he meant by "ode," but no other poet had; his predecessors consequently failed to meet his expectations for the genre.

Thus, the irregular ode has a strange status in the *In Memoriam* review. It is one of "the established metres," and yet it has no real examples. It has an ideal form, but that form has never previously been used. It comes at the end of the historical sequence, but it has not yet arrived. In the context of the discussion of *In Memoriam*, it becomes clear that a perfect irregular ode would borrow some quality from Tennyson's poem that even Wordsworth's magnificent ode lacks. That quality is not beauty, because Wordworth's ode is very beautiful. Instead, it is a "thorough knowledge and pure feeling for metre"—a deliberate rather than fortuitous conjunction between feeling and form.[48]

In 1850, Patmore could only dream. But by the time he wrote and then reissued his "Metrical Law" in 1878, he could describe the irregular ode by generalizing about poems he had already written. By that time, the connection between form and feeling had become even more essential to his idea of the irregular ode:

> The iambic ode, erroneously called "irregular," of which there exist few legitimate examples in our language, is, if I mistake not, a tetrameter, with almost unlimited liberty of catalexis, to suit the variations of the high and stately lyrical feeling which can alone justify the use of this measure. The existence of an amount of catalectic pause varying from the time of two to fourteen syllables—for the line, in this kind of metre, may change at once to that extent—is justified by the analogy of the pauses, or stops, in a similar style of music; and the fact of this amount of catalexis being of the essence of this metre, seems to have

> been unconsciously felt and acknowledged by almost all who have written or attempted to write in it; for almost all have tried to represent the varying pauses, and to prepare the ear for them, by printing the lines affected with catalexis with shorter or longer blank spaces at the beginning; a precaution which seems to me to be unnecessary; for, if the feeling justifies the metre, the ear will take naturally to its variations; but if there is not sufficient motive power of passionate thought, no typographical aids will make anything of this sort of verse but *metrical nonsense*—which it nearly always is, even in Cowley, whose brilliant wit and ingenuity are strangely out of harmony with most of his measures. (27–28)

In the "Metrical Law," then, the irregular ode has found its prosodic principle. Whereas earlier English odes either followed their models too closely or indulged in irregularity for irregularity's sake, Patmore sees each syllable and pause contributing to the poem's orchestration of feeling. For this to be possible, the scientific approach he praises in the *In Memoriam* review is required. A poet needs to understand how a line, a pause, a rhyme might express emotion. The varying meter depends entirely on variations of "lyrical feeling"; the feeling has to "justif[y] the metre." The poet, in short, must be motivated by "passionate thought," and his verse must be organized in such a way as to convey that feeling-thought transparently.[49]

The trouble with previous irregular odes in English was that they leaned too heavily on unhelpful models. Obviously, Patmore did not subscribe to Gosse's notion of strophic and triadic fidelity. Nor did he approve of Cowley's attempt to find an English translation for Pindaric irregularity. In Patmore's view, both of these approaches mistook the nature of the ode. The English ode is not a Greek melody played on a "homelier lyre"; it is an altogether different melody played on a different instrument. For Patmore, there had been no great ode "in the language," because there had never been an ode that engaged seriously enough with the special prosodic conditions of English. This had to be the case, because nobody had yet articulated those conditions in a satisfactory way. In believing that he was, with the "Metrical Law," explaining the mechanism of English verse "for the first time" (26), Patmore also believed that he was for the first time describing the materials out of which a true English ode might be made. Without a scientific knowledge of modern English's ways of conveying feeling—distinct from those of other languages and other times—the English ode had to be impossible.

"WHAT IS ODE?"

Instead of one long line of deviations from Pindar, then, Patmore sees ode history as multiple: each poetic culture must have its own form of ode. Patmore's concept of the ode was not his alone. Before Gosse's late-century historiography became definitive, "ode" was used to denote a range of lyric forms, many of which had no clear causal connection to the poetry of antiquity. William Jones in 1772 published a book of translations of "odes" from a diverse set of literary cultures, with the aim of demonstrating parallels among them, despite their prosodic differences. Here, "The First Nemean Ode of Pindar" is not the ur-ode, but one ode among many more: "An Ode of Petrarch" (canzone 27); "An Ode of Jami in the Persian Form and Measure"; "A Chinese Ode Paraphrased"; "A Turkish Ode of Mesihi."[50]

After Jones, a prevalent use of the word was as a synonym or English approximation for the Italian word *canzone*. Many late-eighteenth- and nineteenth-century collections of Petrarch's poems used the word "ode" for the poems that Petrarch had called *canzoni*, beginning with John Nott's *Petrarch Translated; in a Selection of His Sonnets, and Odes* (1777; 1808)—the preface of which refers to Petrarch's "49 Odes (CANZONI, some of which are denominated SESTINE, BALLATE, or MADRIGALI)."[51] R. G. Macgregor's 1851 collection of *canzoni* was called, simply, *Odes of Petrarch*. The same phenomenon could be observed in Petrarch criticism. Susannah Dobson's *Life of Petrarch* (1775) opted for "ode" instead of "canzone," while Ugo Foscolo, in his influential *Essays on Petrarch* (1823), was clearly torn between the two terms. He defines the Petrarchan *canzone* as "a species of composition partaking of the ode and the elegy, the character and form of which are exclusively Italian,"[52] and then proceeds to use the two words interchangeably: he discusses Petrarch's "political odes" in his text but reproduces one of them with the title "Canzone."[53] In *Select Sonnets of Petrarch* (1822), James Caulfeild, Earl of Charlemont uses "ode" to explain not the canzone but the sonnet: "Probably *suono,* among the early Italian poets, was taken nearly in the same sense as eidos or ode was among the Greeks and Romans; and thus *sonetto,* being a diminutive of *suono,* will properly signify a short ode."[54]

The analogous thinking above points to the practical and conceptual difficulties involved in describing foreign prosodies. These difficulties were perhaps most acutely felt by general literary historians. For them, the substitution of "ode" for "canzone" was often an explanatory expedient, a means to help the reader understand an unfamiliar form or genre by way of reference to one that was known. So in Sismondi's effort, for instance, to bring together the various literatures of the South under a romantic banner, he is often tempted by the explanatory power of "ode"—thus, the Persian *ghazal* "is an amatory ode."[55] But this kind of explanation seems to trouble Sismondi, for it prompts a curious reflection on the limits of both analogy and translation. Of Petrarch Sismondi writes,

> The other form of his lyrical compositions, the *canzone,* is not unknown to us, although we have no express word for it, in the French; that of *chanson,* derived from it, signifying a poem of a totally different kind. We have seen that, amongst the Troubadours and the Trouvères, the chansons were odes divided into regular stanzas, longer than those of the odes of antiquity. There are some of Petrarch's *Canzoni,* in which we find stanzas of twenty lines.... This extraordinary length, which perhaps renders the harmony less perceptible to the ear, has given a peculiar character to the *canzoni,* and distinguishes the romantic from the classical ode.... The translation of a *canzone* of Petrarch could never be confounded with the translation of an ode of Horace. We are obliged to class them both under the head of lyrical poems; but we immediately perceive that such a division includes very different kinds of compositions.[56]

Here, Sismondi questions the catchall nature of the word "ode," and addresses the danger of merging—as Jones pointedly did—diverse poetic systems into the same genre for the sake of comparison.[57] (Sismondi's English translator, Thomas Roscoe, must have found this a particularly strange passage to translate.) Sismondi finally settles on a useful distinction: even if we must consider the canzone a kind of ode, we can acknowledge a basic difference between the "classical ode" and the "romantic ode." Sismondi's taxonomy offers another way around the genealogical question that has dogged the criticism of Patmore's odes: the poems may be both Petrarchan canzoni and "odes" with no historical contradiction, if Patmore had in mind this *romantic* ode.

Although the word "ode" presents some linguistic obstacles to Sismondi, it also enables his comparative historiography: it allows him to make broad distinctions between classical and modern literatures, and fine distinctions among the modern ones. Not surprisingly, Hegel also conceived of two large categories of ode, writing in the *Aesthetics* of "those kinds of lyric poetry that may be called by the general name of 'Odes' in the newer sense of that word." This ode is a "new form" with a new "manner of expression." In contrast to the classical ode, it takes as its subject the poet's own subjectivity as it encounters some external theme. And while the classical ode has "a measure fixed by rule," this new ode has a more expressive form. As the poet's subjectivity wrestles with his topic, his poem acquires its shape: "the swing and boldness of language and images, the apparent absence of rule in the structure and course of the poem, the digressions, gaps, sudden transitions, etc." In Hegel, the modern ode is not to be confused with the canzone, which gets its own treatment (it is not as elevated as the ode, and its form internalizes melody to a greater extent). But the ode nonetheless expresses Hegel's conviction that lyric poetry, more than any other art form, is materially shaped by "a particular period and nationality and the individuality of the poet's genius."[58]

Hegel's theory of poetry was extremely important to Patmore. It was the philosophical basis of his "Metrical Law" essay, and Patmore continued writing about Hegel through his prose-writing career. But the aesthetic historian whose vision of the ode was most in keeping with Patmore's own was J. G. Herder, who was in the background of Hegel's *Aesthetics*—and who had been so influential for nineteenth-century genetic formalism more broadly.[59] Herder was also interested in the organic relationship between a people and its poetry, and he saw the ode as key. It was not a subset of lyric but the original and essential literary form: "the fountainhead of poetic art, and the germ cell of its life."[60] In Herder's theory, the ode had a crucial anthropological and historical function.[61] As a result, the hallmark of the genre was, perhaps counterintuitively, *difference.* In his "Fragments of a Treatise on the Ode" (1765), Herder describes the ode's special position in the literary history of the world: "If any one genre of poetic art has become a Proteus among nations, judged on the basis of sensibility, subject matter, and language, the ode has so altered its spirit and countenance and pace, that perhaps only the aesthetician's magic mirror will recognize the same living essence among such varied manifestations. Nevertheless, there is yet a certain general unity of sensibility, of expression, and of harmony, which makes possible the drawing of a parallel among all of them" (36–37). Herder's ode is not recognizable by one form or one tone, and it is a genre only in the loosest sense of the word. It is more properly an idea about how poetry, culture, and history interact.

Because each of the varied manifestations of ode had its own formal and tonal characteristics, a special kind of openness and attention is demanded by the literary historian. In "Essay on a History of Lyrical Poetry" (1766), Herder makes the question "What is ode?" a hermeneutic one:

> There have been efforts to determine a concept of the ode; but, what is ode? The Greek, the Roman, the Middle Eastern, the Skaldic, the ode of more recent origin, they are not quite like one another; which of them is the finest, the others merely being deviations? I could easily demonstrate that most investigators have decided the question in accordance with their own favorite notions, because each one draws his concepts and standards from only *one* kind, manifested by *one* people, and declared the others deviations. The impartial investigator will consider all kinds equally worthy of his commentary, and he therefore will seek first to create for himself a totality of history, subsequently to render judgment upon everything individually. (71)

Herder objected not only to the privilege accorded the classical ode but also to any reading of other odes with reference to that type. The Middle Eastern ode and the Skaldic ode should not be understood as approaching or departing from the aesthetics of the Greek or Latin ode. To answer the question "What is ode?," the historian must decenter the dominant model and look with fresh eyes.

For Herder, the ode is endemic to all peoples and therefore differentiated according to the temper, language, climate, history, tastes, and folk culture of each. An ode belonging to another culture should *feel* foreign and *be* untranslatable, because it emerges from that culture and not ours. In a section of "Fragments" called "Of Various Odic Rhythms," Herder describes the prosodic differences that characterize each nation. The Hebrews' ode melody was "splendid in its simplicity" with "frequent short pauses," because their language was simple and drum-like. The Greeks' odic cadences "were *more drawn out*," because their "language was for the most part polymetric, their sound more protracted than ours, their tongue more flexible, and their melody the zither." Horace's cadences were different from Pindar's because "he wrote for Roman ears" and the Roman lyre (42). The German ode should not be Horatian, because German folk poetry is "ingeniously and pleasingly monotonous"; its instrument is "the flute or the trumpet"; at its best, it has "relatively sizable caesurae, the meter grows short, the rhyme [becomes] a beauty in its monotony" (42–43). Herder bemoans the German obsession with Horace, which comes at the expense of producing a true German ode—one made from properly German feelings and rhythms, for "German ears" (38, 42).

Ultimately, it seems that Herder's historiographic and anthropological investigation into the nature of the ode is directed toward the problem of German poetry. Germans have understood the German ode to be a classical ode translated, rather than its own particular thing. By looking too closely at the form of the Horatian model, by trying too hard to imitate it, the German people have blocked all the sources of inspiration that lead to the true ode.[62] They have failed to recognize that the basis of their favorite foreign models was "a *thread of passion*"; that classical odes exhibit a "logic of affect" that eludes translation; and that "the driving motive of the true poet is *frenzy*, his words are arrows, his target the whole heart" (44–46). As Patmore will do, Herder yearns for a passionate modern ode in his own idiom.

Through Herder, we can see Patmore's poetic intention with more clarity. In his wish to make a new form of ode, he was not turning his back on literary history. On the contrary, his ode was profoundly historical. He knew that classical prosody was unavailable to the modern English poet and, with Herder, saw the ode as a tool for thinking about—and feeling—literary-historical change. He believed that writing a true ode involved not a mastery of older ode forms (though a genetic study of these forms was desirable), but a sharp recognition of the difference between past and present, there and here. Instead of a relic of classical antiquity or the European Renaissance, Patmore saw his ode as the best possible elaboration of the English prosodic law that he sought and believed he found.

"THE AZALEA"

By way of illustration, I want to examine the formal feeling in one of Patmore's odes: what Herder called the "logic of affect," what Patmore called the "complete metrical science and feeling," what Ezra Pound would call, at the beginning of the twentieth century, "equations for the human emotions."[63] Given Patmore's admiration for *In Memoriam* and its acutely sensitive form, it is not surprising that Patmore's odes are also often elegies. The emotional intensity of elegy offers him an opportunity to test his expressive prosodic system against Tennyson's. It is this intensity, this Herderian "thread of passion," that I track in the following pages.

Among Patmore's odes is a set of elegies written about the death of his first wife Emily, the woman exalted in *The Angel in the House* (and the dead mother in "The Toys"). These poems also idealize Emily, but they are not sentimental in the same way as *The Angel in the House* is. As the best elegies do, they make the loss felt as a visceral shock, by minutely investigating some all-too-real detail that seems to enfold a world of previously unrecorded pain. In "The Azalea," the speaker wakes from a dream that his wife has died, is relieved to find that it was just a dream, and then realizes that the dream was right: he has confused the scent of a flower in the room with the scent of his wife. The details are few—a potted plant, a bedroom, a widower, morning—but in the course of twenty-five lines Patmore produces the elegiac shock at least twice:

> There, where the sun shines first
> Against our room,
> She train'd the gold Azalea, whose perfume
> She, Spring-like, from her breathing grace dispersed.
> Last night the delicate crests of saffron bloom,
> For this their dainty likeness watch'd and nurst,
> Were just at point to burst.

At dawn I dream'd, O God, that she was dead,
And groan'd aloud upon my wretched bed,
And waked, ah, God, and did not waken her,
But lay, with eyes still closed,
Perfectly bless'd in the delicious sphere
By which I knew so well that she was near,
My heart to speechless thankfulness composed.
Till 'gan to stir
A dizzy somewhat in my troubled head—
It *was* the azalea's breath, and she *was* dead!
The warm night had the lingering buds disclosed,
And I had fall'n asleep with to my breast
A chance-found letter press'd
In which she said,
"So, till to-morrow eve, my Own, adieu!
Parting's well-paid with soon again to meet,
Soon in your arms to feel so small and sweet,
Sweet to myself that am so sweet to you!" (1–25)

It is certainly possible that there are readers who don't respond to this poem the way I do, but I imagine my reaction to be something like the kind of reaction that Patmore was trying to provoke. I have read "The Azalea" many times, and it always makes me feel the same way. Even typing it up, my breath catches in my throat, and I notice my heart beating a little bit harder. The ending of the poem doesn't affect me much—Emily's ventriloquized voice sounds relatively artificial—but I will admit that the rest of it almost hurts. One of Patmore's favorite readers, the poet and essayist Alice Meynell, described the impact of the odes thus: "In *The Unknown Eros* the poet's intention, single, separate, strikes unique strokes against which the reader's human heart is all unarmed by custom."[64] In the case of "The Azalea," I agree.

There are many narrative and semantic details that help generate pathos. The death is obviously recent enough to seem a perverse disturbance of reality rather than an integrated part of reality (it is still "our room"), and it is recent enough to have happened within the time span of a particular flower's budding and blooming. It is also recent enough for the speaker to remember the sensory experience of his wife's nearness, especially her smell. There is the wife's loss, too. She has tenderly cultivated the plant but has just missed its flowering—an elegant shorthand for everything else the young mother will now miss. And of course, the poem's terrible voltas: the dream of her death, the relieved waking, and then the realization of her death more terrible than (and more terrible because of) the dream. Word choices also manipulate the reader. As the speaker lies "with eyes still closed / Perfectly bless'd in the delicious sphere / By which I knew so well that she was near," the reader accepts the verb "knew" as confirmation that the dream was wrong. As a result, the creeping insight of the lines that follow—"Till 'gan to stir / A dizzy somewhat in my troubled head"—dawns on the reader in distressing real time.[65]

But this accounting of the poem's pathetic details fails to capture its total effect, because it misses the role of prosody. Patmore's theoretical writing suggests that a poet uses prosody to put feelings into poems. In a carefully written catalectic ode, a pause is at syllabic minimum "a long-drawn sigh" and at syllabic maximum a "passionate cataract."[66] Rhyme's appeal to memory and hope also becomes, for Patmore, an applicable formula. "[U]pon this saying," he writes, "we would found the rule that rhymes which recur at irregular and unexpected intervals ought always to be increased in number, in order to make up for the effect of their irregularity in weakening the force of that appeal."[67] By Patmore's metric of pause, the most emotionally intense parts of the poem may be the shortest lines—"Against our room" (1); "Till 'gan to stir" (15); and "In which she said" (21)—and of these isochronous lines, the most intense one of all might be the one embedded in the densest network of rhymes: "In which she said." This line is the fifth among five C rhymes that are distributed across the length of the poem, and presumably it is haunted by the memory of the other four: "dead," "bed," "head," and "dead." This moment at the edge of prosopopoeia, when the *now definitely dead* wife is about to speak but is not yet speaking (as the passionate cataract of pause roars on), may be the prosodic climax of the poem.

In Meynell's opinion, Patmore's law was imperfect, and imperfectly observed by even himself. Nonetheless, she writes, "A more lovely dignity of extension and restriction, a more touching sweetness of simple and frequent rhyme, a truer impetus of pulse and impulse, English verse could hardly yield than are to be found in his versification."[68] And whether or not the feelings of "The Azalea" are quantifiable in the ways that Patmore suggests, the poem certainly does make powerful use of pause and terminal rhyme. The first four lines demonstrate those effects undeniably at work:

> There, where the sun shines first
> Against our room,
> She train'd the gold Azalea, whose perfume
> She, Spring-like, from her breathing grace dispersed.

Patmore's lineation controls the way we encounter this bit of verse. Were he not working deliberately with the experiences of terminal rhyme and pause, and against conventional ideas about metrical regularity, these four jagged lines would almost certainly appear as three even ones:

> **There**, where the **sun** shines **first** a**gainst** our **room**,
> She **train'd** the **gold** Aza**lea**, **whose** per**fume**
> She, **Spring**-like, **from** her **breath**ing **grace** dis**persed**.

This arrangement throws the lines into something very like iambic pentameter, and the gravitational pull of that pattern noticeably coerces our reading. We are off to a galloping start with the first line, and by the third line the momentum is strong: the "She" at its beginning is barely registered (despite the comma), and the beat falls heavily on "Spring" and "from," and every other alternating syllable. Patmore is pushing against this rhythmic pull. By separating the first two lines, he slows them all the way down. The first line becomes heavily spondaic; the second line seems to demand an extended pause. No longer compelled by iambic pentameter regularity, the fourth line falls differently, so that "She" weighs more heavily on the ear.[69]

Such lineal disruption might not immediately read as sad, but upon rereading, the lines' slow and heavy beats seem to invite a mimetic interpretation. We can infer that Patmore wished it so, because it is precisely this lineal disruption that enables a familiar rhyme pattern to shape the poem's opening lines: ABBA. This rhyme pattern, which also closes the poem (and which closes "The Toys," too), is Tennyson's elegiac stanza—the form that Patmore helped identify in his 1850 review as uniquely moving, as a perfect instantiation of rhyme's "Memory and Hope." While Tennyson's stanza fits the ABBA rhymes into extremely regular iambic tetrameter quatrains, Patmore's verse does not. He extricates the rhymes from both the rhythmic and the stanzaic frame, sharpening the affective power of Tennyson's rhymes with a motivated irregularity.[70]

By invoking the formal sorrows of *In Memoriam*, Patmore is also addressing that poem's relationship to his own prosodic project. In 1850, Patmore saw *In Memoriam* as a "high water-mark" in the development of modern poetry, and he was just beginning to imagine an English form that might be more expressive still.[71] By the time of "The Azalea" and "The Toys," Patmore had found a meter of his own, one that combined the emotional rhyme science of Tennyson with the great pauses of Wordsworth's yet-imperfect ode. Eschewing the old symmetries of the classical strophe and the romantic stanza, Patmore's ode pointed forward into the twentieth century.[72] As Herder had, he saw in ode form the "germ cell" of a whole new kind of poetry. I'll quote one more time from the 1868 letter in which Patmore describes the joy of finding his new meter. Here, he confesses the hope that one day the ode he discovered might grow and bloom into something else, a resource for future poets:

> The beauty and incomparable variety of the metre opens up quite a new prospect to me of the possibilities of poetry. In the hands of a Goethe, for example, what might not be done with it. Fancy a drama full of power and tenderness in which the persons should speak their passions in that splendid and delicate torrent of music, instead of in stupid blank verse. But far be it for me to dream of such a work. I must content myself with "brief swallow-flights of song."[73]

Patmore's prosodic dream is not, ultimately, the dream of elegiac expressiveness, of Tennyson's "short swallow-flights of song." It is the dream of something less personal, but more versatile, more passionate, and larger: a poetic language whose powerful expressiveness is—as Arthur Hallam suggested—"contained in itself." Patmore finds no prototype for this form in the history of literature, but the theory of literary history shows the way.

Conclusion

THE SPIRIT OF ROMANCE

One subject of this book has been the loss of a way of reading, a critical capacity for feeling and thinking about history and form together. I have argued that Victorian genetic formalism—as a view of literature, as a competency derived from scholarly knowledge and fantasy that are no longer ours—was lost to New Critical formalism, and I've suggested that the value of rhyme and the intricacy of Victorian poetry were lost with it. It is not the case that eighteenth- and nineteenth-century European writers did literary history better than we do. Their generalist work was necessarily full of second- and third-hand knowledge, especially of non-European cultures, and that distance from their literary materials sometimes resulted in misunderstanding, factual error, oversimplification, or outright caricature. Nevertheless, their efforts to think both deeply and broadly about literature—to think about the interconnectedness and interdependence of literary cultures and literary histories—allowed unfamiliar kinds of poetics to emerge. Recognizing the imperfect historical knowledge that work produced, we can nonetheless ask what it made intellectually and artistically possible.[1]

At the beginning of this book, I showed how the possibilities of genetic formalism were foreclosed by New Criticism, which developed its own critical categories in negative relation to its historicist precursors. But there's another twentieth-century story to tell, too: the story of its rhyme practice. I cannot tell that story in full, but I can make some generalizations. As early as T. S. Eliot's 1917 insistence that free verse's "liberation from rhyme might be as well a liberation *of* rhyme," it has been understood that free verse isn't actually free of meter or rhyme; it simply takes those prosodic techniques in new directions, toward expressively irregular rather than fixed forms.[2] I don't need to rehearse here all the ways rhyme structures the apparently free lines of free verse.[3] The early *vers-librists* make that case: Ezra Pound's use of Provençal, early Italian, and Pre-Raphaelite verse patterns in *A Lume Spento* (1908) and *Canzoni* (1911), for instance; H. D.'s use of irregular, internal, and long-distance rhyming in *Sea Garden* (1916); T. S. Eliot's use of couplets, alternating rhymes, and refrains in *Prufrock and Other Observations* (1917). We can take it for granted that in a period when rhyme was loudly disparaged, it continued to structure verse in essential ways.[4]

In my view, a more interesting question than the presence or absence of rhyme in modernist poetry is the continuity of Victorian *conceptions* of rhyme, especially the model of romantic rhyme I've been exploring in this book. If we allow rhyme to mean what it meant to Victorian poets, we can discern a much richer legacy for Victorian rhyming in twentieth-century poetry. Instead of seeing free verse as rhyming *nonetheless*, we can start to see it as one more variety of rhyme practice: an extension of the historiographic experiments of the nineteenth century. For Arthur Hallam, who was thinking about the difference between classical and medieval poetics, rhyme meant the "diffused resemblances" that befit a modern "soul susceptible of musical impression."[5] For Tennyson, who was thinking with Hallam about the relationship between Arabic and Provençal poetry, rhyme was a way to theorize the adjustment of poetic sound and shape to feeling; it was a formula for inventing entirely new forms. For Elizabeth Barrett Browning, who was thinking about medieval Spanish assonance and the Elizabethan convergence of blank verse and sonnet form, rhyme meant organic rather than mechanical prosody, the sweet and irregular sonic patterns that made blank verse also a kind of rhyme. For William Morris, who was thinking about the association of rhyme and love in romantic literary history, rhyme brings an embodied vitality and eroticism to poetry. For Coventry Patmore, thinking with Hegel, Hallam, and the Herderian tradition, rhyme works with pause to generate poetic feelings and make a new prosodic language for the present, and the future.

The claims made on behalf of free verse were often claims about its unprecedented expressivity, its perfect adjustment of form to content, its organic beauty and vitality, its singular fittedness to modern experience—and, of course, its novelty in relation to Victorian practices of meter and rhyme.[6] This suggests, as Meredith Martin and Ben Glaser have persuasively argued, that the discourse of free verse as a break from Victorian prosody (in their studies, Victorian meter) was always in conflict with the reality of its continuity.[7] I want to emphasize, though, not just the persistence of rhyme but the persistence of the aesthetic and poetic values that derived from Victorian genetic formalism—values that also motivated the *vers-librists'* experiments, even as those poets began to position themselves against Victorian poetry.[8] In other words, "free verse" was a new name for the possibilities inherent in Victorian rhyme.

I'll close by suggesting another way that genetic formalism reached into the twentieth century: as an underappreciated—and positive—influence on the practice of close reading. I don't mean, in this case, how the New Critics used genetic formalism as a foil for their ahistorical formalism. I mean how modernist concepts of form, of the autonomous poem, of poetry's apparently intrinsic aesthetic effects emerged from the scholarly tradition of literary historiography.

In Ezra Pound's *Spirit of Romance* (1910), we witness once more the uneven transition from nineteenth-century literary historiography to twentieth-century close reading methods. Pound's first prose work was adapted from a lecture series he delivered at the London Polytechnic titled "The Development of Literature in Southern Europe." Its chronological scheme begins with the corruption of Latin at the start of the first millennium CE and then moves through a series of subjects related to Southern European poetry: the Provençal troubadours, early French romances, Tuscan poetry before Dante, Dante's poetry, Villon, Lope de Vega and Spanish poetry, Camoens and Portuguese poetry, and the revival of Latin poetry at the Renaissance.[9] If a century were a poem, we would hear a rhyme between Pound's book and Sismondi's *Historical View*. Like Sismondi's book, Pound's was a lecture series first. Like Sismondi's book, Pound's offered many examples of medieval verse forms, as well as observations on various prosodic cultures and reflections on the enigmatic operations of poetic form.

Despite Pound's obvious debts to nineteenth-century general literary historians such as Sismondi and Henry Hallam (whom he cites on Portuguese literature), he heartily disavows literary-historical scholarship. His preface begins, "This book is not a philological work. Only by courtesy can it be said to be a study in comparative literature. I am interested in poetry."[10] And it proceeds with similar refusals: "There is no attempt at historical completeness" (6); "contrary to the custom of literary historians . . . all critical statements are based on a direct study of the texts themselves and not upon commentaries" (7); "the scholars have not known anything about poetry" (23). Pound sees philology and literary historiography as already outmoded and looks eagerly toward "the time when it will be possible for the lover of poetry to study poetry—even the poetry of recondite times and places—without burdening himself with the rags of morphology, epigraphy, *privatleben* and the kindred delights of the archaeological or 'scholarly' mind" (5).

Yet Pound has an unmistakable affinity for those archaeological delights. For instance, of Dante he writes, "Ignorance of most of the data of Dante's life is no bar to the understanding of his works. The life itself is, however, most interesting. . . ."; two pages of biographical summary follow (118). Pound's style oscillates between the sweeping historiographic proclamation ("The Troubadours, Dante and Apuleius, all attempt to refine or to ornament the common speech") and the sweeping formalist aphorism ("Poetry is a sort of inspired mathematics, which gives us equations, not for abstract figures, triangles, spheres, and the like, but equations for the human emotions") (13–14). And even the formalist aphorism has a distinctly genetic character. When he describes poetry as a set of equations for feelings, Pound is making a point about the old historiographic categories of "classic" and "romantic" art. Bringing the grand narrative into contact with the math and magic of poetry, he enters the scholarly tradition he claims to leave behind.[11] Pound thus articulates his formalist aesthetic just as the Victorians did: historiographically.

Ezra Pound's vision of a future when the lover of poetry might study "*poetry as poetry*" did come to pass.[12] Indeed, we are still living in that future insofar as our conception of form remains unburdened by genetic fantasy. But it has also become more difficult for the lover of poetry to *theorize* a love of the poem. In Pound's argument, the delights of poetry can't quite be separated from the "delights of the archaeological or 'scholarly' mind." For the young poet-scholar, just out of the nineteenth century, poetic form is still vibrant with the spirit of romantic rhyme.

Acknowledgments

This book has been enabled by so many people and institutions and some extraordinary gifts of generosity. To begin with: the book is dedicated to Greg Ellermann, my partner and co-thinker for twenty years. Greg has been the book's most consistent and insightful reader. It has been enriched by his deep knowledge of Romanticism; his impeccable judgment about what works and what doesn't; his example of scholarly passion and integrity; his endless encouragement; and our long, soul-sustaining conversation about poetry and ideas. In the final stages, he also did the editorial work of several research assistants and kept me fed and caffeinated, while taking on even more childcare than usual. This book would have been impossible without Greg's many contributions. Thank you, Greg.

Work toward *The Burden of Rhyme* began at Rutgers University. My time in the doctoral program there was incredibly happy: full of wonderful teachers and the sheer joy of intellectual community. At Rutgers, I found models of scholarly delight and commitment that have continued to motivate me. I thank my dissertation committee—Carolyn Williams, Jonah Siegel, Meredith McGill, and Meredith Martin—for years of feedback and support. Carolyn and Jonah have both shaped my thinking in ways that I know I can't even see. Carolyn believed in my work, and gave me wise guidance, intellectual inspiration, and the right amount of freedom to think my way toward this project, and she has been an advocate ever since. Jonah's brilliant questions and prompts, his suggestions for reading, and his warm humor and continued mentorship have been so important to me. Meredith McGill introduced me to historical prosody, and conversations

I had with her about poetics were formative. Meredith Martin was officially an external reader, but she has been a generous mentor for years, offering valuable advice and responding thoughtfully to every document I sent her way. Thank you to my other nineteenth-century teachers and advisors at Rutgers—Kate Flint, Billy Galperin, Colin Jager, John Kucich, David Kurnick, and Dianne Sadoff—and thanks to Cheryl Robinson and Courtney Borack for making a graduate program feel like a family. Thank you to my Rutgers friends, including Brian Becker, Josh Gang, Amanda Kotch, John Miller, Brian Pietras, Bill Ryan, Debapriya Sarkar, Matt Sherrill, and Mimi Winick. Mark DiGiacomo, Vivian Kao, and Emily Crossen gave me great feedback in a writing group we had. And Anne Terrill deserves special mention for a friendship that has deepened over the years. I would also like to thank Victorianist friends from elsewhere, including Veronica Alfano, Ronjaunee Chatterjee, Maggie Deli, Letitia Henville, Simon Reader, and Bea Sanford Russell. Justin Sider and Michael Hansen have been indispensable Victorian poetry interlocutors.

My book has benefited substantially from the generous feedback it received from scholars I admire. A manuscript colloquium allowed me to discuss a draft of the book with Erik Gray, Stefanie Markovits, Seamus Perry, and Yopie Prins; I'm so grateful to those readers for their comments and interventions, and for seeing what the book could be. (Extra thanks to Stefanie for her supportive mentorship at Yale.) I thank the Faculty of Arts and Sciences at Yale University for the opportunity to convene the colloquium, and Sarah Harford for organizing it. Thanks to V. Joshua Adams, Marshall Brown, Joel Calahan, Michael Hansen, and Charles LaPorte for comments on an earlier version of chapter 4. Thanks to Jonathan Kramnick for comments on chapter 1 and much sage advice. Mary Ellis Gibson read a manuscript draft (entirely voluntarily!) at a crucial moment and sent me excellent notes. Two anonymous readers at the University of Chicago Press (as well as several other anonymous readers in my field) made suggestions that mattered enormously to the final shape of the book. I am grateful to Alan Thomas and Randolph Petilos for taking on this book and for soliciting such helpful peer reviews, to Adriana Smith and Meredith Nini at the press, and to Susan Olin for her meticulous copyediting. My sincere thanks to Diane Berrett Brown at the Whitney Humanities Center as well. And many thanks to my friend Ali Qadeer for designing the rhyme-scheme diagram in chapter 3.

Over the years, I've presented many pieces of this book as conference papers or talks. Thanks to audiences at the ACLA, INCS, and NAVSA, and at colloquia at Harvard, Princeton, Rutgers, Yale, and CUNY for questions that have strengthened my arguments. Thanks to those who invited me to share my work and gave helpful feedback, including Nathan Brown, yasser elhariry, Sophia Hsu, Petar Milat, Olivia Loksing Moy, Simon Reader, and Liesl Yamaguchi. For their assistance, thanks to the staff at the Archivio di Stato di Pescia, the Armstrong Browning Library, and the Beinecke Rare Book and Manuscript Library; and thanks to Letizia Pagliai and Jacqueline de Molo Veillon of the Associazione di Studi Sismondiani for their expertise and hospitality in Pescia. For their support of my work at various points, I would also like to thank Stephen Arata, Dino Felluga, Danny Hack, Beth Helsinger, Linda Hughes, David Hensley, Virginia Jackson, George Levine, Tricia Lootens, Adela Pinch, Jonathan Sachs, Marjorie Stone, and Beverly Taylor. And many thanks to the collective thinking of the Historical Poetics group.

I deeply appreciate my junior colleagues in the English Department (and beyond) at Yale. Thanks to Felisa Baynes-Ross, Tasha Eccles, Marcel Elias, Joanna Fiduccia, Marta Figlerowicz, Ben Glaser, Alanna Hickey, Jonathan Howard, Elleza Kelley, Tim Kreiner, Katja Lindskog, Ernest Mitchell, Priyasha Mukhopadhyay, Joe North, Juno Richards, Claire Roosien, Rasheed Tazudeen, and Sunny Xiang. I want especially to extend my love and gratitude to Ben, Tasha, Alanna, and Priyasha (and Melissa Winders, Morgan Day Frank, Andy Bruns, and Zack Barnett-Howell) for heroic acts of friendship. Thanks also to Ernest, Robyn Creswell, and Sam Hodgkin for well-timed discussions about poetry. For their conversation and encouragement, I thank Jessica Brantley, Leslie Brisman (champion of poetry!), David Bromwich, Ardis Butterfield, Jill Campbell, Joe Cleary, Richard Deming, Lanny Hammer, Cajetan Iheka, Heather Klemann, Cathy Nicholson, Meghan O'Rourke, John Durham Peters, Marc Robinson, Emily Thornbury, Katie Trumpener, Ruth Yeazell, and Cynthia Zarin. My gratitude to Jane Bordiere, Sarah Harford (again), Jamie Morris, Doreen Neelans, and Erica Sayers for being amazing colleagues in the undergraduate office. Thanks to Yale graduate students who have thought with me about poetry, including Marcus Alaimo, Julia Chin, Julian Durkin, Clay Greene, Lacey Jones, Jessica Modi, Josy Raheem, Talin Tahajian, Colton Valentine, and Celine Vezina. And profound thanks, again, to Ben Glaser for sustaining a meaningful poetics community in the department.

I still can't believe my good fortune to have spent two years at the Harvard Society of Fellows. My project developed significantly while I was in Cambridge, partly because of the luxury of time and partly because of the fast friendship, interdisciplinary conversation, and feedback of Alex Bevilacqua, Daniel Blank, Gabriella Boulting, Stephanie DeGooyer, Stephanie Dick, Len Gutkin, Anna Henchman, Daniel Hochbaum, Kevin Holden, Anthony Abraham Jack, Abhishek Kaicker, Kelly Katz, Madhav Khosla, Marika Knowles, Jed Lewinsohn, Ana Novak, Andrew Ollett, Matthew Spellberg, Paris Spies-Gans, William Todd, Hannah Walser, Moira Weigel, and Daniel Williams.

My heartfelt appreciation to the teachers at the Edith B. Jackson Childcare Center.

Dear friends have given me a life outside of this project. Thanks to Laura Fisher, Heather Hayes, Rochelle Ross, Aylin Ross, Claire Hurtig, Josh Katz-Rosene, Morel McMaster, Christine Paglialunga, Gesa Sophia Borgeest, Emily Cohodes, Selena Ross, Kate Pulman, Ron Blumer, Muffie Meyer, François Dansereau, Cynthia Mitchell, Nathan Brown, Shirley Wong, Cee Strauss, and Bronwen Agnew. Thanks to my wonderful Montreal and Prince Edward Island family: Joah Levine, Hubert Trahan, Sora Trahan-Levine, Laura MacDonald, and Harry Herbert. I can't thank my parents and siblings enough for their interest in my work and the long-distance care that makes me feel less far away from them. My father Norman Levine has been so encouraging of my research. His love of poetry, his inexhaustible willingness to generate book title ideas, and his own passion for knowledge have been invaluable to me. My stepmother Penny Cousineau-Levine has also been a source of loving encouragement and an important example to me of an academic. Thanks to my beloved stepsiblings Zoë and Dylan Cousineau and my in-laws Marti, Ray, Jon, Kate, and Xavier Ellermann for their love and support. My brilliant and generous siblings Handy and JJ are my best friends. I am so grateful for our closeness, which has been a precious constant in my life. It has helped me write this book and do so much else.

This book is filled with the memory and influence of my mother, Susan Schouten Levine.

And to my little Abe: thank you for all the innumerable ways you beautify the world. When it comes to you, my words run out.

❋

An earlier version of chapter 4 appeared in *Modern Language Quarterly* 77, no. 1 (2016): 81–104. An earlier version of a portion of chapter 2 appeared in *Victorian Literature and Culture* 46, nos. 3/4 (2018): 844–47, © Cambridge University Press 2018, all rights reserved. My thanks to Duke University Press and Cambridge University Press for permission to republish.

Notes

INTRODUCTION

1 On the historicist character of the nineteenth century and the emergence of historically oriented disciplines and methods, see, e.g., Suzy Anger's introduction to *Knowing the Past*. Anger writes, "Questions of historical knowledge were central to Victorian intellectual debate, as was the Victorians' sense of themselves as historical beings (which [John Stuart] Mill famously called 'the dominant idea' of the age)" ("Introduction," 3).

2 Wellek and Warren, *Theory of Literature*. For a more detailed discussion of the intrinsic/extrinsic binary that structures Wellek and Warren's book, see chap. 1.

3 White, *Metahistory*, xxvi, xxx.

4 For an in-depth treatment of the history of literary history as a method (and the role of desire in the narration of literary history), see Perkins, *Is Literary History Possible?* See, too, Perkins's edited collection *Theoretical Issues in Literary History*; and White, "Literary History: The Point of It All." For more on Romantic and Victorian models of literary history, see Wellek, "English Literary Historiography during the Nineteenth Century" and "The Concept of Evolution in Literary History."

5 Some recent books that have been valuably extending the cultural and national horizons of Victorian poetics include Reynolds, *Realms;* Jamison, *Poetics*; Gibson, *Indian Angles*; Keirstead, *Victorian Poetry*; Drury, *Translation*; Rudy, *Imagined Homelands*.

6 There are also canonical Victorian poets whom I don't consider to be part of this dominant tradition, whose poetry and prosody are obviously historiographic but whose experiments tend away from the particular romantic story I focus on here (e.g., Gerard Manley Hopkins, with his studious interest in Anglo-Saxon prosody). Historical attention to rhythm and meter bring other theories and histories of poetry into view. On the cultural meanings attached to Victorian metrics, see, e.g., Blair, *Culture of the Heart*; Martin, *Rise and Fall of Meter*; Phelan,

Music of Verse; Prins, "Victorian Meters" and *Victorian Sappho*; and Rudy, *Electric Meters*.

7 On Gilbert and Sullivan's overt parody of Victorian poetic forms, especially the prosodic characteristics of Tennyson, Patmore, and the Pre-Raphaelites, see Williams, *Gilbert and Sullivan*, 174–86. As for Browning: his thinking was profoundly historical (see Gibson, *History*, for a book-length study of his poetic historicism); he had read the literary histories I treat here (his poem *Sordello* drew on Sismondi's work); he corresponded with Elizabeth Barrett Browning about her experiments with rhyme; he also himself experimented with Italianate forms like terza rima. But as Oscar Wilde observed in "The Critic as Artist," Browning often intentionally undermined rhyme's affective tendencies. Wilde's satirical appraisal is worth quoting at length, because in addition to observing that Browning "passed not from emotion to form, but from thought to chaos," Wilde perfectly illustrates the nineteenth-century conflation of rhyme *theory* with rhyme *history*: "Rhyme, that exquisite echo which in the Muse's hollow hill creates and answers its own voice; rhyme, which in the hands of the real artist becomes not merely a material element of metrical beauty, but a spiritual element of thought and passion also, waking a new mood, it may be, or stirring a fresh train of ideas, or opening by mere sweetness and suggestion of sound some golden door at which the Imagination itself had knocked in vain; rhyme, which can turn man's utterance to the speech of gods; rhyme, the one chord we have added to the Greek lyre, became in Robert Browning's hands a grotesque, misshapen thing, which at times made him masquerade in poetry as a low comedian, and ride Pegasus too often with his tongue in cheek. There are moments when he wounds us by monstrous music. Nay, if he can only get his music by breaking the strings of his lute, he breaks them, and they snap in discord" (*Complete Works*, 1012).

8 See Herder, *Philosophical Writings*, 292: "In order to share in feeling this, do not answer on the basis of the word but go into the age, into the clime, the whole history, feel yourself into everything—only now you are on the way towards understanding the word." As Michael Forster explicates this famous moment from "This Too a Philosophy of History for the Formation of Humanity," Herder is not prescribing "some sort of psychological self-projection onto texts" but rather "an arduous process of historical-philological inquiry" in relation to "radical difference" (Forster, "Introduction," xvii).

9 Vernon Lee turned critical empathy into an even more psychological and embodied method of "aesthetic responsiveness." Lee uses the term *Einfühlung* in the introduction to her *Gallery Diaries* of 1901–4, connecting it to the contemporary psychological aesthetics of Theodor Lipps and Karl Groos (rather than Herder). See Lee, *Psychology*, 47–49. On the formalist quality of Lee's theory of aesthetic empathy and its relationship to the development of close reading, see B. Morgan, *Outward Mind*, 219–54; Morgan convincingly presents Lee's *Einfühlung* as a methodological provocation to current literary studies. For an illuminating argument about the usefulness of nineteenth- and twentieth-century theories

of *Einfühlung* for theorizing transgender feeling and for understanding Virginia Woolf's *Orlando*, see Crawford, "Woolf's *Einfühlung*." On the aesthetics of "tact" and "handling" in the Victorian essay, see Russell, *Tact*.

10 For the significance of the self in aestheticist theory, see, for example, Friedman, who argues that the writings of queer aesthetes "demonstrate how encounters with art could be crucial for gaining sexual self-knowledge and, in turn, how queer desire could bring into being radically new ways of perceiving the self and the world in and through art" (2).

11 Pater, *The Renaissance*, 3, 10.

12 Auerbach, *Time, History, and Literature*, 7, 260. In "The Philology of World Literature," Auerbach argues that a philological method appropriate to the task of world literature would reach for synthesis without homogenization (253–66).

13 For his appreciative discussion of Auerbach's method and the "creative" aspect of philology, see Said, *Orientalism*, xxiv–xxv (that's the preface to the twenty-fifth anniversary edition; for a more ambivalent treatment of "sympathetic identification," see Said's earlier remarks about historicism on 118). Said was an early cotranslator of "The Philology of World Literature" (first published as "Philology and *Weltliteratur*"); see Porter, *Time, History, and Literature*, 274. See also Mufti, *Forget English!*, 203–42, for a detailed discussion of Auerbach's view of world literature and Said's role in Auerbach's reception. Mufti's subtle appraisal of Herder and his later detractors is also worth attending to (61–62). For an influential postcolonial critique of the European historicist tradition of which Herder is a part, see Chakrabarty, *Provincializing Europe*.

14 On the turn in Victorian studies from "knowing" to "feeling," and a new critical interest in "what nineteenth-century readers and writers *thought* they were doing" when they were reading, see Ablow, *Feeling of Reading*, 3.

15 Pater, *The Renaissance*, 3; Auerbach, *Time, History, and Literature*, 260.

16 See Dames for a suggestion analagous to mine about the way another "vanished theoretical configuration"—Victorian physiological novel theory—might "offe[r] possibilities of renewal for our own considerations of the social meaning of the novel form, and ope[n] up areas of investigation that have been successively foreclosed by the author-centered novel theory of the past century" (*Physiology*, 3–4).

17 Forms are not usually understood as having feelings. But see Brinkema, *Forms*, for a recent argument for bringing formalism to bear on questions of affect in cinema studies (though she is more interested in the forms of affects than the affects in forms). Brinkema writes, "Reading affects as having forms involves de-privileging models of expressivity and interiority in favor of treating affects as structures that work through formal means, as consisting in their formal dimensions (as line, light, color, rhythm, and so on) of passionate structures" (37). In relation to the Victorian novel, Alicia Mireles Christoff has suggested that "feeling is not simply produced in and by individual subjectivity, but instead in and through literary form" (*Novel Relations*, 17); and in relation to the Victorian ballad, Justin Sider

has described the "aesthetic feelings" such genres solicited from their readers ("Modern-Antiques," 461). Isobel Armstrong, responding to Simon Jarvis's account of "musical thinking" in Hegel, writes of rhyme that "form and structure think and feel" ("Hegel," 125). For the broader historiographic context to which Hegel's affective rhyme theory belonged, see my argument in chap. 2.

18 I want to insist, though, that empathizing with forms isn't the same thing as empathizing with historical human poets. There are moments when I feel for the poets I discuss; it's hard not to share in the scholarly thrills and frustrations registered in EBB's marginalia, or to condole with the catastrophes of grief recorded in Tennyson's and Patmore's elegies. But there are plenty of biographical and historical reasons not to want to feel with these poets all the way, and it's not necessary that we do. Confusing empathy for form with empathy for a poet would mean ignoring something Victorian poets themselves believed about poetic form: at an elemental level, it doesn't really belong to the poet, because it has its own historical and affective life.

19 In a footnote to *Touching Feeling*, Eve Kosofsky Sedgwick remarks on a crucial shift—that she had helped bring about—in the "common usage" of *affect* for literary studies: "So far, I have been following common usage in using 'affect' and 'emotion' interchangeably. In the rest of this section, however, I focus on 'affects' in Tomkins's sense. For Tomkins, a limited number of affects—analogous to the elements of a periodic table—combine to produce what are normally thought of as emotions, which, like the physical substances formed from the elements, are theoretically unlimited in number" (24n1). On affect as "force" and "a gradient of bodily capacity," see Gregg and Seigworth, "Inventory," 2.

20 A. Hallam, *Writings*, 195.

21 Subsequent chapters offer many examples of the coordination of feeling with specific genetic narratives about poetry. But I'm thinking here in particular of the orientalist philologist William Jones's theorization of the expressive hypothesis that influenced so much nineteenth-century poetry. Jones routes his theory of poetic feeling through stories about the origins of poetry and of Arabic and Persian poetics. See Abrams, *Mirror*, 84–88; and Mufti, *Forget English!*, 67–69. Mufti writes, "The essay on the poetic practices of the 'Eastern nations' thus provides the ground for the elaboration of the broader ideas about poetry and expressiveness, with a view to their lessons for poetry and poetics in the European languages" (69).

22 *Oxford English Dictionary*, s.v., "burden." On the idea of "undersong" in modern poetic theory, see Helsinger, *Poetry and the Thought of Song*, 4–5.

CHAPTER ONE

1 See, e.g., Felski, *Limits*, 153–54: "Literary studies seem destined to swing between these two ends of the pendulum, with opposing sides rehashing the same argu-

ments"; Felski proposes actor-network theory, and ultimately, "postcritical reading" as alternatives. See also North, *Literary Criticism*, 141, for an analysis of the pendulum metaphor in histories of the discipline. North has argued that literary criticism continues to be dominated by the "historicist/contextualist paradigm" that succeeded the more properly critical paradigm initiated by I. A. Richards. See Buurma and Heffernan, *Teaching Archive*, for a study that "rejects the idea that our discipline has been pulled in two directions"; their book argues that classroom practices tell a different, and truer, story about the discipline than do critical manifestos (9).

2 For an overview of New Formalism in literary studies, see Levinson, "What Is New Formalism?" Heather Dubrow's 1990 *A Happier Eden* and Susan Wolfson's 1997 *Formal Charges* were important early contributions to the range of methods "New Formalism" came to name. Related approaches bridge formalist and historical-cultural criticism by showing either that formalist attention helps us understand historical and political realities or that a historical perspective helps us understand genres and forms. In 1999, Herbert Tucker envisioned a "neoformalist" cultural studies; for a description of that method and its relationship to the history of the discipline, see Tucker, "Fix of Form." In 2006, Caroline Levine coined "strategic formalism" to denote the somewhat different relationship between formalist close reading and cultural analysis that motivates her 2015 *Forms*. The 2015 V21 Manifesto positioned itself against "positivist historicism" and "bland antiquarianism" in favor of new investigations into (among other things) "the politics of form" ("Manifesto"). On the formalist character of the method of "surface reading" (Best and Marcus, "Surface Reading") and the broader "descriptive turn" (Love, "Close but not Deep"), see Kramnick and Nersessian, "Form and Explanation," 653–54. For a critical assessment of the unexamined politics of the return to form in Victorian studies, see Chatterjee, Christoff, and Wong, "Introduction: Undisciplining."

3 Just a few examples: in *Professing Literature*, Gerald Graff refers to "the New Criticism put[ting] the old historicism out of its misery" (11); in the introduction to *Reading for Form*, Susan Wolfson writes that American formalist criticism "itself emerged in revolt against another moribund critical institution, old historicism" (8); in "The Historicization of Literary Studies and the Fate of Close Reading," Jane Gallop writes, "When the New Critics introduced the methodology called close reading in the years just before and after World War II, what it replaced was literary history (the old historicism, we might call it)." Gallop also argues here for the continuity between New Criticism and deconstruction (182–83).

4 T. S. Eliot's "Reflections on Vers Libre" (first published in the *New Statesman* in 1917) describes "absence of rhyme" as an accepted criterion for modernist free verse, though he takes pains to explain that modern poetry's unfixed forms can exhibit "liberation *of* rhyme" rather than freedom *from* rhyme. In the same essay, the taste for free verse is aligned with anti-Victorianism, even as Eliot notes Matthew Arnold's pioneering role in the development of the form (518–19).

5 Toward the end of this chapter, I explain how the New Critic W. K. Wimsatt enshrined rhyme as the paradigmatic poetic "technique." However, there is a much longer history of treating rhyme as exemplary. On the post-Renaissance understanding of rhyme as "synecdochic . . . for form" (as well as for "verse structure" and "poetic convention"), see Hollander, *Vision and Resonance*, 117–19; see also Wesling, *The Chances of Rhyme*, x.

6 In contrast to my study, Peter McDonald's *Sound Intentions: The Workings of Rhyme in Nineteenth-Century Poetry* takes a deliberately unhistoricist approach to the subject of Victorian rhyme. In his introduction, McDonald makes the following case for a study of rhyme based on "judgement" and "appreciation" rather than nineteenth-century rhyme theory: "A comprehensive catalogue of nineteenth-century rhyme words, and a collection of everything put into writing on the subject in the period, would not go very far towards answering any of the questions which rhyme posed to the poets themselves. Theories of rhyme, likewise, do not in this sense constitute primary critical evidence, just as they cannot explain the major poems in any very useful ways—ways, that is, that allow us to deepen an appreciation of the actual poems, rather than of the theory by which they are encompassed" (14). My book insists, rather, on the explanatory value of such theories.

7 Leighton, *On Form*, 2–3. This way of accounting for form predates the New Formalist moment. René Wellek began his 1963 essay "Concepts of Form and Structure in Twentieth-Century Criticism" by remarking on the "hundreds of definitions of 'form' and 'structure'" that one could collect. "The temptation is great," he admitted, "to throw up one's hands in despair, to pronounce the case another instance of the Babylonian confusion of tongues which seems to be a characteristic of our civilization" (54).

8 Zitin, *Practical Form*, 2.

9 C. Levine, *Forms*, 2.

10 Kramnick and Nersessian, "Form and Explanation," 664.

11 Levinson, "What Is New Formalism," 559; Wolfson, *Formal Charges*, 1.

12 Macpherson, "A Little Formalism," 385.

13 Although the terms "form" and "genre" are sometimes used interchangeably, an important theoretical distinction is that "genre" has not been—and could not be—subject to the same dehistoricization effort. Genre's association with "historical kinds" and its involvement in dynamic and diachronic processes of influence, "evolution," reception, and parody have been central to its theorization in the twentieth century and beyond. See, e.g., Wellek and Warren's chapter "Literary Genres," in *Theory of Literature*; Fowler, "Life and Death of Literary Forms"; Jauss, *Toward an Aesthetic of Reception*; Williams, *Gilbert and Sullivan*; and R. Cohen, *Genre Theory and Historical Change*. Stefanie Markovits notes, however, that "*genre* has long been recognized as a category every bit as slippery as . . . *form*." See "Form Things," 593.

14 Brooks, *Well Wrought Urn*, x.

15 Wolfson, *Formal Charges*, 8. The New Critics often defended themselves against charges of antihistoricism. In "Literary Theory, Criticism, and History," Wellek (who was reluctant to identify as a New Critic himself) describes attacks on Brooks and Robert Penn Warren's *Understanding Poetry* and his own and Austin Warren's *Theory of Literature* thus: "a straw man is set up: the New Critic, who supposedly denies that a work of art can be illuminated by historical knowledge at all" (6–7). Brooks makes a similar complaint in "My Credo," 72–74.

16 Although the essay was only published in this form posthumously in 1846, it is considered an articulation of his (quite diffuse) philosophical program and especially of the method that was so important an influence on the Schlegels and others. For the publication history of this fragmentary document, see Menze and Menges's editorial notes in *Selected Early Works*, 261.

17 Herder, *Selected Early Works*, 70.

18 Wellek, *History of Modern Criticism*, 1.183.

19 Ruskin, *Selected Writings*, 38, 34, 51.

20 Pater, *The Renaissance*, 36, 32, 34.

21 This permanent feature of rhyme marks a distinction from the architectural historicism in Ruskin: unlike the gothic cathedral, whose medieval spirit may be lost in the Gothic Revival, rhyme's history continues to inflect its modern usage.

22 A. W. Schlegel, *Lectures*, 11, 16; emphasis mine.

23 De Staël, *Germany*, 198, 190–91.

24 Sismondi helped popularize the "Arabist" or "Hispano-Arabic" theory of rhyme among nineteenth-century readers. This particular historiographic theory—and its significance for Hallam and Tennyson—is the subject of chaps. 2 and 3.

25 Sismondi, *Historical View*, 1.116–17.

26 Brooks and Warren, *Understanding Poetry*, 251, vii–viii.

27 A. Hallam, *Writings*, 222, 194, 192.

28 Patmore, "*In Memoriam*," 545; "Metrical Law," 31.

29 For two particularly influential twentieth-century treatments of nineteenth-century genetic historicism (specifically, Nietzsche's), see Foucault, "Nietzsche, Genealogy, History" (1971); and de Man, "Genesis and Genealogy" (1979). For a discussion of Foucault's critique of continuous history and the status of genetic claims in literary studies today, see Underwood, *Why Literary Periods*, 133–34, 162–63. On the history of the term *genetic fallacy* in philosophy, a history that aligns with the literary-critical chronology I present here, see Margaret Crouch, "A 'Limited' Defense," 230 ff.: "The fallacy is not mentioned in any of the well-known British logic texts of the 19th century.... The first quotation in the OED under the term 'genetic fallacy' is from Cohen and Nagel's *Introduction to Logic and Scientific Method*, published in 1934. It would seem, then, that the term 'genetic fallacy' is of rather recent invention." Crouch also finds an earlier usage of the term (interestingly, in relation to the history and evaluation of art) in Morris Cohen's *Reason and Nature* (1931), as well as the suggestion there—familiar to literary scholars—that Romanticism is to blame for the genetic errors of

"psychologism" and historicism (233–34). For a more recent deployment of "the genetic fallacy" and a discussion of its meaning for epistemology, see Kramnick, "Interdisciplinary Fallacy." Kramnick objects there to the notion that the origins of a discipline can explain away its methodological richness.

30 Eichenbaum, "Formal Method," 119.

31 While this is Eichenbaum's overt claim, Jessica Merrill has argued for overlooked continuities between Veselovsky's historical work and the Formalists' idea of poetic language (reorienting conventional intellectual-historical narratives that emphasize links between formalism and structuralism). See Merrill, "Historical Poetics," 520. For another counterintuitive genealogy of formalism—this time routed through novelistic sentimentalism, see Eccles, "Formalism and Sentimentalism." Eccles writes that "the imperative to repress its own origins" is "one of the basic operations of formalism" (541).

32 Eichenbaum, "Formal Method," 117. Before his recent recuperation as the nineteenth-century inventor of Russian "Historical Poetics," Veselovsky was associated with genetic logic and its problems. In his landmark book on Russian Formalism (the first full-length study in English), Victor Erlich writes with hindsight, "Veselovskij's explorations of literary craft were . . . hampered by what some modern critics call the Genetic Fallacy" (31). On the relationship between the Russian Formalists and the American New Critics, see Erlich, *Russian Formalism*, 273–76. In "The Concept of Evolution in Literary History," Wellek writes of Veselovsky's "genetic inquiry into the dim origins of poetry" (47). For a major translation and study of Veselovsky's writings, see Kliger and Maslov, eds., *Persistent Forms*.

33 Eichenbaum, "Formal Method," 117.

34 Brooks, *Well Wrought Urn*, 228–36.

35 Pottle, *Idiom of Poetry*, xiii.

36 Pottle, "A Method," 326.

37 Decades later, in "The Fall of Literary History" (1979), Wellek reflected that "The possibly oversharp distinction between extrinsic and intrinsic methods which organizes the order of the chapters in my and Austin Warren's *Theory of Literature* may have contributed to the singling out of the work of art as an isolated object outside history, even though the last chapter of our book is expressly devoted to a program of literary history" (421).

38 Scholars of historical prosody have been challenging the intrinsic/extrinsic binary as it applies to prosodic form. Meredith Martin's work on the history and politics of meter argues that because of its involvement in national identity and patriotic pedagogy, "meter is at once intrinsic and extrinsic to a formal reading of a poem." See *Rise and Fall of Meter*, 4.

39 Wellek and Warren, *Theory of Literature*, 139, 73, 139.

40 Wimsatt, *Verbal Icon*, xi; subsequent references to this book appear parenthetically.

41 Beardsley pursued this argument further in *Aesthetics* (1958), and Wimsatt con-

tinued it in "Genesis: An Argument Resumed" in *Day of the Leopards* (1976). In the latter essay, Wimsatt describes the motivation behind the "intentional fallacy" thus: "It was against a background of triumphantly prevalent genetic studies in various modes, and in an effort to give assistance in what seemed a badly needed program to rescue poems from the morass of their origins" (12).

42 Simon Jarvis, in "Why Rhyme Pleases," calls Wimsatt's essay "one of the peaks of that range" of "canonical rhyme-theory" (31). The essay is also a key reference in the rhyme theories of Hollander (*Vision and Resonance*); Wesling (*Chances*); Kenner ("Rhyme"); Fried ("Rhyme Puns"); G. Stewart (*Reading Voices*); and Hunter ("Seven Reasons").

43 Lanz relies on Hermann von Helmholtz's idea of melody as "a *variety of desire*, a longing or craving" (Lanz's words) for his account of the emotional element of rhyme. See Lanz, *Physical Basis*, 34.

44 This is not to say that the emotional aspect of rhyme disappears completely from Wimsatt's account. But he does reserve aesthetic value for poetry's intellectual aspect: "It is within the scope of my argument to grant the alogical character of rhyme, or rather to insist on it, but at the same time to insist that the alogical character by itself has little, if any, aesthetic value" (165).

45 On Tennyson's New Critical reception and for another perspective on the relationship between historicity and emotion in his poetry, see Tucker, *Tennyson and the Doom of Romanticism*, 7–8.

46 Brooks, *Modern Poetry*, 239–40.

47 Brooks, *Well Wrought Urn*, 223–24, 167.

48 Tennyson, *Tennyson's Poetry*.

49 H. Tennyson, *Memoir*, 253.

50 Tennyson and his nineteenth-century critics (including Patmore) commented on the strange impression of rhymeful rhymelessness (or rhymeless rhymefulness) generated by this poem, with T. S. Eliot and Graham Hough later pointing out the emotive vowel sounds. See Eliot, "In Memoriam," 214; and Hough, "Tears," 188. Eric Griffiths attempted to analyze those sounds, explaining that "cadence and refrain combine to give a sense of formal stability which we have in the past found with rhyming stanzas, and which leads us now to imagine rhymes where there are rhymes no more. The sound of 'Tears, idle tears' is the sound of prosodic days that are no more" ("Tennyson's Idle Tears," 52). For related discussions of the form of "Tears, Idle Tears" and the question of absence and presence, see Tucker (*Tennyson and the Doom of Romanticism*); Perry (*Alfred Tennyson*); McDonald (*Sound Intentions*); and Wolfson ("Tennyson's Tears"). See Kozicki, "Case for Violet," for a history of the poem's reception up to 1986; and Wolfson, "Tennyson's Tears," for a study of Brooks's career-long struggle with "Tears, Idle Tears."

51 Brooks and Warren, *Understanding Poetry*, vii–viii.

52 Hough, "Tears," 188. For Eliot's reading of "Tears, Idle Tears," see his "In Memoriam," 214.

53 For more on the devaluation of Victorian poetry, see N. Levine, "Understanding

Poetry Otherwise." Important earlier accounts of the problem include Christ, *Victorian and Modern Poetics*; Armstrong's monumental reassessment of the field, *Victorian Poetry*; and Psomiades, "The Lady of Shalott." Psomiades writes that "Literary criticism [was] founded on Victorian poetry's devaluation" (25–26). In an interesting counterpoint to the argument I have been making here, Armstrong cites genetic historiography as a *cause* of Victorian poetry's neglect in the twentieth century: "The Victorian period has always been regarded as isolated between two periods, Romanticism and modernism.... It is situated between two kinds of excitement, in which it appears not to participate. What has been called the 'genetic' history of continuous development through phases and periods, a form of history which the Victorians themselves both helped to create and to question, sees Victorian poetry as a gap in that development" (*Victorian Poetry*, 1). In a 2003 special issue of *Victorian Poetry* convened by Linda Hughes and dedicated to the future of the field, Stephanie Kuduk Weiner wrote, "It has become almost customary to begin discussions of Victorian poetry with a lament," citing the arguments of Christ and Armstrong. Twenty years later, the lament continues to ring true (Kuduk, "Victorian Poetry," 513).

54 Over the last three decades, scholars in queer theory have significantly bridged the methodological divide between history and feeling (though not often in relation to poetry). See, e.g., Love, *Feeling Backward*, on the affective conditions of queer historicism and "cross-historical desire" (31). On formalism and affect theory, see Brinkema, *Forms*.

CHAPTER TWO

1 On the terms "general," "universal," and "world" as modifiers for literary historiography, see Wellek and Warren, *Theory of Literature*, 46–53. See also Henry Hallam's introduction to his *Literature of Europe* for a historical account of the genre and his sense of his most important predecessors. See D'haen et al., *World Literature*, 1, on the difference between this descriptive and critical historiographic tradition (as represented by Juan Andrés's eighteenth-century effort to tell the story of "all literature") and Goethe's future-oriented understanding of "world literature" (*Weltliteratur*).

2 Wellek and Warren, *Theory of Literature*, 50–51, 49. See Curtius, *European Literature and the Latin Middle Ages* (1948); and Auerbach, *Mimesis* (1946). Although *Theory of Literature* was a collaboration, Wellek was the primary author of this chapter. His thoughts on the genealogy of general literary history are vastly elaborated in his magisterial *History of Modern Criticism, 1750–1950* (1955–92). As I noted in the previous chapter, Wellek saw Herder as part of this tradition, too.

3 Wellek and Warren, *Theory of Literature*, 50.

4 Moretti, *Distant Reading*, 48. In the essay "Conjectures on World Literature," Moretti writes that the kind of literary historiography he is proposing "will [be]

very different from what [literary historiography] is now: it will become 'second hand': a patchwork of other people's research, *without a single direct textual reading*. Still ambitious, and actually even more so than before (world literature!); but the ambition is now directly proportional *to the distance from the text*: the more ambitious the project, the greater must the distance be" (*Distant Reading*, 48; Moretti's emphasis). Pascale Casanova's *World Republic of Letters*, on the other hand, seeks to transcend the intrinsic/extrinsic binary with a model of "international literary space" that enables a "reading and interpretation of literary texts that may be at once, and without any contradiction, internal (textual) and external (historical)." Although Casanova was originally writing in the context of the French academy, and in relation to "the French critical tradition," in the preface to the English-language edition, she identified internal criticism with New Critical "close reading" (xii–xiii). As Jahan Ramazani has observed, the contemporary field of world literature has strongly favored readings—close or distant—of the novel, perhaps because lyric poetry challenges the frameworks of "translatability" (see Damrosch, *What Is World Literature?*) and "untranslatability" (Apter, *Against World Literature*) that have been so important to the field's theorization (Ramazani, "Persian Poetry," 213–15). Ramazani's own work in twentieth-century transnational poetics shows how "poetic analysis in particular—attentive to figure, rhythm, allusion, stanza, line, image, genre, and other such resources—can foster an aesthetically attuned transnational literary criticism" (*Transnational Poetics*, xi).

5 Jonah Siegel has argued, regarding the Victorian "culture of art," that British artists and writers cannot be understood apart from their Continental influences and interlocutors: "Images, texts, and ideas, as well as individual critics and artists crossed the channel with great facility in this period. It is not simply the case that British writers were very often looking at foreign art, ancient and modern; they were also following the achievements of philosophers, historians, and curators abroad, authors whose works were translated and engaged with at a level of detail that really should embarrass the contemporary" (*Material Inspirations*, xiii). For a related argument about how the scholarly "division between Continental and British culture" limits Victorian studies as a field, see Jamison, *Poetics*, 4. See also Hughes, *Victorian Women Writers and the Other Germany*.

6 Eileen Tess Johnston makes this Wordsworthian point explicitly ("Hallam's Review," 6), but it is a basic assumption of Tennyson studies. As many critics have observed, Tennyson—unlike Wordsworth, Coleridge, Shelley, Keats, and others—has no critical writing of his own; he left the theorizing and manifesto writing to others. See Lang and Shannon, *Letters*, xxvi; Miller, "Temporal Topographies," 277; and Douglas-Fairhurst, *Tennyson*. McLuhan argues that Hallam's aesthetic theory was basically Tennyson's aesthetic theory from 1828 to about 1842 ("Tennyson," 262). Helsinger (*Poetry and the Thought of Song*) and Hansen ("Arthur Hallam's 'Characteristics'") have suggested that Hallam's review may have been less well-known during the middle years of the nineteenth century

than has generally been assumed. See Helsinger, *Poetry and the Thought of Song*, 15–16; and Hansen, 899.

7 A. Hallam, *Writings*, 191; cited parenthetically in what follows.

8 See Leighton, *On Form*, 57–58.

9 The earliest editions were private printings. The *Remains* was subsequently reprinted in an 1862 edition published by John Murray.

10 Yeats, "Spiritual Art," 34; Le Gallienne, *Poems*, xxxiv.

11 McLuhan, "Tennyson," 262; Johnston, "Hallam's Review," 1.

12 Armstrong, *Victorian Poetry*, 60. See also Christ, *Victorian and Modern Poetics*.

13 Isobel Armstrong's chapter on Hallam in *Victorian Poetry* takes a wide-ranging approach to his prose and poetry, but she doesn't address this particular essay. Some scholarship on the Victorian reception of Dante and nineteenth-century nationalism (e.g., Milbank, *Dante and the Victorians*; and Reynolds, *Realms of Verse*) gives brief consideration to the "Oration." Reynolds, rather than connecting the "Oration" to an earlier culture of Romantic literary historiography, positions it "at the very beginning of a widespread surge of interest in English etymology and its relation to national history" (238). See Hansen, "Arthur Hallam's 'Characteristics,'" for an unusually in-depth treatment of Hallam's essay in relation to "Characteristics" (as well as Hartleyan mind science).

14 For a fuller account of these circumstances, see Blocksidge, *"A Life Lived Quickly,"* 169–70, which I follow here.

15 Motter, *Writings*, 213.

16 A. Hallam, *Letters*, 512, 498.

17 William Hazlitt's article appeared in the June 1815 *Edinburgh Review*, several years before the English translation. This review article is considered "one of the most penetrating assessments of Dante written by any early nineteenth-century British critic" (Cignatta, "William Hazlitt," 69).

18 Perhaps the closest thing was Thomas Warton's *History of English Poetry* (1774–81), which, like the "Oration," considered external influences on English literature, especially in its appended "dissertations." Hallam references Warton directly in the "Oration."

19 Wellek and Warren, *Theory of Literature*, 50–51.

20 This process has sometimes been described as plagiarism, but such borrowing was an acknowledged convention of the genre (compare with Moretti's description, above, of distant reading as necessarily "second-hand" and "a patchwork of other people's research" [*Distant Reading*, 48]). Robert Macfarlane, in *Original Copy*, describes a similar idea of authorship—"the ability to assimilate and to transform rather than spontaneously to produce"—as a late nineteenth-century reaction against Romantic ideas of original genius (45). But, as I argue in this chapter and elsewhere, assimilative creativity was a value espoused in Romantic-era literary historiography and a crucial criterion of the revaluation of authors like Dante, Petrarch, Boccaccio, Shakespeare, and Chaucer (see N. Levine, "Tirra-Lirrical Ballads").

21 Compare to Blair's 1783 *Lectures on Rhetoric and Belles Lettres*: "But these disadvantages [of irregularity], if they be such, of a compound Language, are balanced by other advantages that attend it; particularly, by the number and variety of words with which such a Language is likely to be enriched. Few Languages are, in fact, more copious than the English" (93). Armstrong sees connections to Herder and Schiller in this passage of Hallam's. For her discussion of Hallam's engagement with language theory and the field of comparative philology, see *Victorian Poetry*, 65–66.

22 This claim may have prompted the "general guffaw" that the critic John Wilson associated with the review (quoted in Motter, *Writings*, 183). Wilson's review of *Poems, Chiefly Lyrical*, published under the pseudonym "Christopher North," was even more critical of Hallam's review than of Tennyson's poems; Wilson suggested that the "pomposity" of Hallam's writing had been responsible for the folding of *Englishman's Magazine* (Jump, *Tennyson: The Critical Heritage*, 51). Tennyson retaliated with a satirical poem entitled "To Christopher North."

23 For the economic conception of world literature, see Casanova, *World Republic*, 12–14; and Mufti, 77–78.

24 In a January 1818 notebook entry, Coleridge used an even more explicit version of this chemistry metaphor to describe the formation of early European culture: "The Gothic Tribes fought their way down Southward; the Romans upward North—met in collision—which ended in a chemical Union" (*Notebooks*, entry 4379).

25 Throughout this book, I use the capitalized "Romantic" to refer to European Romanticism, and I follow Hallam in using the lower-case "romantic" to refer to the medieval Romance-language cultural formation.

26 See Friedrich Schlegel's similar remark in *Lectures on the History of Literature* (1815): "Of the three early Italian poets, Dante was, unquestionably, at once the most copious, dignified, and inventive: his work embraces the whole compass of knowledge open to that age" (198).

27 On the nineteenth-century idea of Italy (and the European South more generally) as a desired origin of culture and "the natural home of genius," see Siegel, *Haunted Museum*, 6.

28 The characterization of Tennyson as an "assimilative" poet—for better or for worse—followed him for his whole career. See J. C. Collins's "Tennyson's Assimilative Skill" (1891), in Jump, *Tennyson: The Critical Heritage*, 447; and Douglas-Fairhurst's introduction to *Tennyson*.

29 The first of these significations has been thoroughly explored by Roberto Dainotto in his illuminating work on the historiography of Europe and the origin of rhyme. Summarizing the position of Juan Andrés (an indirect source for Hallam's historiography, as I will discuss later in this chapter), Dainotto writes, "poetic rhyme [was] a mere synecdoche" of "modern European culture" ("Arab Origin," 282–83).

30 The story of the Dark Ages is dramatically expounded by Henry Hallam in *View*

of the State of Europe during the Middle Ages (1818): "We begin in darkness and calamity; and though the shadows grow fainter as we advance, yet we are to break off our pursuit as the morning breathes upon us, and the twilight reddens into the lustre of day." In elaborating on the spiritual and cultural darkness of this period, he writes, "In the shadows of this universal ignorance, a thousand superstitions, like foul animals of night, were propagated and nourished" (304, 338).

31 Hallam and many other historians of his period use *Provençal* and *Langue d'Oc* interchangeably. *Occitan* is the less geographically specific term that is used most commonly now to denote the endangered language group to which Provençal belongs. I will be using "Provençal" here for the sake of consistency.

32 Boase names Thomas Rymer as the first English proponent of this theory, citing Rymer's 1693 comment that "'all our Modern Poetry' comes from Provence" (*Origin*, 2).

33 Hallam makes a similar point in his 1832 review of an Italian translation of *Paradise Lost*, in addressing the problem of translating English blank verse into Italian. In this instance, Hallam seems to emphasize the robustness of Northern languages: "[The languages] of the South, however uniformly pleasing in the language of common life, and however exquisitely beautiful their mellifluous expression of simple feeling, have not that range of power, that variety of resources, that flexure, and, as it were, muscularity of sound, which seem to belong exclusively to dialects more rich in consonants" (*Writings*, 237).

34 Boase traces the Arabist theory back to Giovanni Barbieri's *Rimario* (ca. 1560); Menocal and Dainotto follow his chronology. See also Wellek, *Rise*, for rhyme theories up to Thomas Warton.

35 Said, *Orientalism*, 115–17, 123; Chakrabarty, *Provincializing Europe*, 27. Chakrabarty is referring most immediately to the study of history in the contemporary university, but his argument engages historicism more broadly. Here is the fuller quotation: "Insofar as the academic discourse of history—that is, 'history' as a discourse produced at the institutional site of the university—is concerned, 'Europe' remains the sovereign, theoretical subject of all histories, including the ones we call 'Indian,' 'Chinese,' 'Kenyan,' and so on. There is a peculiar way in which all these other histories tend to become variations on a master narrative that could be called 'the history of Europe'" (27).

36 Phelan, "Empire and Orientalisms," 807.

37 Drury, *Translation*, 5, 102.

38 Menocal, *Arabic Role*, 81–85, 1–2, 85.

39 Boase, *Origin*, 63.

40 Dainotto, "Arab Origin," 274.

41 De Staël, *Germany*, 190–91.

42 Seamus Perry finds related thoughts in Coleridge's *Biographia Literaria* and *The Friend*, which Hallam had read. Perry writes that Coleridge's "intelligence is repeatedly stirred by the 'particular pleasure' that is to be 'found in anticipating the recurrence of sounds and quantities'"; he also cites a passage about Cimarosa's

music that describes the way "retrospection blends with anticipation, and Hope and Memory (a female Janus) become one power with a double aspect" (quoted in Perry, "Hallam and Coleridge," 442–43). Hallam's social group, the Apostles, was described by R. C. Trench as a "'Wordsworthian-Germano-Coleridgian' group" (Blocksidge, "*A Life Lived Quickly*," 119), and Hallam's *Remains* includes many references to Coleridge's work and to Hallam's personal acquaintance with him. For a discussion of resonances between Hallam's rhyme theory and Coleridge's and August Schlegel's ideas of organic form, see chap. 4.

43 The presence of rhyme in pre-Christian Latin poetry (as well as Christian Latin poetry, as Leonine rhymes) was a well-known and oft-repeated fact. Ovid and Horace were frequently cited in literary historiography as sporadic, rather than systematic, users of end rhyme (e.g., in Campion, Henry Hallam, and Hegel).

44 Simon Jarvis summarizes eighteenth-century criticism's prevailing attitudes toward rhyme in the following discussion of Edward Young and Thomas Sheridan: "Young's and Sheridan's verdicts [against rhyme] are only the most vehement deployments of a repertoire of rhyme-hating which expanded rapidly (though by no means uncontestedly) just in the epoch of rhyme's most complete domination of English verse-practice. The lexicon itself also carries the double character evident in Young. Rhyme is an idol, it is witchcraft, it is contemptible, it is depraved, it is a prostitute, it is a mercenary, it is a barbarian, it is stupefaction. Yet rhyme is also a toy, a bawble [*sic*], a gewgaw, a trifle; it jingles, it tinkles, it rattles and babbles. In short, it is something of absolutely no importance whatever, which must therefore be destroyed without further delay, because it is so deeply evil" ("Why Rhyme Pleases," 18–19).

45 Milton, "The Verse," 2.

46 Campion, *Songs*, 236.

47 In the *In Memoriam* review, Patmore suggests that Hallam's line expresses a law that has *always* guided the best prosodists: "It has been excellently said that rhyme owes much of its charm to the fact of its containing a continual appeal to memory and expectation: and upon this saying we would found the rule that rhymes which occur at irregular and unexpected intervals ought always to be increased in number, in order to make up for the effect of their irregularity in weakening the force of that appeal. Great metrists have always felt and acted upon this principle" (545). In chap. 6, I examine Patmore's rule more closely.

48 Ricks, *Tennyson*, 314. Ricks found Hallam's comment on rhyme resonant enough to apply elsewhere, too—including in a book on Bob Dylan and an essay on Milton, where he invokes "Arthur Hallam's profound restatement of the nature of rhyme" (*Force of Poetry*, 77). For more on the comment's elegiac suggestiveness, see Douglas-Fairhurst, *Victorian Afterlives*, 180. Peter McDonald's study of Victorian rhyme also uses the "Memory and Hope" construction in the same way (indeed, his Tennyson chapter is called "Alfred Tennyson: Memory and Hope"). McDonald proposes that the phrase "contain in itself" "foreshadows, perhaps, the self-containments of Tennyson's stanza" (*Sound Intentions*, 174).

49 Perry, *Tennyson*, 136. For an earlier version of this argument, see Perry, "Elegy"; and for a more sustained treatment of the source of Hallam's statement, and a hypothesis about its relationship to Coleridge's thought, see "Hallam and Coleridge."

50 Hunter, "Seven Reasons," 189–90. For another account of the relationships among rhyme, melody, and feeling, see Henry Lanz, *The Physical Basis of Rime* (1931), which I discussed in relation to Wimsatt in chap. 1. Lanz's background was in logic, and he approached these questions in a particularly unsentimental way: "Musical emotions are all based on the psycho-physical fact that when we hear a harmonic deviation from a given tone we feel a peculiar tendency to go back to the original." Lanz differentiates between the emotions produced by music and more familiar emotions, like love: "*No other 'emotions' are expressed by melodies except those which are produced by the tones themselves, owing to their ability to please or to offend the ear*" (35, Lanz's emphasis).

51 The 2012 edition of the *Princeton Encyclopedia of Poetry and Poetics* describes the two broadest positions in the origin-of-rhyme debate as *derivationist* versus *natural/linguistic,* with Sharon Turner arguing for the former (on behalf of Chinese and Sanskrit) in 1808 and Theophilus Swift arguing for the latter in 1803 (Brogan et al., "Rhyme"). In his popular *Amenities of Literature* (1841), which includes the chapter "The Origin of Rhyme," Isaac Disraeli attempts to close the subject once and for all. After surveying genetic theories of rhyme, he declares, "To deduce the origin of rhyme from any particular people, or to fix it at any stated period, is a theory no longer tenable. The custom of rhyming has predominated in China, in Hindustan, in Ethiopia; it chimes in the Malay and Javanese poetry, as it did in ancient Judea: this consonance trills in the simple carol of the African women; its echoes resounded in the halls of the frozen North, in the kiosque of the Persian, and in the tent of the Arab, from time immemorial. RHYME must therefore be considered *as universal as poetry itself*" (273, Disraeli's emphasis). When George Saintsbury wrote about origin-of-rhyme theories in his 1906–10 *History of English Prosody,* he quipped, "The beauty of it is that you never *can* find it out" (1.413). Among the rare (anglophone) twentieth-century investigations into the subject is Michael McKie's 1997 article "The Origins and Early Development of Rhyme in English Verse." McKie concludes, with the natural/linguistic camp, that rhyme likely "emerged in several cultures at differing times" (820); after a preliminary treatment of the first-origin debate, the remainder of the essay focuses on possible routes of transmission into English.

52 The *Aesthetics* lectures (also known as *Lectures on Fine Art*) were roughly contemporaneous with Arthur Hallam's brief career. Hegel's lectures were delivered between 1820 and 1829 and printed in German in 1835 by H. G. Hotho. Hallam's general familiarity with Hegel's thought is evident in a footnote to his 1832 essay, "Remarks on Professor Rossetti's 'Disquisizioni Sullo Spirito Antipapale,'" where he writes, "Hegel, who died last year of Cholera at Berlin, has been for some years undoubted occupant of the philosophic throne, at least in the North

of Germany" (*Writings*, 250). Although Hallam read German (well enough to translate several poems from Schiller), it isn't obvious from the "Oration" that he knew Hegel's work on rhyme; it is more likely that both writers were working from the same sources, especially the Schlegels and Sismondi.

53 Hegel, *Aesthetics*, 1023; cited parenthetically in what follows.

54 "Leonine verse" is the name for hexameter or hexameter-and-pentameter lines governed by internal rhyme (one rhyme at the middle of the line and one rhyme at its end). The form flourished in medieval Latin poetry (Brogan, "Leonine"). Tennyson's 1830 volume included a poem in the form, called "Leonine Elegiacs."

55 Jarvis, "Musical Thinking," 61–64.

56 Armstrong, "Hegel," 133, 135, 136.

57 According to Henry Hallam's biographer Peter Clark, *View of the State of Europe during the Middle Ages* was "one of the first major historical works to use the phrase 'the Middle Ages'" (*Henry Hallam*, 34; Hallam's work hereafter referred to as *Middle Ages*). Beatrice Corrigan writes that "Hallam's book was so widely read that he became one of the most frequently quoted authorities on the Italian poets" (*Italian Poets*, 13).

58 H. Hallam, *Remains*, xxxvi, xii.

59 H. Hallam, *Middle Ages*, 3.563; cited parenthetically in what follows.

60 H. Hallam, *Literature of Europe*, 1.43; cited parenthetically in what follows.

61 A. W. Schlegel, *Observations*, 67–68, my translation.

62 Quoted in A. Hallam, *Letters*, 505.

63 H. Hallam, *Remains*, xxiv.

64 Patrick Conner writes, "At Lucca, [Ruskin's] breakfast consisted of 'coffee, eggs, and a volume of Sismondi,' while at Pisa Sismondi helped him 'feel what I had to look for in the Campo Santo'" (*Savage Ruskin*, 101). J. B. Bullen argues that Sismondi was much more important to Ruskin's thinking about architecture than was Pugin: "We know that Ruskin studied Sismondi attentively, and Sismondi sketched the connection between builder and building. 'Of all the fine arts,' he said, 'architecture is that which most immediately conveys the character of the century, and best makes known the grandeur, energy or pettiness of the nation in which it flowered.' 'It is the art,' he continued, 'which best passes down the inheritance of previous generations'" ("Ruskin and the Tradition of Renaissance Historiography," 68).

65 Warton used specimens, too. So much so, in fact, that Wellek writes, "Warton's *History* became less a work of history than, for instance, Gibbon's or Winckelmann's books, to mention only two of the great achievements of eighteenth-century historiography. It was, first of all, an accumulation of materials, a bibliography and anthology, and only secondarily a history.... Warton thus combines practically all the older forms of literary history: the catalogue, the anthology with explanatory notes, the biography (though there is least of this)" (*Rise*, 174–76).

66 Sismondi, *Historical View*, 1.13n; cited parenthetically in what follows.

67 Dainotto, *Europe (in Theory)*, 161. For substantial discussions of Sismondi's

relationship to Andrés, see Dainotto, *Europe (in Theory)*; and Mazzeo, *Abate Juan Andrés*. Dainotto emphasizes (along with such copyings) Sismondi's fundamental divergence from Andrés's Arabist theory, arguing that Sismondi limits the Arab influence to Southern Europe rather than Europe as a whole. I understand many of the passages Dainotto cites as evidence differently. For instance, when Sismondi writes that "Arab poetry is rhymed *like* ours" (Dainotto's emphasis), he is making a technical point, referring illustratively to the French couplet form (in relation to the *ghazal* couplet) rather than insisting on the separate origin of Northern European rhyme (*Europe (in Theory)*, 162–63). Elsewhere, Sismondi is adamant that the troubadours learned rhyme from Arabic poetry and then disseminated it to "all the other nations of modern Europe" (*Historical View*, 1.108).

68 The manuscript notes for Sismondi's lectures are held at the archives of the Associazione di Studi Sismondiani in Pescia, Italy. I am grateful to the staff at the Archivio di Stato di Pescia and the Associazione di Studi Sismondiani for their assistance during my visit to the archive.

69 Blocksidge, *"A Life Lived Quickly,"* 18. Sismondi was the brother-in-law of Henry Hallam's close friend, the historian and politician Sir James Mackintosh, through Sismondi's wife, Jessie Allen.

70 A. Hallam, *Letters*, 27, 31.

71 William Jones, one of Sismondi's most important sources, writes similarly of Persian poets, "This delicacy of their lives and sentiments has insensibly affected their language, and rendered it the softest, as it is one of the richest, in the world" (*Poetical Works*, 2.219–20).

72 Sismondi's grim fantasy of modern Islamic culture forms part of a conjecture about the rise and fall of civilizations: just as Arab countries have declined from a golden age into barbarity, so might Europe "in a few ages, become as wild and deserted as the hills of Mauritania, the sands of Egypt, and the valleys of Anatolia," with future philologists from the Americas and Australia combing through the cultural ruins of Europe, just as European orientalist scholars have had to do for the Orient (1.76–77). For a discussion of Andrés's similar treatment of "the progress of literature," see Dainotto, *Europe (in Theory)*, 131–32. On the European orientalist as "a hero rescuing the Orient from the obscurity, alienation, and strangeness which he himself had properly distinguished," see Said, *Orientalism*, 121.

73 Sismondi, *Midi de l'Europe*, 1.115.

74 "The consonants held a very important place in the languages of the North, which abound in them, as do the vowels in those of the South. Alliteration, therefore, which is but a repetition of the consonants, is the ornament of the Northern tongues; while *assonance*, or the rhyming of the termination vowels, is peculiar to the popular verses of the nations of the South, although the practice has been reduced into a system only amongst the Spaniards" (Sismondi, *Historical View*, 1.102).

75 Patmore, "Essay on English Metrical Law," 31.

76 Roth, Editor's notes, 88.

77 Roscoe translates "l'espérance" as "expectations," rather than the more spiritually inflected and emotionally resonant (and accurate) "hope." Hallam's choice of "hope" restores the connotations of the original; it also suggests that perhaps he was familiar with Sismondi in French. As I noted in the introduction, Hallam's formulation also chimes with August Schlegel's description of romantic literature (which "hovers betwixt recollection and hope" [*Lectures*, 16]), as well as de Staël's description of rhyme as "the image of hope and of memory" (*Germany*, 190–91). Interestingly, Patmore's earliest allusion to Hallam's idea of rhyme, in 1850, uses the word "expectation" rather than hope ("a continual appeal to memory and expectation")—either a coincidence of paraphrase or a sign that he first met the sentence in Roscoe's translation of Sismondi, before attributing it to Hallam in 1857.

78 The character of Rudel appears in Robert Browning's "Rudel to the Lady of Tripoli" (1842) and Algernon Charles Swinburne's "The Triumph of Time" (1866), as well as two poems not published in Swinburne's lifetime, "The Death of Rudel" and "Rudel in Paradise." Ezra Pound later alludes to Rudel in his *Cantos* (1917–62). Stendhal retells Rudel's story in his fascinating theoretical work *De l'amour* (1822); and Pater uses Rudel as an example of delirious and impossible medieval love in his 1868 "Poems by William Morris." See Passerini, *Europe in Love*, 207, on the Rudel fad in relation to the emergence of Romance philology and associated ideas of European identity.

79 Thanks to Ben Glaser and Stefanie Markovits for hearing this rhyme.

80 Here is Sismondi's description of the *ghazal* form: "Both [the 'ghazele' and the 'casside'] are compositions in couplets, and the second lines of each couplet rhyme with one another throughout the whole poem. The first lines are not rhymed." See Sismondi, *Historical View*, 1.61.

81 Sismondi's version is no longer considered part of Rudel's corpus; see the variants in Pickens, *Songs of Jaufré Rudel*, which follow a different rhyme scheme. On the unreliability of Rudel's sixteenth-century editor, Jean de Nostredame, see Anglade, introduction to *Les vies*, 63–65; and Boase, *Origin*, 11–12. Boase points out that even at the time of Sismondi's writing, the Rudel material in Nostredame's collection was known to have been partially fabricated. Sismondi's contemporary, the Romance philologist François Just Marie Raynouard, reproduced the more accurate seven-line stanza form in his important edition of troubadour poetry (Raynouard, *Choix*, 3.101). That Sismondi chose to use the less accurate but more convenient version of Rudel's poem suggests a tension between the wishful historiographic narrative and the historical document.

CHAPTER THREE

1 In addition to his passionate scholarly interest in Dante and Petrarch, Hallam wrote sonnets in both English and Italian. *In Memoriam* records these preoccupations of Hallam's when it narrates his companions' delight "To hear him, as

he lay and read / The Tuscan poets on the lawn" (89.21–24). In an essay on the history of the *In Memoriam* stanza in English poetry, Denise Gigante describes the emotional dynamics of Petrarchan quatrains that are "not fully executed as sonnets" and therefore arrive at neither volta nor resolution ("Forming Desire," 496). Her broader argument, relevant here, concerns "how the particular 'lost desire' that Tennyson laments in *In Memoriam* is materially cathected in form" (481). Seamus Perry has likewise described the poem as "a sequence of disappointed sonnets" (*Tennyson*, 136).

2 Tennyson, *In Memoriam*, 117.1–8; cited parenthetically in what follows.

3 Quoted in Shannon, "Pinnacle," 116; Jump, *Tennyson: The Critical Heritage*, 183. For an excellent survey of critical comments on Tennyson's ABBA stanza form, in the context of a study of Cambridge verse culture, see Mazel, "Age of Rhyme," 375–76, n3.

4 As Gigante and Gray ("Introduction") have both pointed out, he didn't actually invent it. It had been used previously by Ben Jonson, Philip Sidney, and D. G. Rossetti; and many have argued (as noted above) that the ABBA stanza is the quatrain of a Petrarchan sonnet, isolated from the rest of the scheme. Tennyson wrote *In Memoriam* over a period of seventeen years, which means that the form belongs as much to the beginning of his career as to its maturity. For more on this issue, and Tennyson's decision to reserve the ABBA stanza for his elegies, see Ricks, *Poems*, 2.311–12.

5 The *Divine Comedy* wasn't the model for the form of *In Memoriam*, but Tennyson cited its comedic structure it as a major influence on his poem. See Ricks, *Poems*, 2.312; and Milbank, *Dante*, 185.

6 Volumes of Dante had passed between Tennyson and Hallam as early as 1828. On Tennyson's early familiarity with Dante in the original Italian, see Pattison, *Tennyson and Tradition*, 115–16; and Milbank, *Dante*, 186. Hallam refers knowledgeably to *De vulgari eloquentia* in his prose. See A. Hallam, *Writings*, 248; cited parenthetically in what follows.

7 Dante, *De vulgari*, 82, 85, 83.

8 For more on the relationship between anatomy and stanzaic form in Dante and the troubadours, see Agamben, *End of the Poem*.

9 Dante, *Vita nuova*, 79.

10 A. Hallam, *Writings*, 237. In his Gabriele Rossetti essay, Hallam writes, "In Dante . . . the form and spirit perfectly correspond as if adapted to each other by preëstabished harmony" (*Writings*, 278).

11 Carlyle was drawing on Coleridge's Dante criticism. Rather than an "allegory," Carlyle saw the *Divine Comedy* as a "sublime embodiment" (*On Heroes*, 97). Here is Carlyle's language in 1842: "I give Dante my highest praise when I say of his *Divine Comedy* that it is, in all senses, genuinely a Song. In the very sound of it there is a *canto fermo*; it proceeds as by a chant. The language, his simple terza rima, doubtless helped him in this. One reads along naturally with a sort of *lilt*. But I add, that it could not be otherwise; for the essence and material of the

work are themselves rhythmic. Its depth, and rapt passion and sincerity, makes it musical;—go *deep* enough, there is music everywhere. A true inward symmetry, what one calls an architectural harmony, reigns in it, proportionates it all: architectural; which also partakes of the character of music" (91). Christina Rossetti makes a related point when she writes in praise of Charles Cayley's 1851 terza rima translation, "[W]e feel that to strip Dante to prose, or chasten him into blank verse, or deform him by couplets or any other unauthorized vehicle, is as indefensible ... as it would be to deprive organ music of its majestic swelling and sinking continuity of sound, substituting for this the disconnectedness of pianoforte notes, or the monotonous jog of a drum" ("Dante," 200–201).

12 Motter, *Writings*, 115.

13 See Lang and Shannon, *Letters*, xxvi.

14 Quoted in Shannon, "Pinnacle," 116.

15 I use "valedictory" in the modal sense specified by Justin Sider: as a kind of inverted elegy, uttered by the departing figure ("Framing Tennyson's Farewells," 488). Tennyson figures prominently in Sider's theorization of the valedictory mode; see his *Parting Words* for the full presentation of the argument.

16 Eliot, "In Memoriam," 207, 209, 214.

17 Jump, *Tennyson: The Critical Heritage*, 96; Coleridge, Table Talk, 85.

18 Coleridge, *Table Talk*, 85.

19 In "Tennyson's Dying Fall," Peter McDonald makes a related point, emphasizing "cadence" over meter (37–38). For more on Tennyson's metrical irregularity, see Pyre, *Formation*; Ostriker, "Three Modes"; and Nabi, "Tennyson with the Net Down." Alicia Ostriker discerns three prosodic modes in Tennyson's early verse: "ode" or "irregular," "stanzaic," and "sustained." In proposing this system, she is refuting Pyre's previous claim that the early poems are "strangely and rashly anarchic" ("Three Modes," 273). It should be noted that the stanzaic variety of *Poems, Chiefly Lyrical* is a marked departure from the more predictable stanzas and meters (often ABAB quatrains or couplets) of the poems Tennyson wrote before meeting Hallam in 1829. Many of these more regular early poems were published in *Poems by Two Brothers* (1827).

20 Eliot, "In Memoriam," 215. Eliot's use of "lyrical" seems very similar to Hallam's, and his reading of Tennyson's forms has much in common with Hallam's reading of the same. The striking similarities between Eliot's and Hallam's poetic theory have been discussed at length in Christ, *Victorian and Modern Poetics*.

21 On "lyric" as a contested term with a long critical history and a particularly powerful methodological utility for New Critical interpretation, see Jackson and Prins, *Lyric Theory Reader*; in their argument, "lyric" has become an abstraction more or less equivalent to "poetry." My own argument is narrower, limited to what "lyric" and "lyrical" meant to Tennyson and Hallam in the early 1830s. For another perspective on Tennyson's early conception of lyric see Peterson, "Sappho," which argues that Sappho was Tennyson's main lyric model. Robert Pattison reports that toward the end of Tennyson's career, when Francis Palgrave was

compiling a selection of the poet's lyrics, the two disagreed about the meaning of "lyric." Palgrave wanted to exclude sonnets, because they did not fit a Greek idea of lyric; Tennyson objected to this criterion (*Tennyson and Tradition*, 17). This quarrel may be related to a distinction that Eileen Tess Johnston makes between the Wordsworth-Coleridgean idea of poetry (based on sincerity) and the Hallam-Tennysonian one (based on craft) (18–19).

22 Of course, there have been several other serious treatments of Hallam's essay, both before and after Armstrong's. See, e.g., Johnston, "Hallam's Review," which considers Hallam's debts to the prose work of Romantic poets (especially Coleridge, Wordsworth, and Shelley). Steven Dillon, in "Canonical and Sensational," argues that Hallam is borrowing the rhetoric of sensation and reflection from the philosophy of Hume and Berkeley, but that "neither would posit a mind that exhibited a single faculty; reflection and sensation are caught up in one another" (97); so he sees Hallam's division of faculties as an original move.

23 Armstrong, *Victorian Poetry*, 67.

24 Armstrong, 66.

25 A. Hallam, *Writings*, 190. Compare with Sismondi, *Historical View*, 1.6; cited parenthetically in what follows.

26 For Keats's famous phrase, see "Letter," 426.

27 This latter example describes a Persian *divan* (a collection of *ghazals*). For his descriptions of the poetry of the medieval Middle East, Sismondi relies on the work of orientalist philologists William Jones, Friedrich Wilken, and Barthélemy d'Herbelot, confessing that he is unable to read the poems in the original languages. Though he describes the prosody, his specimens here tend to be in prose. It's worth noting, also, that his discussion of Arabic poets is uncharacteristically thin on biographical and textual detail. Andrés is his major source for the historical narrative of Arabic and Persian culture. By "Al-Monotabbi of Cufa," Sismondi seems to mean al-Mutanabbi. Of Arabic poets from the period of Haroun al-Raschid and after, Sismondi writes, "Their names, which I have vainly attempted to impress upon my memory, since I am unacquainted with their works, would also probably escape the greater part of my readers" (1.54).

28 The Renaissance critic George Puttenham had also associated "more compasses and interweavings" in a stanza with more intense emotional effects, writing that "very large distances be more artificial than popularly pleasant, and yet do give great grace and gravity, and move passion and affections more vehemently, as it is well to be observed by Petrarch's *canzoni*" (*Art*, 177). After Sismondi, Hegel, too, identified "a more ramified figuration of rhyme" and "variously articulated and interlaced rhyme-strophes" as the special property of modern lyric. For Hegel, even when complex rhyming happens in epic, it should be understood as a lyric element (*Aesthetics*, 1137).

29 Hallam's selection and presentation of Tennyson's poems roughly aligns with the romantic chronology he presents in the "Oration." Hallam begins with "Recollections of the Arabian Nights" and comments especially on its fresh and lavish

images—just the qualities that Hallam associates in the "Oration" with the first rhymed poems in Arabic. He then discusses "The Ballad of Oriana," an example of affective prosody that he connects with medieval Romance-language lyric poetry. Then he examines the more "English" specimens—the Shakespearean "Mariana" and "Adeline"—before concluding that "ours is necessarily a compound language" (198). Thus, the order of the close readings helps construe Tennyson as both the culmination and embodiment of the literary-historical route that Hallam describes in the "Oration."

30 See Ricks, *Poems*, 1.225.

31 "The celebrated Haroun-al-Raschid, who reigned from 786 to 809, acquired a glorious name by the protection which he afforded to letters. The historian Elmacin assures us, that he never undertook a journey without carrying with him at least a hundred men of science in his train. The Arabians are indebted to him for the rapid progress which they made in science and literature; for Haroun never built a mosque without attaching to it a school" (Sismondi, *Historical View*, 1.45).

32 Meredith Martin has argued that although the familiar 4-3-4-3 structure was common in English and described by Scott as the dominant form, there were actually many nineteenth-century ballad stanzas: "Variable definitions of the ballad stanza persist throughout the eighteenth and nineteenth centuries and do not solidify into the notion we have now (a quatrain of alternating iambic tetrameter and trimeter) until the turn of the twentieth century" ("Imperfectly Civilized," 351).

33 In addition to Galland's *Arabian Nights* and Jones's *Works*, other documented sources include Charles Rollin's *Ancient History* and Claude Étienne de Savary's *Letters on Egypt* (Ricks, *Poems*, 1.113, 1.148, 1.157, 1.225). The orientalist poems by Tennyson that predate *Poems, Chiefly Lyrical* include "Written by an Exile of Bassorah," "Persia," "The Expedition of Nadir Shaw into Hindostan," "Thou Camest to Thy Bower, My Love," "Love [Almighty Love]," and "The Ganges"; the majority were published in *Poems by Two Brothers*, 1827. As I noted above, most poems in that volume have comparatively simple rhyme schemes (e.g., AABB or ABAB).

34 Phelan, "Empire and Orientalisms," 801, 811.

35 Tennyson, *Poems, Chiefly Lyrical*, 1.1–11; in what follows, cited parenthetically by stanza and line. All spellings per the 1830 version of the poem.

36 Although a few of Tennyson's rhymes are questionably "allowable" from the perspective of nineteenth-century rhyming dictionaries, my calculation of the rhyme scheme generally takes half-rhymes as rhymes. I agree with Herbert Tucker that there is a rhyme-scheme repetition in two of the stanzas (4 and 9). For Tucker that repetition only serves to emphasize the effect of intentional variety, "as if to show that even the pattern of fresh stanzaic invention is an obligation that can be thrown off at whim" (*Tennyson and the Doom of Romanticism*, 79).

37 A. Hallam, *Writings*, 193.

38 Arthur Hallam used the compound "citron-shadow" in a dramatic poem he wrote while traveling to the Rhine with Tennyson (Motter, *Writings*, 106). As Ricks

notes (likewise citing the Motter edition of Hallam's work), Hallam also used the phrase "the tide of time" in his poem "A Farewell to the South" (Ricks, *Poems*, 1.226; Motter, 24).

39 Tucker, *Tennyson and the Doom of Romanticism*, 80.

40 Sismondi, *Historical View*, 1.60.

41 Compare these lines to Sismondi's prose rendering of the Persian poet Ferduzi's "Schah-Namah" (which, by the time it reached English readers, had been translated from Ferduzi's Persian to Frederick Wilken's Latin to Sismondi's French to Roscoe's English): "Behold! how the fields glitter with the red and the yellow rays! . . . How beautiful are the stars! How sweetly does the water murmur! Is not this the garden of an emperor's palace? The colours of the earth are varied, like the tapestry of the kings of Ormuz." (1.56). Tennyson later changed "breaded blosms" to "braided blooms."

42 See Reynolds, *Realms*, 221; and Haddad, *Orientalist Poetics*, 184, for related discussions of the pattern of nature/craft imagery in this poem. Emily Haddad points out how generic these descriptions are, writing that "'Recollections' closely follows nineteenth-century orientalist poems' tendency to present Middle Eastern nature as artful" (184). She additionally describes Tennyson's archaisms and "verbal preciousness" as features of the poem's decorative orientalist aesthetics. Haddad's discussion of Tennyson is part of a larger thesis about the importance of orientalism to nineteenth-century poetic experimentation—a phenomenon she suggests has been overlooked by scholars of both orientalism and Victorian poetry (1–2).

43 See Hollander, *Vision and Resonance*, 277. By contrast, when Wellek and Warren used the term "graphic prosody," they were referring to scansion, rather than the poem's shape (*Theory of Literature*, 166).

44 For the Arabic and Persian tradition of pattern poetry, and for more on Western associations of ornate surfaces (including textual surfaces) with "Eastern impulses," see Hollander, "The Poem in the Eye," in *Vision and Resonance*, esp. 252. Hollander cites Puttenham's treatment of pattern poetry here.

45 The notation system I'm adapting is not from Puttenham's discussion of pattern poetry; it is from his discussion of stave structure and its sound effects, and the visualization is merely "an ocular example" of what the ear hears. Puttenham justifies the visual representation of an auditory experience on the grounds of a "natural sympathy" between the senses: "I set you down an ocular example, because ye may the better conceive it. Likewise, it so falleth out most times, your ocular proportion doth declare the nature of the audible, for if it please the ear well, the same represented by delineation to the view pleaseth the eye well, and *e converso*. And this is by a natural sympathy between the ear and the eye, and between tunes and colors" (*Art*, 174–75). Recall that Arthur Hallam made the sensitivity of ear and eye a hallmark of the sensation poet: "Mr. Tennyson belongs decidedly to the class we have already described as Poets of Sensation. He sees all the forms of nature with the 'eruditus oculus,' and his ear has a fairy fineness" (191).

46 Sismondi, *Historical View*, 1.62, 1.107.

47 As I discuss in chap. 5, Walter Pater described the "aesthetic poetry" of Morris with a similar sense of the difference between an antiquarian and a more richly historicist orientation toward literary history. Morris's poetry is "like some strange second flowering after date, it renews on a more delicate type the poetry of a past age, but must not be confounded with it" ("Poems by William Morris," 144). Morris's is not a "vain antiquarianism" but a "profounder medievalism," because his poetry takes account of the "composite experience of all the ages" that have passed since the medieval era. Pater writes, "It is one of the charming anachronisms of a poet, who, while he handles an ancient subject, never becomes an antiquarian, but vitalizes his subject by keeping it always close to himself" (144–46). Carolyn Williams's reading of this Pater essay offers a helpful gloss on Hallam's sense of history, too. Of Pater she writes, "The very quality that makes it 'aesthetic' … is its poetic involvement in the question of whether (and how) a past age can be represented in the present. Pater argues that aesthetic poetry imitates a former age and poetic style, not with the mimetic aim of reproducing the former age, but with the antithetical aim of differentiating it *from*, and the synthetic aim of comprehending it *within*, the present" (*Transfigured World*, 58).

48 Hallam's claim about Tennyson's immediate source is corroborated by Ricks: "[Edward] FitzGerald, in his copy of *1842* (*Trinity College*), says that the poem was 'in some measure inspired' by the ballad of Helen of Kirkconnell. T. knew it by heart (*Mem.* I 48), presumably in the version given in Scott's *Minstrelsy*" (*Poems*, 1.270).

49 In the twentieth century, Ezra Pound made a remarkably similar observation about the expressiveness of "pure sound" in Dante's verse: "Dante has the advantage [over Shakespeare] in points of pure sound; his onomatopoeia is not a mere trick of imitating natural noises, but is a mastery in fitting the inarticulate sound of a passage to the mood or to the quality of voice which expresses that mood or passion which the passage describes or expresses" (*Spirit of Romance*, 160). In the essay "How to Read," he calls this condition "MELOPOEIA, wherein the words are charged, over and above their plain meaning, with some musical property, which directs the bearing or trend of that meaning" (*Polite Essays*, 170).

50 Scott, *Complete Works*, 2.5–8.

51 Scott, 2.1–4.

52 Tennyson, *Poems, Chiefly Lyrical*, 1.1–9; in what follows, cited parenthetically by stanza and line.

53 Tennyson toyed with an even stronger pattern of O's; in an early draft, the "wasted" in line 1 was instead "hollow" (see Ricks, *Poems*, 1.271).

54 Scott, *Complete Works*, 2.26–28.

55 Barton, *Tennyson's Name*, 24.

56 Hollander remarks that, in contrast to French and even Chaucer's Middle English, "In [modern] English, *rime très riche* is always in a sense, *rime pauvre*" (*Vision and Resonance*, 118).

57 Ruskin, *Selected Writings*, 38.

CHAPTER FOUR

1 Barrett Browning, *Sonnets from the Portuguese*, 2.8–14, in *Works*.

2 Barrett Browning, *Aurora Leigh*, 1.1–8; cited parenthetically in what follows.

3 Milton, "The Verse," 2.

4 Addison, *Works*, 2.41.

5 Johnson, *Dictionary*; Murray, *New English Dictionary*, 902.

6 See the current entries on "blank verse" in Abrams and Harpham, *Glossary*, 33; and in the *Princeton Encyclopedia of Poetry and Poetics* (Weismiller et al., "Blank Verse," 145).

7 Smith, "Mrs. Browning's Rhymes," records dozens of examples of Victorian critics complaining of EBB's terrible rhymes. For extensive analyses of EBB's "odd" rhymes, see Morlier, "Sonnets"; and Hayter, "Experiments." See also Stone and Taylor, *Works*, xi. In terms that seem to satirize Arthur Hallam's bon mot, George Saintsbury wrote that the rhymes in "Lady Geraldine's Courtship" "are horrible and heartrending. They make the process of reading Mrs. Browning something like that of eating with a raging tooth—a process of alternate expectation and agony" (*Prosody*, 3.244). For an important account of EBB's reception more broadly, see Lootens, *Lost Saints*.

8 "Aurora Leigh," 182.

9 Saintsbury, *Criticism*, 293.

10 René Wellek and Austin Warren still credited Hallam—with the Schlegels, Sismondi, and Bouterwek—as a founder of literary history (*Theory of Literature*, 49). However, David Perkins downplays Hallam's contribution, arguing that his books were "essentially compendia. They rehearsed what was known about authors in the various fields of belles lettres, history, philosophy, classical philology, theology, and so forth, and if the authors were arranged in chronological series, this was what Hallam understood by 'history'" ("Literary History," 338).

11 Donaldson, *Works*, 3.xi.

12 Poe, *Works*, 3.420.

13 *Brownings' Correspondence*, 9.26, 96.

14 A notable exception to the pattern of selective attention is Donald Hair's study of Barrett Browning's language, *Fresh Strange Music*. Robert Stark, in "[Keeping] Up the Fire," also briefly but productively reads "The Book of the Poets" in relation to EBB's metrical and rhythmic choices in *Aurora Leigh*. See, too, Freiwald, "World of Books," on EBB's critical prose.

15 See Donaldson, *Works*, 4.443.

16 *Brownings' Correspondence*, 6.16–19.

17 Barrett Browning, "Book of the Poets," in *Works*, 4.445; cited parenthetically in what follows.

18 Donaldson, *Works*, 4.479n27.

19 Warton, *History*, 1.i.

20 Griffin, *Wordsworth's Pope*, discusses the role of both Thomas and Joseph Warton in developing a lasting Romantic historiography predicated on the rejection

of Pope. See also Brooks and Wimsatt, *Literary Criticism*, 530. Warton saw his Arabian-Nordic theory as a synthesis of Warburton, Mallet, and Percy (Wellek, *Rise*, 189).

21 H. Hallam, *Literature of Europe*, 1.48; cited parenthetically in what follows. Hallam was vindicated when the philologist Richard Garnett condemned Warton's dissertation as "extremely illogical and unsatisfactory" in 1840 (Supplementary Notes, 1.lvi).

22 See Wellek, *History of Modern Criticism*, 3.90; Clark, *Henry Hallam*, 95–96; and T. Lang, "Hallam, Henry."

23 This is not to imply that Hallam was EBB's only source of information about literary history. For instance, she owned the 1824 edition of Warton (now held at the Beinecke Library), but she annotated its pages very minimally.

24 "Hallam's *Literature*," *New York Review*, 2.

25 "Hallam's *Literature*," *London Quarterly Review*, 209, 185.

26 Hallam addresses the contributions and limitations of many of these historians in his introduction. He also cites Juan Andrés's history of ancient and modern literature (1782–99) as an important precedent.

27 For a discussion of EBB's exclusion from university education on the basis of her sex (and EBB's amateur and amatory relationship to classical learning, in particular), see Prins, *Ladies' Greek*, 1–8.

28 *Browning's Correspondence*, 6.173.

29 Volumes 2–4 have an inscription on the title page with EBB's name and a note that her uncle Robert Hedley presented those volumes to her at Torquay in 1839. Volume 1 has a different inscription—"Robert & Elizabeth Barrett Browning" (Item A1127)—but this married inscription seems to postdate her acquisition of the volume by several years. I am grateful to the staff at the Armstrong Browning Library, Baylor University, for their assistance in the archive. When citing EBB's marginalia, I use the page numbers from Hallam's edition.

30 *Brownings' Correspondence*, 9.26.

31 See Jarvis, "Why Rhyme Pleases," 17–18.

32 Later in life EBB dismissed her Pope imitations as "a girl's exercise," the product of "that disastrous monster a precocious child" (*Brownings' Correspondence*, 9.52). For more on EBB's early love and subsequent repudiation of Pope, see Morlier, "Sonnets," 101; and Tucker, "Ebbigrammar."

33 A. Hallam, *Writings*, 222.

34 Carlyle, *On Heroes*, 91.

35 Some detail about this web of influence: Carlyle cites Coleridge in this discussion of terza rima in *On Heroes, Hero-Worship and the Heroic in History* (1841). For the influence of Coleridge on Arthur Hallam (and for Henry Hallam's personal acquaintance—and intellectual disagreement—with Coleridge), see Perry, "Hallam and Coleridge." EBB was attracted to Schlegel's thought as early as 1832 (see *Brownings' Correspondence*, 3.70). Schlegel's Shakespeare lectures were first translated into English by John Black in 1815, and the 1840 reissue included an introduction by EBB's friend and collaborator, Richard Hengist Horne. EBB greatly

admired Carlyle; she wrote an essay on him for Horne's *A New Spirit of the Age* (1844), and she cites his *On Heroes* in bk. 5 of *Aurora Leigh.*

36 Coleridge, *Collected Works,* 5.1.494–95.

37 A. W. Schlegel, *Lectures,* 340.

38 A. W. Schlegel, 377–78.

39 Hallam's best remembered remarks on Shakespeare are about the sonnets: "It is impossible not to wish that Shakspeare [*sic*] had never written them" (3.504). Hallam's reservations about Shakespeare actually set him against a growing culture of what Charles LaPorte terms "bardology"; by the middle of the nineteenth century, Shakespeare had become the object of quasi-religious devotion, as well as "an index of value and a shibboleth of cultural literacy akin to the Bible itself" (*Victorian Cult,* 10).

40 Barrett Browning, "Book of the Poets," 4.469–70; A. Hallam, *Writings,* 230.

41 See Billington, *Elizabeth Barrett Browning,* 90–92.

42 The *spirit/spirit* and *form/more* pairings are both controversial rhymes for opposite reasons: one rhymes too much, the other rhymes too little. The former is an identical rhyme, a variant (common in both blank verse and rhymed verse) that is considered either a nonrhyme or a more-than-perfect-rhyme, depending on the reader and verse culture (Brogan et al., "Identical Rhyme"); the *form/more* pairing is a clear example of the assonantal rhyme that EBB champions. The scheme may continue into the subsequent line, too, if *spirit/art* is allowed as a consonant rhyme. Monique Morgan also notes the sonnet structure apparent in this passage and catalogs several of its rhyme-like sound effects in her argument about lyric and narrative (*Narrative Means,* 151). Matthew Reynolds points to other moments of "virtual rhyme" and lines that "nearly rhyme" in *Aurora Leigh* to demonstrate how EBB's prosody adapts to Aurora's movement through English and Italian locations (*Realms,* 119–21).

43 Dorothy Mermin describes EBB's "fusion of two apparently incompatible genres" as a "generic anomaly" (*Elizabeth Barrett Browning,* 184–85). For more on the generic hybridity of *Aurora Leigh,* see Stone, "Genre Subversion." EBB herself used the phrase "a sort of novel-poem" to describe her project (*Brownings' Correspondence,* 10.102–3).

44 Of course, there have been eloquent defenses of the couplet on just these grounds. Jarvis, e.g., detects similar constellations of sound in Pope's verse ("Why Rhyme Pleases," 34–39). For more contrapuntal accounts of couplet rhyme, see Wimsatt, *Verbal Icon*; Kenner, "Pope's Reasonable Rhymes"; and Hunter, "Formalism and History."

45 The mobile pause is a striking feature of EBB's sonnets. Josie Billington connects it persuasively to Shakespearean form in particular (*Elizabeth Barrett Browning,* 59, 98–104). Medial caesuras are also apparent in the sonnets of Petrarch, Milton, Wordsworth, and others. For the role of caesuras in the blank verse of *Aurora Leigh,* see Stark, "[Keeping] Up the Fire."

46 *Brownings' Correspondence,* 7.137. EBB wrote to Horne that she loved "the beauty of the figure used to illustrate my *rhymatology*" (9.26).

47 Hallam's Continental pioneers of blank verse—Juan Boscán Almogávar, Giovanni di Bernardo Rucellai, Gian Giorgio Trissino—are probably among the "Spanish and Italian poets of prime note [who] have rejected rhyme in both shorter and longer works" referenced by Milton as models in "The Verse," 2.

48 H. Hallam, *Literature of Europe*, 1.56.

CHAPTER FIVE

1 It seems plausible to me that an inspiration for *Monna Innominata* was Arthur Hallam's review of Gabriele Rossetti's Dante study, which included a translated poem about an Unnamed Lady. Although Hallam's review was a witty and detailed refutation of Gabriele Rossetti's paranoid reading of Dante's poetry (as encoding an antipapal conspiracy), it was appreciated by Gabriele and known to the Rossetti children (see W. M. Rossetti, *Gabriele Rossetti*, 112). Embedded in a footnote of Hallam's essay was a sonnet translation he had made of a canzone by the troubadour poet Arnaud de Marveil, addressed four times to a "Lady" and declaring at the volta, "I will not name thee" (see Motter, *Writings*, 313, for the poem).

2 I am drawing here on Helsinger's perceptive discussion of C. Rossetti and rhyme. For more on the significance of an "enabling distance" in Rossetti's rhyme practice and the way "relations of rhyme correspon[d] to the distance Rossetti maintained in her personal life from potential lovers and from her poet-brother," see Helsinger, *Poetry and the Thought of Song*, 75.

3 C. Rossetti, *Goblin Market*, 267, in Buckley, *Pre-Raphaelites*. Poems from this edition are cited by line number.

4 For two illuminating readings of *Goblin Market*'s form, see Jamison, *Poetics*, 145–77 (on meter); and Chatterjee, *Feminine Singularity*, 90–123 (on simile and rhyme). For a treatment of Algernon Charles Swinburne's erotic versification and his use of "long-distance rhyming," see Jarvis, "Swinburne."

5 D. G. Rossetti, "The Blessed Damozel," 21–22, in Buckley, *Pre-Raphaelites*.

6 D. G. Rossetti, "Nuptial Sleep," 5–8, in Buckley, *Pre-Raphaelites*.

7 Buchanan, "Fleshly School," 444, 438. Relatedly, see Jerome McGann's assessment: "Rossetti's is—spectacularly—an art of the body" (*Dante Gabriel Rossetti*, 27).

8 On "intensity" as a crucial feature of Pre-Raphaelite aesthetics, see Helsinger, *Poetry and the Pre-Raphaelite Arts*.

9 Morris, "Defence," 133–38.

10 Byron, *Don Juan*, 6.59.

11 Kenner, "Pope's Reasonable Rhymes," 78.

12 Wimsatt, "One Relation of Rhyme to Reason," *Verbal Icon*, 153–66.

13 A. W. Schlegel, "For the Reinstatement of Dante," 423–24.

14 The relevant Byron poem is "Francesca of Rimini" (1830); Browning's is "The Statue and the Bust" (1850). Byron's poem was an English terza rima translation

of Francesca's monologue from *Inferno* 5, highlighting the correspondence between triangulated love and the ternary form. For more on this topic, see N. Levine, "Trebled Beauty."

15 Quoted in Mackail, *Life of William Morris*, 2.275.

16 Caroline Arscott has demonstrated that Morris's ornamental wallpaper patterns, with their "twists and turns and curves of plant forms" generate a number of Ruskinian allegories (*William Morris*, 43, 97). Elizabeth Helsinger has written extensively about the relationship between Morris's poetry and pattern designs, and she sees forms like color and rhythm as expressive in both the poems and the patterns. For Helsinger, too, the form of *The Earthly Paradise* partakes in the "delicate eroticism" that pervades the poem (*Poetry and the Pre-Raphaelite Arts*, 212).

17 Quoted in Arscott, *William Morris*, 157. For more on the relationship between Morris's poetry and his design work, see B. Morgan, 174–75.

18 Erik Gray has also remarked on the formal similarities between kissing and rhyming: "Rhyme is the formal aspect of poetry most obviously akin to a kiss: the outer edges of two separate lines of verse momentarily come together, in a gratifying touch of complementarity and fulfilment" (*Art of Love Poetry*, 88). On couplets as "kissed" (*baciata*) rhymes in early Italian poetry, see Agamben, *End of the Poem*, 115.

19 Johnson, *Major Works*, 741; emphasis mine.

20 Lane's *Thousand and One Nights* was a book that Morris owned and read aloud to his family. Eleonora Sasso writes, "Evidence of his indebtedness to the *Arabian Nights*, which to him 'was a kind of Bible,' can be found in *The Earthly Paradise* whose utopian dreamland and narrative design recall the rare combination between magic and realism, as well as the inner-frame narratives of the *Nights*" ("*Aja'ib*," 66). Sasso also discusses here the tales drawn from Arabic sources.

21 For two influential genealogies of the terms "Romantic" and "Romanticism," see Lovejoy's 1941 "Meaning of Romanticism"; and Wellek's 1949 "Concept of 'Romanticism.'" Wellek's history of the term is an open challenge to Lovejoy's claim that "Romanticism" is too equivocal to be meaningful. For two important studies of the history of romantic love, see Lewis, *Allegory of Love*; and de Rougemont, *Love in the Western World*.

22 In *The Poet's Freedom*, Susan Stewart offers a genetic explanation for the eroticism of Provençal rhyme: "At this moment [1100–1300 in Provence] the erotic and cognitive powers of art seem intensified as poets develop techniques that require inhabiting multiple perspectives and anticipated patterns. . . . Gestures of withholding and release, calculation and surprise, typify a poetics eroticized by its courtly love context, where the metaphorical and imaginative had as much power as the literally realized, and the deferred pleasures of the aesthetic held sway" (147).

23 Pater, "Poems by William Morris," 144.

24 Pater, "Postscript," 214. See also Pater's extended description of "a new music . . .

arising, the music of rhymed poetry" in the first chapter of *The Renaissance* (12). Here, Pater also remarks on the possible "Arabian origin" of the early French romance "Aucassin and Nicolette" (11).

25 Wellek describes the dichotomy of romantic and classic in Warton's *History of English Poetry* as "implied," whereas it is more explicit (if less significant) in Warton's discussion of Dante: "Here the two famous words meet, possibly for the first time, but Warton probably meant little more than that Dante used both classical mythology and chivalric *motifs*" ("Concept of 'Romanticism,'" 4). Lynch, *Loving Literature*, especially chap. 2, also treats Warton's periodization of poetic history. Pascale Casanova argues that Herder was the source of the dichotomy: "the very concept of 'romantic,' in the sense of 'modern'—by contrast with that of 'classic' and 'ancient'—has its origin in Herder's thought, which supplied the basis for the Germans' claim to modernity in their struggle against French cultural hegemony" (*World Republic*, 77).

26 Warton, *History of English Poetry*, 1.i.

27 Warton's theory of romance wasn't uncontested. In addition to Henry Hallam (whose position I discussed in the previous chapter), Warton found a vociferous critic in the antiquarian Joseph Ritson. Where Warton saw disjuncture between classical and medieval European literature, Ritson saw parallel and continuity. For more on the Warton-Ritson dispute, see Lynch, *Loving Literature*, 83.

28 As I suggested above, Pater reformulated de Staël's "classic" and "romantic" into two transhistorical "tendencies" or "tempers" in art that might equally apply to the literature of antiquity and the medieval or modern age (Pater, "Postscript," 209–13).

29 Hegel, *Aesthetics*, 562, 563–64.

30 Hegel, *Aesthetics*, 1025, 1030. See Armstrong on Hegel's erotics of rhyme—and for a comparison between Knox's translation and that of F. P. B. Omaston, who describes the ear as "coquetted with" ("Hegel," 133). See also Jarvis: "Since its origins are *necessary*, rather than external, we may view rhyme, even, as one aspect of the conditions of possibility of that interiority—and this because, as becomes clear, it can in a certain sense be said that the *subject* rhymes" ("Musical Thinking," 63). See chap. 2 for a fuller discussion of both Hegel's versification theory and Jarvis's and Armstrong's responses to it.

31 Keats, "Isabella," 69–72.

32 Pater discusses this scene in the "Winckelmann" chapter of *The Renaissance*: "Goethe illustrates that union of the Romantic spirit, its adventure, its variety, its deep subjectivity, with Hellenism, its transparency, its rationality, its desire of beauty—that marriage of Faust and Helena, of which the art of the nineteenth century is the child" (114). Vernon Lee's 1884 book *Euphorion* borrows its title from Faust and Helena's child, who personifies for her the Renaissance. Goethe's interest in the historical relationship between love and rhyme shaped another of his poems, included in *The West-Eastern Divan*, which is drawn from Persian tradition. The poem begins, "King Behramgur, they say, invented rhyme. . . ." (Goethe, *Selected Poetry*, 169).

33 B. Taylor, *Faust*, x.

34 Goethe, *Faust*, 9368–71.

35 Goethe, 9372–76.

36 Goethe, 9377–84.

37 Tucker, *Epic*, 434.

38 Morris, "The Land East of the Sun and West of the Moon," 846–48, in *Earthly Paradise*; in what follows, individual tales are cited parenthetically by line number.

39 Boos, "Introduction," 14. J. W. Mackail named the problem in his early study of Morris: "It is . . . one of the commonest criticisms made on the Greek stories in 'The Earthly Paradise,' that the atmosphere and treatment are not Greek but medieval; that the feelings, incidents, and decoration are neither those of classical poetry, nor yet of the stories of ancient Greece as interpreted and modernized by the taste of the present day" (*Life*, 1.180).

40 Pater, "Poems by William Morris," 146.

41 On Pater's aesthetic uses of history, see Williams, *Transfigured World*; and "Walter Pater's Impressionism."

42 See definition 3 in the *Oxford English Dictionary*, current in the nineteenth century: "Specifically applied to the period of history before the fall of the Western Roman Empire. In this sense contrasted with *modern*, and *medieval*."

43 My discussion here is informed by Maria DiBattista's theorization of first love in the modern novel; see *First Love*.

44 Richards, *Principles*, 119. For an equally suggestive nineteenth-century theory about the way pronunciation happens in the mouth, see Jamison's discussion of Edwin Guest's 1838 *History of English Meter*, in the context of her chapter on Christina Rossetti's erotic metrics (*Poetics*, 153–54).

45 Buchanan, "Fleshly School," 444.

46 Quoted in Wellek and Warren, *Theory of Literature*, 162.

CHAPTER SIX

1 Patmore, "The Toys," 3, 14–21, in *Unknown Eros*.

2 Patmore, 26, 27.

3 Patmore, 6.

4 See Woolf, "Professions"; and Gilbert and Gubar, *Madwoman*.

5 The current editions of *The Norton Anthology of English Literature: The Victorian Age* (10th ed.) and *The Broadview Anthology of Victorian Literature: The Victorian Era* (3rd ed.) follow this pattern. Both place Patmore alongside the conduct manuals of Sarah Stickney Ellis.

6 See Pinch, "Love Thinking"; Markovits, *Victorian Verse-Novel*; and Gray, *Art of Love Poetry*.

7 Patmore the prosodist features in essays by Jason Hall, Isobel Armstrong, Yisrael

Levin, Meredith Martin, Yopie Prins, and Jason Rudy in the collection *Meter Matters*, ed. Hall. See also, more recently, Jones, "Coventry Patmore's Corpus."

8 Pinch, "Love Thinking," 391.

9 For suggestive discussions of rhyming and ending, see Agamben, *End of the Poem*; and Pinch, "Rhyme's End."

10 Patmore, "Essay on English Metrical Law," 15; cited parenthetically as "Metrical Law" in what follows.

11 Prins, "Patmore's Law," 262.

12 Attridge, *Rhythms*, 90.

13 Patmore, "To the Unknown Eros," 8, 30, in *Unknown Eros*; in what follows, individual poems are cited parenthetically by line number.

14 Patmore's theory of isochrony is of course much more complicated than my simple syllabic notation suggests. He would consider a sixteen-syllable line to be made up of four "dipodic" sections of four syllables each, where each section has a stronger and weaker "iambic foot." The sixteen-voiced-syllables line referenced above would sound like this (assuming "feathering" is elided, as I think he means it to be): Through-**DEL**-i-**CA** | test-**E**-ther-**FEA** | th'ring **SOFT** their **SOL** | . . .

15 Omond, *English Metrists*; quoted in Roth, 84.

16 Patmore, "Francis Thompson," 163, 161–62.

17 Champneys, *Memoirs*, 1.112.

18 See King, "Patmore," for a discussion of Patmore's and Tennyson's disagreement over this poem and its emotive effects.

19 While at first Patmore presents alliteration and rhyme as categorically different, by the end of the essay he describes alliteration as "a sort of rhyme" ("Metrical Law," 47).

20 Patmore, "Preface," v–vi.

21 On the interplay of presence and absence in Patmore's pauses (and Alice Meynell's reading of those pauses), see Prins, "Patmore's Law." See J. C. Reid, *Mind and Art*, for an observation similar to mine about the way rhyme, in his words, "serves to attenuate the pause" (278).

22 See Armstrong, "Meter and Meaning," 33.

23 See, e.g., Rudy, *Electric Meters*, 114.

24 Robert Shafer writes that "the ode is always an address" (*English Ode*, 3), while George Shuster explains that "the element of address is of no especial significance, being merely a reflection of the classical influence." For Shuster, an ode is "a lyric poem derived, either directly or indirectly, from Pindaric models" (quoted in Jump, *The Ode*, 3). John Jump adheres to the same criteria, organizing his study of the genre around the legacies of Pindar and Horace.

25 Gosse, *Patmore*, 128. This wasn't a preposterous suggestion. Like Dante's and Petrarch's canzoni, Patmore's odes are erotic, elegiac, and religious; and like theirs, they use intricate interlacings of rhyme. Patmore was very familiar with both of these poets' work and had identified or been identified at various points in his

life with each. A sonnet he wrote in the early forties begins in Dantean fashion, "At nine years old I was Love's willing Page: / Poets love earlier than other men" (quoted in Gosse, *Patmore*, 19–20); and shortly before Patmore began working on *The Unknown Eros*, he had read the manuscript of Dante Gabriel Rossetti's *Early Italian Poets*, which included a translation of Dante's *Vita nuova* (full of commentary on the canzone) as well as translations of many diverse canzoni by poets in Dante's extended circle. Around the same time, Patmore was termed "the English Petrarch" in a review in *Fraser's Magazine*.

26 Gosse, *English Odes*, xxi.

27 In 1933, Frederick Page also suggested that Patmore's so-called odes might actually be modeled on the Italian *canzone*, derived through Milton and Spenser from Dante (*Patmore*, 150). Reid later found a way to reconcile what seemed to be Patmore's classical ambitions with the Italian lineage that Gosse and Page identified. Drawing on studies of Milton's prosody, he pointed to a form called the "liberated canzone," a later Italian Renaissance development that more directly influenced Milton and Spenser than Dante had (*Mind and Art*, 272–75). This form was less rigorously stanzaic than the medieval canzone and therefore closer to the shape of Patmore's long and irregular single-stanza poems.

28 Fogle and Fry, "Ode."

29 See Gosse, "Ode."

30 Champneys, *Memoirs*, 2.252–53.

31 Gosse, *English Odes*, xiii. Gosse did soften his position on Spenser for the encyclopedia. Gosse also had a fascinating role in the definition of the villanelle as a fixed form. See French, "Edmund Gosse."

32 Gosse, *English Odes*, x–xii.

33 Gosse excludes "the elegy, or funeral ode" from his canon (xiii). This is an obvious divergence from Patmore's position, considering the elegiac tone of so many poems in *The Unknown Eros*.

34 Gosse, *English Odes*, xvii.

35 Gosse, xx.

36 Gosse, xxi.

37 On Patmore's own objections to spasmodic poetry and on the relationship between spasmodic style and *The Angel in the House*, see Rudy, "Cultural Neoformalism." For more on the characteristics of the spasmodic "school," see LaPorte and Rudy, "Editorial Introduction."

38 Gosse, "Plea," 54–56.

39 Cowley, "Preface," 155–56.

40 Gosse, "Greece and England," 1.1–7, in *New Poems*.

41 Gosse, 4.1–7.

42 "Mr. Gosse's New Poems," 240.

43 Champneys, *Memoirs*, 1.252, 258.

44 One unusually ugly poem from *The Unknown Eros*, "1867," protests Benjamin Disraeli's expansion of the franchise in harshly nationalist, antidemocratic, and antisemitic terms. Here, Patmore identifies himself with the mythic past (and

poetry) of a better, more Christian England: "In the year of the great crime, / When the false English Nobles and their Jew, / By God demented, slew / The Trust they stood twice pledged to keep from wrong, / One said, Take up thy Song, / That breathes the mild and almost mythic time / Of England's prime!" (1–7). The "passion" that organizes the prosody of this ode is evidently self-righteous rage rather than sorrow.

45 Patmore, "*In Memoriam*," 532, 543,532, 545.

46 Patmore sees this history as falling into three periods, shaped by greater and lesser degrees of metrical inventiveness. In the first period, "rhymed stanzas seem to have been constructed upon distinct and easily discoverable principles." The second "was characterized by an extreme barrenness in the invention of new metres." The third, he says, "is, as yet, young; but its youth is very promising" ("*In Memoriam*," 535).

47 Patmore, 541, 542.

48 Patmore, 545. Just as important to Patmore as Hegel's observations on the difference between ancient and modern versification were his ideas on "the nature of the relation between the poet's peculiar mode of expression and the matter expressed." Quoting Hegel, Patmore writes, "It is false . . . that versification offers any obstacle to the free outpouring of poetic thought. True genius disposes with ease of sensible materials, and moves therein as in a native element, which instead of depressing or hindering, exalts and supports its flight" ("Metrical Law," 7).

49 The requirement of a "motive power of passionate thought" for meter resembles Emerson's "meter-making argument" in "The Poet" (1844). Patmore's debts to Emerson are well documented. See Reid, *Mind and Art*, for more.

50 See Jones, *Poetical Works*, vol. 2. On Jones's deliberate revision of "the bases of the neo-classic theory of poetry" in this collection, see Abrams, *Mirror*, 84–88. See also Mufti on Jones's influential theorization of feeling in the poetry of "the Eastern nations" in the essays that accompanied the translations (67–69).

51 Nott, *Petrarch*, ix. See Fiske, *Catalogue*, 40–43, for a list of early Petrarch translations in English.

52 Foscolo, *Essays on Petrarch*, 92.

53 Foscolo, 308. Foscolo also includes odes by Sappho and Anacreon alongside Petrarch's poems in an appendix at the back of the book.

54 Charlemont, *Select Sonnets*, xiv.

55 Sismondi, *Historical View*, 1.61.

56 Sismondi, 1.436–37.

57 Jones is nonetheless one of Sismondi's key sources, especially in his chapters on Arabic poetry (see chap. 2).

58 Hegel, *Aesthetics*, 1141, 1142, 1146, 1147.

59 Hegel mentions Herder's anthropological contribution to the study of folksongs in the lyric poetry section of the *Aesthetics*, saying that he "did a great deal in this direction," along with Goethe (1124). For more on Herder's formative influence on Hegel's thought, see Forster, "Introduction."

60 Herder, *Selected Early Works*, 36; cited parenthetically in what follows.

61 See the editorial gloss of Menze and Menges, *Selected Early Works,* 264.

62 This problem resonates with Sismondi's and Arthur Hallam's literary-historical binary of sensation and reflection.

63 Pound, *Spirit of Romance,* 14.

64 Meynell, "Coventry Patmore," 128. Elsewhere, Meynell writes of the defamiliarizing effect of Patmore's diction, "Often the word has a fullness of significance that gives the reader a shock of appreciation" ("Mr. Coventry Patmore's Odes," 93–94). My sense of the elegiac shock accords with this appraisal of Patmore's style.

65 John Maynard describes this real-time reading experience as "deregulating and physical" (*Victorian Discourses,* 221).

66 Patmore, "Francis Thompson," 161.

67 Patmore, "*In Memoriam,*" 545.

68 Meynell, "Mr. Coventry Patmore's Odes," 95.

69 For an altogether different scansion of the same lines, see Pierson, "Coventry Patmore's Ideas," 510.

70 Actually, Patmore thinks that Tennyson's form is not really stanzaic: "The divisions are scarcely to be regarded as stanzas, for the beauty of the measure mainly depends upon its adaptation to lengthy phrases. A stanza ought to contain a completed phrase: stanzas of any but the shortest lengths should terminate in a full stop . . . this metre has the continuity of Dante's *terza rima*" ("*In Memoriam,*" 546).

71 Patmore, "*In Memoriam,*" 547.

72 Patmore's ode form is frequently cited as a precursor to free verse. See, e.g., Kirby-Smith, *Origins*; and Phelan, *Music of Verse.*

73 Champneys, *Memoirs,* 1.258.

CONCLUSION

1 I am inspired by Eve Kosofsky Sedgwick and Adam Frank's argument for returning attentively to the intellectual work of the past (in their case, the affect psychology of Silvan Tomkins): "The moralistic hygiene by which any reader of today is unchallengeably entitled to condescend to the thought of any moment in the past (maybe *especially* the recent past) is globally available to anyone who masters the application of two or three discrediting questions. How provisional, by contrast, how difficult to reconstruct and how exorbitantly specialized of use, are the tools that in any given case would allow one to ask: What was it possible to think or do at a certain moment of the past that no longer is? And how are those possibilities to be found, unfolded, allowed to move and draw air and seek new voices and uses, in the very different disciplinary ecology of even a few decades distance?" (*Touching,* 117–18).

2 Eliot, "Reflections," 519.

3 For a study of the significance of rhyme for twentieth-century poetry, see Wesling, *Chances*.

4 I can't help observing that the modernist story about Victorian rhyme had a genetic logic of its own. The modernists assigned rhyme a new origin—Victorian poetry—and that origin began to condition its meaning. As one partisan of free verse wrote in 1924, "Rhymed verse requires a setting: tea-cups, a darkened room, soft music, and soft hearts. A limitation not easily provided for in these days when man does not wear his greatness in the shape of lace ruffles on a velvet sleeve, but lifts a steel and concrete arm in salute to the watchful heavens" (quoted in Swett, "Free Verse," 129).

5 A. Hallam, *Writings*, 222.

6 See, e.g., Monroe, "Free-Verse"; Swett, "Free Verse"; and Hartman, *Free Verse*.

7 Martin, *Rise and Fall of Meter*; Glaser, *Modernism's Metronome*. See also Kappeler, "Free Verse." See Christ, *Victorian and Modern Poetics*, for a broader treatment of modernism's reception of Victorian poetry and poetic theory.

8 Any account of Pound's and Eliot's anti-Victorianism is bound to be complicated by their utter ambivalence (evident in Pound's debts to D. G. Rossetti and Robert Browning; Eliot's appreciation of Tennyson). But Pound and Eliot remain two of Victorian poetry's most influential detractors. See, e.g., Eliot, "The Metaphysical Poets"; and Pound, "A Retrospect."

9 Pound had been working toward a graduate degree in Romance Languages at the University of Pennsylvania, and he acknowledges in a 1968 "post-postscript" that he based his book on notes he took in the seminars of Hugo Rennert. For more on Pound's study of Romance languages and literatures, see Nadel, *Ezra Pound*, 44–46. On Pound's engagement with nineteenth-century historicism, see Gibson, *Epic Reinvented*.

10 Pound, *Spirit of Romance*, 5; cited parenthetically in what follows.

11 Pound's postscript from 1929 characterizes *The Spirit of Romance* as predominantly historical work: "A good deal of what immediately follows can not be taken as criticism, but simply as information for those wanting a shortish account of the period. The mode of the statement, its idiom or jargon, will have to stand as partial confession of where I was in the year 1910" (8).

12 Brooks, *Well Wrought Urn*, 76.

Bibliography

Ablow, Rachel. Introduction to *The Feeling of Reading: Affective Experience and Victorian Literature*, ed. Rachel Ablow, 1–10. Ann Arbor: University of Michigan Press, 2013.

Abrams, M. H. *The Mirror and the Lamp: Romantic Theory and the Critical Tradition*. New York: Norton, 1958.

Abrams, M. H., and Geoffrey Harpham. *A Glossary of Literary Terms*. Stamford, CT: Cengage, 2014.

Addison, Joseph. *The Works of the Right Honourable Joseph Addison*. Vol. 2. Ed. Richard Hurd. 6 vols. London: Cadell and Davis, 1811.

Agamben, Giorgio. *The End of the Poem: Studies in Poetics*. Stanford, CA: Stanford University Press, 1999.

Agathocleous, Tanya, and Jason Rudy, eds. Introduction to "Victorian Cosmopolitanisms." Special issue, *Victorian Literature and Culture* 38, no. 2 (2010): 389–97.

Anger, Suzy. "Introduction: Knowing the Victorians." In *Knowing the Past*, ed. Suzy Anger, 1–22. Ithaca, NY: Cornell University Press, 2001.

Anglade, Joseph. Introduction to *Les vies des plus célèbres et anciens poètes provençaux* by Jehan de Nostredame. Edited by Camille Chabaneau. Paris: Honoré Champion, 1913.

Apter, Emily. *Against World Literature: On the Politics of Untranslatability*. London: Verso, 2013.

Arata, Stephen. "Rhyme, Rhythm, and the Materiality of Poetry." *Victorian Studies* 53, no. 3 (Spring 2011): 518–26.

Armstrong, Isobel. "Hegel: The Time of Rhythm, the Time of Rhyme." *Thinking Verse* 1 (2011): 124–36.

———. "Meter and Meaning." In Hall, *Meter Matters*, 26–52.

———. *Victorian Poetry: Poetry, Poetics and Politics*. London: Routledge, 1993.

Arscott, Caroline. *William Morris and Edward Burne-Jones: Interlacings*. New Haven, CT: Yale University Press, 2008.

Attridge, Derek. *The Rhythms of English Poetry*. London: Longman, 1982.

Auerbach, Erich. *Mimesis: The Representation of Reality in Western Literature.* Princeton, NJ: Princeton University Press, 1953.

———. *Time, History, and Literature: Selected Essays of Erich Auerbach.* Edited by James I. Porter. Princeton, NJ: Princeton University Press, 2014.

"Aurora Leigh." Unsigned review of *Aurora Leigh*, by Elizabeth Barrett Browning. *United States Magazine* 4 (1857): 182–87.

Barrett Browning, Elizabeth. *Aurora Leigh.* Edited by Margaret Reynolds. New York: Norton, 1996.

———. *The Works of Elizabeth Barrett Browning.* Edited by Sandra Donaldson, Rita Patteson, Marjorie Stone, Beverly Taylor, Simon Avery, Cynthia Burgess, Clare Drummond, and Barbara Neri. 5 vols. London: Pickering and Chatto, 2010.

Barton, Anna. *Tennyson's Name: Identity and Responsibility in the Poetry of Alfred Lord Tennyson.* Burlington, VT: Ashgate, 2008.

Beardsley, Monroe. *Aesthetics: Problems in the Philosophy of Criticism.* New York: Harcourt Brace, 1958.

Best, Stephen, and Sharon Marcus. "Surface Reading: An Introduction." *Representations* 108, no. 1 (Fall 2009): 1–21.

Billington, Josie. *Elizabeth Barrett Browning and Shakespeare: "This Is Living Art."* London: Bloomsbury, 2012.

Blair, Hugh. *Lectures on Rhetoric and Belles Lettres.* Edited by Linda Ferreira-Buckley and S. Michael Halloran. Carbondale: Southern Illinois University Press, 2005.

Blair, Kirstie. *Victorian Poetry and the Culture of the Heart.* Oxford: Oxford University Press, 2006.

Blocksidge, Martin. *"A Life Lived Quickly": Tennyson's Friend Arthur Hallam and His Legend.* Sussex: Sussex Academic Press, 2011.

Bloom, Harold. *The Anxiety of Influence: A Theory of Poetry.* Oxford: Oxford University Press, 1973.

Boase, Roger. *The Origin and Meaning of Courtly Love.* Manchester: Manchester University Press, 1977.

Boos, Florence. Introduction to *The Earthly Paradise.* Vol. 1, 3–41. New York: Routledge, 2002.

Brinkema, Eugenie. *The Forms of the Affects.* Durham, NC: Duke University Press, 2014.

Brogan, T. V. F. "Leonine Rhyme, Verse." Greene et al., *Princeton Encyclopedia.*

Brogan, T. V. F., S. Cushman, K. S. Chang, R. M. A. Allen, W. L. Hanaway, and C. Scott. "Rhyme." Greene et al., *Princeton Encyclopedia.*

Brogan, T. V. F., and E. J. Rettberg. "Identical Rhyme." Greene et al., *Princeton Encyclopedia.*

Brooks, Cleanth. *Modern Poetry and the Tradition.* Chapel Hill: University of North Carolina Press, 1939.

———. "My Credo: The Formalist Critics." *Kenyon Review* 13, no. 1 (Winter 1951): 72–81.

———. *The Well Wrought Urn: Studies in the Structure of Poetry*. New York: Harcourt, Brace, 1947.

Brooks, Cleanth, and Robert Penn Warren. *Understanding Poetry: An Anthology for College Students*. New York: Holt, 1938.

Brooks, Cleanth, and W. K. Wimsatt. *Literary Criticism: A Short History*. London: Routledge and Kegan Paul, 1957.

Brownings' Correspondence. Edited by Philip Kelley, Ronald Hudson, Scott Lewis, Edward Hagan, et al., 29 vols. to date. Winfield, KS: Wedgestone Press, 1984–.

Buchanan, Robert. "The Fleshly School of Poetry." In *The Pre-Raphaelites*, edited by Jerome H. Buckley, 437–60. Chicago: Academy Chicago, 1986.

Buckley, Jerome H., ed. *The Pre-Raphaelites*. Chicago: Academy Chicago, 1986.

Bullen, J. B. "Ruskin and the Tradition of Renaissance Historiography." In *The Lamp of Memory: Ruskin, Tradition, and Architecture*, ed. Michael Wheeler and Nigel Whiteley, 54–76. Manchester: Manchester University Press, 1992.

Buurma, Rachel Sagner, and Laura Heffernan. *The Teaching Archive: A New History for Literary Study*. Chicago: University of Chicago Press, 2021.

Byron, Lord (George Gordon). *Don Juan: Cantos 6–8*. London: Hunt, 1823.

Campion, Thomas. *Songs and Masques, with Observations in the Art of English Poesy*. London: A. H. Bullen, 1903.

Carlyle, Thomas. *On Heroes, Hero-Worship and the Heroic in History*. Lincoln: University of Nebraska Press, 1966.

Casanova, Pascale. *The World Republic of Letters*. Translated by M. B. DeBevoise. Cambridge, MA: Harvard University Press, 2004.

Chakrabarty, Dipesh. *Provincializing Europe: Postcolonial Thought and Historical Difference*. Princeton, NJ: Princeton University Press, 2008.

Champneys, Basil. *Memoirs and Correspondence of Coventry Patmore*. 2 vols. London: George Bell and Sons, 1900.

Charlemont, James, late Earl of [James Caulfeild]. *Select Sonnets of Petrarch*. Dublin: William Folds and Son, 1822.

Chatterjee, Ronjaunee. *Feminine Singularity: The Politics of Subjectivity in Nineteenth-Century Literature*. Stanford, CA: Stanford University Press, 2022.

Chatterjee, Ronjaunee, Alicia Mireles Christoff, and Amy R. Wong. "Introduction: Undisciplining Victorian Studies." *Victorian Studies* 62, no. 3 (Spring 2020): 369–91.

Christ, Carol. *Victorian and Modern Poetics*. Chicago: University of Chicago Press, 1986.

Christoff, Alicia Mireles. *Novel Relations: Victorian Fiction and British Psychoanalysis*. Princeton, NJ: Princeton University Press, 2019.

Cignatta, Maria Cristina. "William Hazlitt and Dante as the Embodiment of 'Power, Passion, Self-Will.'" In *British Romanticism and Italian Literature: Translating, Reviewing, Rewriting*, ed. Laura Bandiera and Diego Saglia, 69–79. Amsterdam: Rodopi, 2005.

Clark, Peter. *Henry Hallam*. New York: Twayne, 1982.

Cohen, Morris R. *Reason and Nature: An Essay on the Meaning of Scientific Method*. New York: Routledge, 2020.

Cohen, Ralph. *Genre Theory and Historical Change: Theoretical Essays of Ralph Cohen*. Edited by John L. Rowlett. Charlottesville: University of Virginia Press, 2017.

Coleridge, S. T. *The Collected Works of Samuel Taylor Coleridge*. Edited by R. A. Foakes. Vol. 5. Princeton, NJ: Princeton University Press, 1987.

———. *Notebooks of Samuel Taylor Coleridge*. Edited by Kathleen Coburn. 5 vols. Princeton, NJ: Princeton University Press, 1957–2002.

———. *Specimens of the Table Talk of the Late Samuel Taylor Coleridge*. Vol. 1. New York: Harper and Brothers, 1835.

Conner, Patrick. *Savage Ruskin*. London: Palgrave Macmillan, 1979.

Corrigan, Beatrice, ed. *Italian Poets and English Critics, 1755–1859*. Chicago: University of Chicago Press, 1969.

Cowley, Abraham. Preface to *Poems*. Edited by A. R. Waller. Cambridge: Cambridge University Press, 1905.

Crawford, Lucas. "Woolf's *Einfühlung*: An Alternative Theory of Transgender Affect." *Mosaic* 48, no. 1 (March 2015): 165–81.

Crouch, Margaret. "A 'Limited' Defense of the Genetic Fallacy." *Metaphilosophy* 24, no. 3 (1993): 227–40.

Curran, Stuart. *Poetic Form and British Romanticism*. Oxford: Oxford University Press, 1986.

Curtius, Ernst Robert. *European Literature and the Latin Middle Ages*. Princeton, NJ: Princeton University Press, 1973.

Dainotto, Roberto. "The Discreet Charm of the Arabist Theory: Juan Andrés, Historicism, and the De-Centering of Montesquieu's Europe." *European History Quarterly* 36, no. 1 (January 2006): 7–29.

———. *Europe (in Theory)*. Durham, NC: Duke University Press, 2007.

———. "Of the Arab Origin of Modern Europe: Giammaria Barbieri, Juan Andrés, and the Origin of Rhyme." *Comparative Literature* 58, no. 4 (Fall 2006): 271–92.

Dames, Nicholas. *The Physiology of the Novel: Reading, Neural Science, and the Form of Victorian Fiction*. Oxford: University of Oxford Press, 2007.

Damrosch, David. *What Is World Literature?* Princeton, NJ: Princeton University Press, 2003.

Dante. *Dante's Vita Nuova*. Edited and translated by Mark Musa. Bloomington: Indiana University Press, 1973.

———. *De Vulgari Eloquentia: Dante's Book of Exile*. Edited and translated by Marianne Shapiro. Lincoln: University of Nebraska Press, 1990.

De Man, Paul. "Genesis and Genealogy (Nietzsche)." In *Allegories of Reading: Figural Language in Rousseau, Nietzsche, Rilke, and Proust*, 79–102. New Haven, CT: Yale University Press, 1979.

De Rougemont, Denis. *Love in the Western World*. Translated by Montgomery Belgion. Princeton, NJ: Princeton University Press, 1983.

de Staël, Germaine. *Germany*. Vol. 1. New York: H. W. Derby, 1861.

D'haen, Theo, César Domínguez, and Mads Rosendahl Thomsen, eds. *World Literature: A Reader*. New York: Routledge, 2013.

DiBattista, Maria. *First Love: The Affections of Modern Fiction*. Chicago: University of Chicago Press, 1991.

Dillon, Steven C. "Canonical and Sensational: Arthur Hallam and Tennyson's 1830 *Poems*." *Victorian Poetry* 30, no. 2 (Summer 1992): 95–108.

Disraeli, Isaac. *Amenities of Literature: Consisting of Sketches and Characters of English Literature*. London: Frederick Warne, 1968.

Dobson, Susanna. *Life of Petrarch*. 2 vols. London: James Buckland, 1775.

Donaldson, Sandra. Editor's notes to vols. 3 and 4, Barrett Browning, *Works of Elizabeth Barrett Browning*, 2010.

Douglas-Fairhurst, Robert. Introduction to *Tennyson Among the Poets: Bicentenary Essays*, ed. Robert Douglas-Fairhurst and Seamus Perry, 1–13. Oxford: Oxford University Press, 2009.

———. *Victorian Afterlives: The Shaping of Influence in Nineteenth-Century Literature*. Oxford: Oxford University Press, 2002.

Drury, Annmarie. *Translation as Transformation in Victorian Poetry*. Cambridge: Cambridge University Press, 2015.

Dubrow, Heather. *A Happier Eden: The Politics of Marriage in the Stuart Epithalamium*. Ithaca, NY: Cornell University Press, 1990.

Eccles, Anastasia. "Formalism and Sentimentalism: Viktor Shklovsky and Laurence Sterne." *New Literary History* 47, no. 4 (2016): 525–45.

Eichenbaum, Boris. "The Theory of the 'Formal Method.'" In *Russian Formalist Criticism: Four Essays*, ed. and trans. Lee T. Lemon and Marion J. Reis, 99–140. Lincoln: University of Nebraska, 1965.

Eliot, T. S. "In Memoriam." In *Critical Essays on the Poetry of Tennyson*, ed. John Killham, 207–15. New York: Barnes and Noble, 1960.

———. "The Metaphysical Poets." In *Selected Essays*, 281–91. London: Faber and Faber, 1951.

———. "Reflections on Vers Libre." *New Statesman* (1917): 518–19.

Erlich, Victor. *Russian Formalism: History—Doctrine*. The Hague: Mouton, 1980.

Frank, Adam, and Eve Kosofsky Sedgwick. "Shame in the Cybernetic Fold: Reading Silvan Tomkins." In *Touching Feeling: Affect, Pedagogy, Performativity*. Durham, NC: Duke University Press, 2003. 93–121.

Felski, Rita. *The Limits of Critique*. Chicago: University of Chicago Press, 2015.

Fiske, Willard. *A Catalogue of Petrarch Books*. Ithaca: University Press of Ithaca, New York, 1882.

Fogle, S. F., and P. H. Fry. "Ode." Greene et al., *Princeton Encyclopedia.*

Forster, Michael, ed. Introduction to *Philosophical Writings,* by Johann Gottfried Herder. Cambridge: Cambridge University Press, 2002.

Foscolo, Ugo. *Essays on Petrarch.* London: John Murray, 1823.

Foucault, Michel. "Nietzsche, Genealogy, History." In *Language, Counter-Memory, Practice,* ed. D. F. Bouchard, 139–64. Ithaca, NY: Cornell University Press, 1977.

Fowler, Alastair. "The Life and Death of Literary Forms." *New Literary History* 2, no. 2 (1971): 199–216.

Freiwald, Bina. "The World of Books Is Still the World: EBB's Critical Prose." *Newsletter of the Victorian Studies Association of Western Canada* 12 (1986): 1–24.

French, Amanda. "Edmund Gosse and the Stubborn Villanelle Blunder." *Victorian Poetry* 48, no. 2 (Summer 2010): 243–66.

Fried, Debra. "Rhyme Puns." In *On Puns: The Foundation of Letters,* ed. Jonathan Culler, 83–99. Oxford: Blackwell, 1988.

Friedman, Dustin. *Before Queer Theory: Victorian Aestheticism and the Self.* Baltimore: Johns Hopkins University Press, 2019.

Gallop, Jane. "The Historicization of Literary Studies and the Fate of Close Reading." *Profession* (2007): 181–86.

Garnett, Richard. Supplementary Notes to Warton, *History of English Poetry,* vol. 1. 1840.

Gibson, Mary Ellis. *Epic Reinvented: Ezra Pound and the Victorians.* Ithaca, NY: Cornell University Press, 1995.

———. *History and the Prism of Art: Browning's Poetic Experiments.* Columbus: Ohio State University Press, 1987.

———. *Indian Angles: English Verse in Colonial India from Jones to Tagore.* Athens: Ohio University Press, 2011.

Gigante, Denise. "Forming Desire: On the Eponymous *In Memoriam* Stanza." *Nineteenth-Century Literature* 53, no. 4 (March 1999): 480–504.

Gilbert, Sandra, and Susan Gubar. *The Madwoman in the Attic: The Woman Writer in the Nineteenth-Century Literary Imagination.* New Haven, CT: Yale University Press, 1984.

Glaser, Ben. *Modernism's Metronome: Meter and Twentieth-Century Poetics.* Baltimore: Johns Hopkins University Press, 2020.

Goethe, J. W. *Faust: Parts 1 and 2.* Translated by Bayard Taylor. London: Sphere Books, 1969.

———. *Selected Poetry.* Translated by David Luke. London: Penguin, 2005.

Gosse, Edmund. *Coventry Patmore.* London: Hodder and Stoughton, 1905.

———, ed. *English Odes.* London: Kegan Paul, 1881.

———. *New Poems.* London: Kegan Paul, 1879.

———. "Ode." *Encyclopedia Britannica.* General editor Hugh Chisholm, 1911.

———. "A Plea for Certain Exotic Forms of Verse." *Cornhill Magazine* 36 (July 1877): 53–71.

Graff, Gerald. *Professing Literature: An Institutional History*. Chicago: University of Chicago Press, 1987.

Gray, Erik. *The Art of Love Poetry*. Oxford: Oxford University Press, 2018.

———, ed. Introduction to *In Memoriam*. New York: Norton, 2004.

———. *Milton and the Victorians*. Ithaca, NY: Cornell University Press, 2009.

Greene, Roland, Stephen Cushman, Clare Cavanagh, Jahan Ramazani, Paul Rouzer, et al., eds. *The Princeton Encyclopedia of Poetry and Poetics*. Princeton, NJ: Princeton University Press, 2012.

Gregg, Melissa, and Gregory J. Seigworth. "An Inventory of Shimmers." In *The Affect Theory Reader*, ed. Gregg and Seigworth, 1–25. Durham, NC: Duke University Press, 2010.

Griffin, Robert J. *Wordsworth's Pope: A Study in Literary Historiography*. Cambridge: Cambridge University Press, 1995.

Griffiths, Eric. "Tennyson's Idle Tears." In *Tennyson: Seven Essays*, ed. Philip Collins, 36–60. London: Macmillan, 1992.

Haddad, Emily A. *Orientalist Poetics: The Islamic Middle East in Nineteenth-Century English and French Poetry*. Aldershot, VT: Ashgate, 2002.

Hair, Donald S. *Fresh Strange Music: Elizabeth Barrett Browning's Language*. Montreal: McGill-Queen's University Press, 2015.

Hall, Jason David, ed. *Meter Matters: Verse Cultures of the Long Nineteenth Century*. Athens: Ohio University Press, 2011.

Hallam, Arthur Henry. *The Letters of Arthur Hallam*. Edited by Jack Kolb. Columbus: Ohio State University Press, 1981.

———. *The Writings of Arthur Hallam*. Edited by T. H. Vail Motter. New York: Modern Language Association of America, 1943.

Hallam, Henry. *Introduction to the Literature of Europe in the Fifteenth, Sixteenth, and Seventeenth Centuries*. 4 vols. London: John Murray, 1837–39.

———, ed. Preface to *Remains in Verse and Prose of Arthur Henry Hallam*. London: John Murray, 1863.

———. *View of the State of Europe during the Middle Ages*. Vol. 3. London: John Murray, 1826.

"Hallam's *Literature of Europe*." Review of *Introduction to the Literature of Europe*, by Henry Hallam. *New York Review* 11 (1840): 1–47.

"Hallam's *Literature of Europe*." Review of *Introduction to the Literature of Europe*, by Henry Hallam. *London Quarterly Review* 65 (1840): 185–209.

Hansen, Michael. "Arthur Hallam's 'Characteristics' and Pleasure's Moral Sense." *Modern Philology* 114, no. 4 (2017): 899–921.

Hartman, Charles O. *Free Verse: An Essay on Prosody*. Princeton, NJ: Princeton University Press, 1980.

Hayter, Alethea. "Experiments in Poetic Technique." In *Critical Essays on Elizabeth Barrett Browning*, ed. Sandra Donaldson, 15–31. New York: G. K. Hall, 1999.

Heath-Stubbs, John. *The Ode*. Oxford: Oxford University Press, 1969.

Hegel, G. W. F. *Aesthetics: Lectures on Fine Art*. Translated by T. M. Knox. 2 vols. Oxford: Clarendon Press, 1975.

Helsinger, Elizabeth K. *Poetry and the Pre-Raphaelite Arts: Dante Gabriel Rossetti and William Morris*. New Haven, CT: Yale University Press, 2008.

———. *Poetry and the Thought of Song in Nineteenth-Century Britain*. Charlottesville: University of Virginia Press, 2015.

Herder, Johann Gottfried. *Philosophical Writings*. Edited by Michael Forster. Cambridge: Cambridge University Press, 2002.

———. *Selected Early Works, 1764–1767*. Edited by Ernest A. Menze and Karl Menges. Translation by Ernest A. Menze with Michael Palma. University Park: Pennsylvania State University Press, 1992.

Historical Poetics. https://www.historicalpoetics.com/about/.

Hollander, John. *Vision and Resonance: Two Senses of Poetic Form*. New York: Oxford University Press, 1975.

Hough, Graham. "Tears, Idle Tears." In *Critical Essays on the Poetry of Tennyson*, ed. John Killham, 186–91. New York: Barnes and Noble, 1960.

Hughes, Linda. *Victorian Women Writers and the Other Germany: Cross-Cultural Freedoms and Female Opportunities*. Cambridge: Cambridge University Press, 2022.

———, ed. "Whither Victorian Poetry?" Special issue, *Victorian Poetry* 41, no. 4 (Winter 2003).

Hunter, J. Paul. "Formalism and History: Binarism and the Anglophone Couplet." *MLQ* 61, no. 1 (2000): 102–29.

———. "Seven Reasons for Rhyme." In *Ritual, Routine, and Regime: Repetition in Early Modern British and European Cultures*, ed. Lorna Clymer, 172–98. Toronto: University of Toronto Press, 2006.

Item A1127. EBB's copy of Henry Hallam's *Literature of Europe*. The Brownings: A Research Guide. Armstrong Browning Library of Baylor University.

Jackson, Virginia, and Yopie Prins. *The Lyric Theory Reader*. Baltimore: Johns Hopkins University Press, 2013.

Jamison, Anne. *Poetics en Passant: Redefining the Relationship between Victorian and Modern Poetry*. New York: Palgrave, 2009.

Jarvis, Simon. "Musical Thinking: Hegel and the Phenomenology of Prosody." *Paragraph* 28, no. 2 (2005): 57–71.

———. "Swinburne: The Insuperable Sea." In *The Oxford Handbook of Victorian Poetry*, ed. Matthew Bevis, 521–35. Oxford: Oxford University Press, 2013.

———. "Why Rhyme Pleases." *Thinking Verse* 1 (2011): 17–43.

Jauss, Hans Robert. *Toward an Aesthetic of Reception*. Translated by Timothy Bahti. Minneapolis: University of Minnesota Press, 1982.

Johnson, Samuel. *A Dictionary of the English Language*. 6th ed. 2 vols. London: Rivington et al., 1785.

———. *Samuel Johnson: The Major Works*. Oxford: Oxford University Press, 2009.

Johnston, Eileen Tess. "Hallam's Review of Tennyson: Its Contexts and Significance." *Texas Studies in Literature and Language* 23, no. 1 (Spring 1981): 1–26.

Jones, Ewan. "Coventry Patmore's Corpus." *ELH* 83, no. 3 (2016): 839–72.

Jones, William. *The Poetical Works of William Jones, with the Life of the Author*. 2 vols. London: Nichols, 1810.

Jump, John D. *The Ode*. London: Methuen, 1974.

———, ed. *Tennyson: The Critical Heritage*. New York: Routledge, 1967.

Kappeler, Erin Joyce. "Free Verse, Historical Poetics, and Settler Time." *Literature Compass* 17, no. 7 (2020): 1–14.

Keats, John. "Isabella; or, The Pot of Basil." In *John Keats: A Longman Cultural Edition*, ed. Susan Wolfson, 312–32. New York: Pearson, 2006.

———. Letter to P. B. Shelley, August 16, 1820. In *John Keats: A Longman Cultural Edition*, ed. Susan Wolfson, 425–27. New York: Pearson, 2006.

Kenner, Hugh. "Pope's Reasonable Rhymes." *ELH* 41, no. 1 (1974): 74–88.

———. "Rhyme: An Unfinished Monograph." *Common Knowledge* 10, no. 3 (2004): 377–425.

Keirstead, Christopher. *Victorian Poetry, Europe, and the Challenge of Cosmopolitanism*. Columbus: Ohio State University Press, 2011.

King, Joshua. "Patmore, Hopkins, and the Problem of the English Metrical Law." *Victorian Poetry* 49, no. 2 (Summer 2011): 31–49.

Kirby-Smith, H. T. *The Origins of Free Verse*. Ann Arbor: University of Michigan Press, 1996.

Kliger, Ilya, and Boris Maslov, eds. *Persistent Forms: Explorations in Historical Poetics*. New York: Fordham, 2015.

Kramnick, Jonathan. "The Interdisciplinary Fallacy." *Representations* 140 (Fall 2017): 67–83.

Kramnick, Jonathan, and Anahid Nersessian. "Form and Explanation." *Critical Inquiry* 43 (Spring 2017): 650–69.

Kozicki, Henry. "Tennyson's 'Tears, Idle Tears': The Case for Violet." *Victorian Poetry* 24, no. 2 (Summer 1986): 99–113.

Kuduk, Stephanie. "Victorian Poetry as Victorian Studies." *Victorian Poetry* 41, no. 4 (Winter 2003): 513–18.

Lang, Cecil Y., and Edgar F. Shannon Jr. *The Letters of Alfred Lord Tennyson*. Vol. 1. Cambridge, MA: Harvard University Press, 1981.

Lang, Timothy. "Hallam, Henry (1777–1859)." *Oxford Dictionary of National Biography*. Oxford: Oxford University Press, 2004.

Lanz, Henry. *The Physical Basis of Rime: An Essay on the Aesthetics of Sound*. New York: Greenwood Press, 1968.

LaPorte, Charles. *The Victorian Cult of Shakespeare: Bardology in the Nineteenth Century*. Cambridge: Cambridge University Press, 2021.

LaPorte, Charles, and Jason Rudy. "Editorial Introduction: Spasmodic Poetry and Poetics." *Victorian Poetry* 42, no. 4 (Winter 2004): 421–28.

Lee, Vernon. *The Psychology of an Art Writer*. New York: David Zwirner Books, 2018.

Le Gallienne, Richard, ed. *The Poems of Arthur Hallam: Together with His Essay on the Lyrical Poems of Alfred Tennyson*. London: Elkin Mathews and John Lane, 1893.

Leighton, Angela. *On Form: Poetry, Aestheticism, and the Legacy of a Word*. Oxford: Oxford University Press, 2007.

Levine, Caroline. *Forms: Whole, Rhythm, Hierarchy, Network*. Princeton, NJ: Princeton University Press, 2015.

———. "Strategic Formalism: Toward a New Method in Cultural Studies." *Victorian Studies* 48, no. 4 (Summer 2006): 625–57.

Levine, Naomi. "Tirra-Lirrical Ballads: Source Hunting with the Lady of Shalott." *Victorian Poetry* 54, no. 4 (Winter 2016): 439–54.

———. "Trebled Beauty: William Morris's Terza Rima." *Victorian Studies* 53, no. 3 (Spring 2011): 506–17.

———. "Understanding Poetry Otherwise: New Criticism and Historical Poetics." *Literature Compass* 17, no. 7 (2020): 1–11.

Levinson, Marjorie. "What Is New Formalism?" *PMLA* 122, no. 2 (2007): 558–69.

Lewis, C. S. *The Allegory of Love: A Study in Medieval Tradition*. Oxford: Oxford University Press, 1936.

Lootens, Tricia A. *Lost Saints: Silence, Gender, and Victorian Literary Canonization*. Charlottesville: University of Virginia Press, 1996.

Love, Heather. "Close but not Deep: Literary Ethics and the Descriptive Turn." *New Literary History* 41, no. 2 (Spring 2010): 371–91.

———. *Feeling Backward: Loss and the Politics of Queer History*. Cambridge, MA: Harvard University Press, 2007.

Lovejoy, Arthur O. "The Meaning of Romanticism for the Historian of Ideas." *Journal of the History of Ideas* 2, no. 3 (1941): 257–78.

Lynch, Deidre Shauna. *Loving Literature: A Cultural History*. Chicago: University of Chicago Press, 2015.

Macfarlane, Robert. *Original Copy: Plagiarism and Originality in Nineteenth-Century Literature*. Oxford: Oxford University Press, 2007.

Macgregor, R. G. *Odes of Petrarch*. London: Smith, Elder, 1851.

Mackail, J. W. *The Life of William Morris*. Toronto: Dover, 1995.

Macpherson, Sandra. "A Little Formalism." *ELH* 82, no. 2 (Summer 2015): 385–405.

Markovits, Stefanie. "Form Things: Looking at Genre through Victorian Diamonds." *Victorian Studies* 52, no. 4 (Summer 2010): 591–619.

———. *The Victorian Verse-Novel: Aspiring to Life*. Oxford: Oxford University Press, 2017.

Martin, Meredith. "Imperfectly Civilized: Ballads, Nations, and Histories of Form." *ELH* 82, no. 2 (Summer 2015): 345–63.

———. *The Rise and Fall of Meter: Poetry and English National Culture, 1860–1930*. Princeton, NJ: Princeton University Press, 2012.

Maynard, John. *Victorian Discourses on Sexuality and Religion*. Cambridge: Cambridge University Press, 1993.

Mazel, Adam. "The Age of Rhyme: The Verse Culture of Victorian Cambridge." *Nineteenth-Century Literature* 72, no. 3 (December 2017): 374–401.

Mazzeo, Guido Ettore. *The Abate Juan Andrés, Literary Historian of the XVII Century*. New York: Hispanic Institute in the United States, 1965.

McDonald, Peter. *Sound Intentions: The Workings of Rhyme in Nineteenth-Century Poetry*. Oxford: Oxford University Press, 2012.

———. "Tennyson's Dying Fall." in *Tennyson Among the Poets*, ed. Robert Douglas-Fairhurst and Seamus Perry, 14–38. Oxford: Oxford University Press, 2009.

McGann, Jerome. *Dante Gabriel Rossetti and the Game that Must Be Lost*. New Haven, CT: Yale University Press, 2000.

McKie, Michael. "The Origins and Early Development of Rhyme in English Verse." *Modern Language Review* 92, no. 4 (October 1997): 817–31.

McLuhan, M. H. "Tennyson and Picturesque Poetry." In *Critical Essays on the Poetry of Tennyson*, ed. John Killham, 67–85. New York: Barnes and Noble, 1960.

Menocal, María Rosa. *The Arabic Role in Medieval Literary History: A Forgotten Heritage*. Philadelphia: University of Pennsylvania Press, 2004.

Menze, Ernest A., and Karl Menges. Editors' notes to Herder, *Selected Early Works*.

Mermin, Dorothy. *Elizabeth Barrett Browning: The Origins of a New Poetry*. Chicago: Chicago University Press, 1989.

Merrill, Jessica. "Historical Poetics and Poetic Language: Rethinking the Concept of Autonomy for Modern Literary Theory." *Poetics Today* 3, no. 38 (2017): 519–48.

Meynell, Alice. "Coventry Patmore." In *The Second Person Singular, and Other Essays*, 126–36. Freeport, NY: Books for Libraries Press, 1968.

———. "Mr. Coventry Patmore's Odes." In *The Rhythm of Life and Other Essays*, 89–96. London: John Lane, 1897.

Milbank, Alison. *Dante and the Victorians*. Manchester: Manchester University Press, 1998.

Miller, J. Hillis. "Temporal Topographies: Tennyson's Tears." *Victorian Poetry* 30, nos. 3/4 (Autumn/Winter 1992): 277–89.

Milton, John. "The Verse" in *Paradise Lost*. Edited by Gordon Teskey. New York: Norton, 2005.

Monroe, Harriet. "The Free-Verse Movement in America." *English Journal* 13, no. 10 (December 1924): 691–705.

Morgan, Benjamin. *The Outward Mind: Materialist Aesthetics in Victorian Science and Literature.* Chicago: University of Chicago Press, 2017.

Morgan, Monique. *Narrative Means, Lyric Ends: Temporality in the Nineteenth-Century Long Poem.* Columbus: Ohio State University Press, 2009.

Morlier, Margaret M. "Sonnets from the Portuguese and the Politics of Rhyme." *Victorian Literature and Culture* 27, no. 1 (1999): 97–112.

Morris, William. "The Defence of Guenevere." In *The Pre-Raphaelites and Their Circle,* ed. Cecil Y. Lang, 161–70. Chicago: University of Chicago Press, 1975.

———. *The Earthly Paradise.* Edited by Florence Boos. 2 vols. New York: Routledge, 2002.

Motter, T. H. Vail, ed. *The Writings of Arthur Hallam.* New York: Modern Language Association of America, 1943.

Moretti, Franco. *Distant Reading.* London: Verso, 2013.

"Mr. Gosse's New Poems." *The Spectator* 53 (February 1880): 239–40.

Mufti, Aamir. *Forget English! Orientalisms and World Literatures.* Cambridge, MA: Harvard University Press, 2016.

———. "Orientalism and the Institution of World Literatures." *Critical Inquiry* 36 (Spring 2010): 458–93.

Murray, James, ed. *A New English Dictionary on Historical Principles.* Oxford: Clarendon, 1887.

Nabi, Jason. "Tennyson with the Net Down: His 'Freer' Verse." *Victorian Poetry* 51, no. 2 (Summer 2013): 177–200.

Nadel, Ira. *Ezra Pound in Context.* Cambridge: Cambridge University Press, 2010.

North, Joseph. *Literary Criticism: A Concise Political History.* Cambridge, MA: Harvard University Press, 2017.

Nott, John, ed. *Petrarch Translated; in a Selection of His Sonnets, and Odes.* London: J. Miller, 1808.

Omond, T. S. *English Metrists.* New York: Phaeton Press, 1968.

Ostriker, Alicia. "The Three Modes in Tennyson's Prosody." *PMLA* 82, no. 2 (1967): 273–84.

Page, Frederick. *Patmore: A Study in Poetry.* Oxford: Oxford University Press, 1970.

Passerini, Luisa. *Europe in Love, Love in Europe: Imagination and Politics between the Wars.* New York: New York University Press, 1999.

Pater, Walter. "Poems by William Morris." *Westminster Review* 178 (October 1868): 144–49.

———. "Postscript (Romanticism)." In *Selected Writings of Walter Pater,* ed. Harold Bloom. New York: Columbia University Press, 1974.

———. *Studies in the History of the Renaissance.* Edited by Matthew Beaumont. Oxford: Oxford University Press, 2010.

Patmore, Coventry. *Coventry Patmore's "Essay on English Metrical Law":*

A Critical Edition with a Commentary. Edited by Sister Mary Augustine Roth. Washington, DC: Catholic University of America Press, 1961.

———. "Francis Thompson, A New Poet." *Courage in Politics and Other Essays, 1885–1896*, 157–66. London: Oxford University Press, 1921.

———. "*In Memoriam*." *North British Review* 13 (1850): 532–55.

———. Preface to Patmore, *The Unknown Eros*, v–vi.

———. *The Unknown Eros*. London: George Bell, 1890.

Pattison, Robert. *Tennyson and Tradition*. Cambridge, MA: Harvard University Press, 1979.

Perkins, David. *Is Literary History Possible?* Baltimore: Johns Hopkins University Press, 1993.

———. "Literary History and Historicism." In *Romanticism*, vol. 5 of *The Cambridge History of Literary Criticism*, ed. Marshall Brown, 338–61. Cambridge: Cambridge University Press, 2000.

———, ed. *Theoretical Issues in Literary History*. Cambridge, MA: Harvard University Press, 1991.

Perry, Seamus. *Alfred Tennyson*. Tavistock, UK: Northcote House, 2005.

———. "Elegy." In *A Companion to Victorian Poetry*, ed. Richard Cronin, Alison Chapman, and Antony H. Harrison, 115–33. Oxford: Blackwell, 2002.

———. "Hallam and Coleridge." *Tennyson Research Bulletin* 9, no. 5 (2011): 434–44.

Peterson, Linda. "Sappho and the Making of Tennysonian Lyric." *ELH* 61, no. 1 (Spring 1994): 121–37.

Phelan, Joseph. *The Music of Verse: Metrical Experiment in Nineteenth-Century Poetry*. New York: Palgrave, 2012.

———. "Empire and Orientalisms." In *The Oxford Handbook of Victorian Poetry*, ed. Matthew Bevis, 800–816. Oxford: Oxford University Press, 2013.

Pickens, Rupert T., ed. *The Songs of Jaufré Rudel*. Toronto: Pontifical Institute of Mediaeval Studies, 1978.

Pierson, Robert. "Coventry Patmore's Ideas Concerning English Prosody and 'The Unknown Eros' Read Accordingly." *Victorian Poetry* 34, no. 4 (Winter 1996): 493–518.

Pinch, Adela. "Love Thinking." *Victorian Studies* 50, no. 3 (Spring 2008): 379–97.

———. "Rhyme's End." *Victorian Studies* 53, no. 3 (Spring 2011): 485–94.

Poe, Edgar Allan. *The Works of Edgar Allan Poe*. Vol. 3. New York: W. J. Widdleton, 1849.

Porter, James I. Editor's notes to Auerbach, *Time, History, and Literature*, 2014.

Pottle, Frederick A. "A Method for Teaching." *Wordsworth Circle* 9, no. 4 (1978): 325–30.

———. *The Idiom of Poetry*. Ithaca, NY: Cornell University Press, 1946.

Pound, Ezra. "A Retrospect." In *Literary Essays of Ezra Pound*, 3–14. New York: New Directions, 1968.

———. *Polite Essays*. Freeport: Books for Libraries Press, 1966.

———. *The Spirit of Romance*. New York: New Directions, 1968.

Prins, Yopie. "Historical Poetics, Dysprosody, and 'The Science of English Verse.'" *PMLA* 123, no. 1 (January 2008): 229–34.

———. *Ladies' Greek: Victorian Translations of Tragedy*. Princeton, NJ: Princeton University Press, 2017.

———. "Patmore's Law, Meynell's Rhythm." In *The Fin-de-Siècle Poem*, ed. Joseph Bristow, 261–84. Columbus: Ohio University Press, 2005.

———. "Victorian Meters." In *The Cambridge Companion to Victorian Poetry*, ed. Joseph Bristow, 89–113. Cambridge: Cambridge University Press, 2000.

———. *Victorian Sappho*. Princeton, NJ: Princeton University Press, 1999.

Psomiades, Kathy Alexis. "'The Lady of Shalott' and the Critical Fortunes of Victorian Poetry." In *The Cambridge Companion to Victorian Poetry*, ed. Joseph Bristow, 25–45. Cambridge: Cambridge University Press, 2000.

Pyre, J. F. A. *The Formation of Tennyson's Style: A Study, Primarily, of the Versification of the Early Poems*. Madison: University of Wisconsin, 1921.

Puttenham, George. *The Art of English Poesy: A Critical Edition*. Edited by Frank Whigham and Wayne A. Rebhorn. Ithaca, NY: Cornell University Press, 2007.

Ramazani, Jahan. *A Transnational Poetics*. Chicago: University of Chicago Press, 2009.

———. "Persian Poetry, World Poetry, and Translatability." *University of Toronto Quarterly* 88, no. 2 (Spring 2019): 210–28.

Raynouard, François Just Marie. *Choix des poésies originales des Troubadours*. Vol. 3. Paris: Firmin Didot, 1818.

Reid, J. C. *The Mind and Art of Coventry Patmore*. London: Routledge, 1957.

Research Services, Beinecke Library, New Haven, CT. Personal Correspondence. August 4, 2014.

Reynolds, Matthew. *The Realms of Verse 1830–1870: English Poetry in a Time of Nation-Building*. Oxford: Oxford University Press, 2001.

Richards, I. A. *Principles of Literary Criticism*. New York: Harcourt, Brace, and World, 1965.

Ricks, Christopher. Editor's notes to Tennyson, *Poems of Tennyson*.

———. *The Force of Poetry*. Oxford: Clarendon Press, 1995.

———. *Tennyson*. Berkeley: University of California Press, 1989.

Ritson, Joseph. *A Dissertation on Romance and Minstrelsy*. Edinburgh: E. and G. Goldsmid, 1891.

Rossetti, Christina. "Dante, an English Classic." *Churchman's Shilling Magazine and Family Treasury* 2 (1867–68): 200–205.

Rossetti, William Michael, trans. and ed. *Gabriele Rossetti: A Versified Autobiography*. London: Sands, 1901.

Roth, Sister Mary Augustine. Editor's notes to Patmore, *Coventry Patmore's "Essay."*

Rudy, Jason. *Electric Meters: Victorian Physiological Poetics*. Columbus: Ohio University Press, 2009.

———. *Imagined Homelands: British Poetry in the Colonies*. Baltimore: Johns Hopkins University Press, 2017.

———. "Material Patmore." In Hall, *Meter Matters*, 135–53.

———. "On Cultural Neoformalism, Spasmodic Poetry, and the Victorian Ballad." *Victorian Poetry* 41, no. 4 (Winter 2003): 590–96.

Ruskin, John. *Selected Writings*. Edited by Dinah Birch. Oxford: Oxford University Press, 2004.

Russell, David. *Tact: Aesthetic Liberalism and the Essay Form in Nineteenth-Century Britain*. Princeton, NJ: Princeton University Press, 2018.

Said, Edward. *Orientalism*. New York: Random House, 2003.

Saintsbury, George. *A History of Criticism and Literary Taste in Europe: From the Earliest Texts to the Present Day*. Vol. 3. Edinburgh: Blackwood, 1904.

———. *A History of English Prosody: From the Twelfth Century to the Present Day*. 3 vols. London: Macmillan, 1906–10.

Sasso, Eleonora. "*Aja'ib, mutalibun* and *hur al-ayn:* Rossetti, Morris, Swinburne, and the *Arabian Nights*." In *Late Victorian Orientalism: Representations of the East in Nineteenth-Century Literature, Art, and Culture from the Pre-Raphaelites to John La Farge*, ed. Eleonora Sasso, 51–78. London: Anthem Press, 2020.

Schiller, Friedrich. *Naive and Sentimental Poetry, and On the Sublime*. Translated by Julius A. Elias. New York: Frederick Ungar, 1966.

Schlegel, A. W. *A Course of Lectures on Dramatic Art and Literature*. Translated by John Black. Vol. 1. London: Baldwin, Cradock, and Joy, 1815.

———. "For the Reinstatement of Dante." In *Dante: The Critical Heritage*, ed. Michael Caesar, 420–26. London: Routledge, 1989.

———. *Observations sur la langue et la littérature provençales*. Paris: La Libraire Grecque-Latine-Allemande, 1818.

Schlegel, Friedrich. *Lectures on the History of Literature, Ancient and Modern*. London: G. Bell and Sons, 1876.

Scott, Walter. *The Complete Works of Sir Walter Scott*. Vol. 1. New York: Connor and Cooke, 1833.

Sedgwick, Eve Kosofsky. *Touching Feeling: Affect, Pedagogy, Performativity*. Durham, NC: Duke University Press, 2003.

Shafer, Robert. *The English Ode to 1660: An Essay in Literary History*. New York: Haskell House, 1966.

Shannon, Edgar Finley. "The Pinnacle of Success: *In Memoriam*." In *In Memoriam*, ed. Erik Gray, 110–21.

Sider, Justin. "Framing Tennyson's Farewells: Authority and Materiality in 'Morte d'Arthur.'" *Victorian Poetry* 51, no. 4 (Winter 2013): 487–509.

———. "'Modern-Antiques,' Ballad Imitations, and the Aesthetics of Anachronism." *Victorian Poetry* 54, no.4 (Winter 2016): 455–75.

———. *Parting Words: Victorian Poetry and Public Address.* Charlottesville: University of Virginia Press, 2018.

Siegel, Jonah. *Haunted Museum: Longing, Travel, and the Art-Romance Tradition.* Princeton, NJ: Princeton University Press, 2005.

———. *Material Inspirations: The Interests of the Art Object in the Nineteenth Century and After.* Oxford: Oxford University Press, 2020.

Sismondi, J. C. L. Simonde. *De la littérature du Midi de l'Europe.* Vol. 1. Paris: Treuttel et Würtz, 1813.

———. *Historical View of the Literature of the South of Europe.* Translated by Thomas Roscoe. 4 vols. London: Henry Colburn, 1823.

Smith, Fred Manning. "Mrs. Browning's Rhymes." *PMLA* 54, no. 3 (1939): 829–34.

Stark, Robert. "'[Keeping] Up the Fire': Elizabeth Barrett Browning's Victorian Versification." *Journal of Browning Studies* 1 (2010): 49–69.

Stewart, Garrett. *Reading Voices: Literature and the Phonotext.* Berkeley: University of California Press, 1990.

Stewart, Susan. *The Poet's Freedom: A Notebook on Making.* Chicago: University of Chicago Press, 2011.

Stone, Marjorie. "Genre Subversion and Gender Inversion: *The Princess* and *Aurora Leigh.*" *Victorian Poetry* 25, no. 2 (Summer 1987): 101–27.

Stone, Marjorie, and Beverly Taylor. Editors' notes to vol. 2 of *The Works of Elizabeth Barrett Browning.*

Strier, Richard. "How Formalism Became a Dirty Word, and Why We Can't Do without It." In *Renaissance Literature and Its Formal Engagements,* ed. Mark Rasmussen, 207–15. New York: Palgrave, 2002.

Stuart, J. Montgomery. "England's Literary Debt to Italy." *Fraser's Magazine* (December 1859): 697–708.

Swett, Margery. "Free Verse Again." *Poetry* 25, no. 3 (Dec. 1924): 153–59.

Symonds, John Addington. *Sketches and Studies in Italy.* London: Smith, Elder, 1879.

Taylor, Bayard. Editor's notes to Goethe, *Faust: Parts 1 and 2,* 1969.

Taylor, Dennis. *Hardy's Metres and Victorian Prosody.* Oxford: Clarendon Press, 1988.

Tennyson, Alfred. *In Memoriam.* Edited by Erik Gray. New York: Norton, 2004.

———. *Poems, Chiefly Lyrical, 1830.* Oxford: Woodstock Books, 1991.

———. *The Poems of Tennyson.* Edited by Christopher Ricks. 3 vols. Harlow: Longman, 1987.

———. *Tennyson's Poetry.* Edited by Robert W. Hill, Jr. New York: Norton, 1999.

Tennyson, Hallam. *Alfred Lord Tennyson: A Memoir.* London: Macmillan, 1897.

Tucker, Herbert F. "An Ebbigrammar of Motives; or, Ba for Short." *Victorian Poetry* 44, no. 4 (Winter 2006): 445–65.

———. *Epic: Britain's Heroic Muse, 1790–1910*. Oxford: Oxford University Press, 2008.

———. "The Fix of Form: An Open Letter." *Victorian Literature and Culture* 27, no. 2 (1999): 531–35.

———. *Tennyson and the Doom of Romanticism*. Cambridge, MA: Harvard University Press, 1988.

Underwood, Ted. *Why Literary Periods Mattered: Historical Contrast and the Prestige of English Studies*. Stanford, CA: Stanford University Press, 2013.

V21 Collective. Manifesto of the V21 Collective. http://v21collective.org/manifesto-of-the-v21-collective-ten-theses/.

Warton, Thomas. *History of English Poetry: From the Close of the Eleventh Century to the Commencement of the Eighteenth Century*. Vol. 1, 1824. London: Thomas Tegg, 1840.

Weismiller, E. R., T. V. F. Brogan, R. B. Shaw, G. T. Wright, H. J. S. Alves, C. Küper, E. Lilja, and N. Friedberg. "Blank Verse." Greene et al., *Princeton Encyclopedia*.

Wellek, René. "The Concept of Evolution in Literary History." In *Concepts of Criticism*, 37–53. New Haven, CT: Yale University Press, 1963.

———. "The Concept of 'Romanticism' in Literary History I: The Term 'Romantic' and Its Derivatives." *Comparative Literature* 1, no. 1 (Winter 1949): 1–23.

———. "Concepts of Form and Structure in Twentieth-Century Criticism." In *Concepts of Criticism*, 54–68. New Haven, CT: Yale University Press, 1963.

———. "English Literary Historiography during the Nineteenth Century." In *Discriminations: Further Concepts of Criticism*, 143–63. New Haven, CT: Yale University Press, 1970.

———. "The Fall of Literary History." In *New Perspectives in German Literary Criticism*, ed. Richard E. Amacher and Victor Lange, 418–31. Princeton, NJ: Princeton University Press, 1979.

———. *A History of Modern Criticism*. 8 vols. New Haven, CT: Yale University Press, 1955–92.

———. "Literary Theory, Criticism, and History." In *Concepts of Criticism*, 1–20. New Haven, CT: Yale University Press, 1963.

———. *The Rise of English Literary History*. Chapel Hill: University of North Carolina Press, 1941.

Wellek, René, and Austin Warren. *Theory of Literature*. New York: Harcourt, Brace and World, 1962.

Wesling, Donald. *The Chances of Rhyme: Device and Modernity*. Berkeley: University of California Press, 1980.

White, Hayden. "Literary History: The Point of It All." *New Literary History* 2, no. 1 (1970): 173–85.

———. *Metahistory: The Historical Imagination in Nineteenth-Century Europe*. Baltimore: Johns Hopkins University Press, 1975.

Wilde, Oscar. *The Complete Works of Oscar Wilde*. New York: Harper Perennial, 2008.

Williams, Carolyn. *Gilbert and Sullivan: Gender, Genre, Parody*. New York: Columbia University Press, 2010.

———. *Transfigured World: Water Pater's Aesthetic Historicism*. Ithaca, NY: Cornell University Press, 1989.

———. "Walter Pater's Impressionism and the Form of Historical Revival." In *Knowing the Past: Victorian Literature and Culture*, ed. Suzy Anger, 77–99. Ithaca, NY: Cornell University Press, 2001.

Wimsatt, W. K. *Day of the Leopards: Essays in Defense of Poems*. New Haven, CT: Yale University Press, 1976.

———. *The Verbal Icon: Studies in the Meaning of Poetry*. Lexington: University of Kentucky Press, 1954.

Winters, Yvor. *In Defense of Reason*. Denver: Swallow, 1947.

Wolfson, Susan J. *Formal Charges: The Shaping of Poetry in British Romanticism*. Stanford, CA: Stanford University Press, 1997.

———. "Introduction: Reading for Form." In *Reading for Form*, ed. Marshall Brown and Susan J. Wolfson, 3–24. Seattle: University of Washington Press, 2006.

———. "Tennyson's Tears, Brooks's Motivations." In *The Question of the Aesthetic*, ed. George Levine, 221–39. Oxford: Oxford University Press, 2022.

Woolf, Virginia. "Professions for Women." In *Virginia Woolf: Selected Essays*, ed. David Bradshaw, 140–45. Oxford: Oxford University Press, 2008.

Yeats, W. B. "John Eglinton and Spiritual Art." In *Literary Ideals in Ireland*, ed. John Eglinton, W. B. Yeats, A. E., and W. Larminie. London: T. Fisher Unwin, 1899.

Zitin, Abigail. *Practical Form: Abstraction, Technique, and Beauty in Eighteenth-Century Aesthetics*. New Haven, CT: Yale University Press, 2020.

Index

Made in the USA
Las Vegas, NV
19 January 2025

16670794R00144